NAVY DEPARTMENT
OFFICE OF NAVAL RECORDS AND LIBRARY
HISTORICAL SECTION

Publication Number 1

GERMAN SUBMARINE ACTIVITIES ON THE ATLANTIC COAST OF THE UNITED STATES AND CANADA

Published under the direction of
The Hon. JOSEPHUS DANIELS, Secretary of the Navy

WASHINGTON
GOVERNMENT PRINTING OFFICE
1920

ERRATA

Page 50, "Cruise of U-156" 1st paragraph, strike out von Oldenburg and substitute Richard Feldt.

Page 38, paragraph 2, line 5: change J.A. Fasset to read Thomas D. Packard.

Page 104, paragraph 5, line 9: change to read one man was mortally wounded.

GERMAN SUBMARINE ACTIVITIES ON THE ATLANTIC COAST OF THE UNITED STATES AND CANADA

Publication No. 1, Historical Section, Navy Department

ERRATA

Page 7, in table bottom of page, in fifth column, lines 6 and 7, strike out words "about Nov. 15" and insert *Sept. 22.* In line 12, strike out "15" and insert *14.*

Page 22, line 39, strike out "Strathmore" and insert "*Strathdene.*"

Page 23, line 10, strike out "Kapitan Van Nostitz und Janckendorf" and insert *Korvettenkapitän (Lieutenant Commander) von Nostitz und Jaenckendorf.*

Page 24, after line 15, insert *Note: The British steamship "Crenella" was formerly the Canadian steamship "Montcalm." The two names were confused in the dispatches and consequently the discrepancy.*

Page 30, after line 14, insert *Note: While it would have been possible for "U-151" to have been in the vicinity of the battleships on June 1, it is improbable that the attack of the battleships was on that submarine. The prisoners from the "Hattie Dunn," "Hauppauge," and "Edna" were not released from "U-151" until June 2, and they do not make any mention of the encounter and would most likely have known of it.*

Page 34, line 37, strike out "United Shipping States Board" and insert *United States Shipping Board.*

Page 36, after line 5 insert a new paragraph, viz:

The loss of the "Texel" had a direct bearing upon the plan of operations for the "United States Naval Railway Batteries in France." That ship was one of those chosen to transport a cargo of material for that remarkable enterprise, and her loss necessitated the selection of another vessel.

Page 38, strike out lines 11 to 26 (both inclusive) and insert in lieu thereof after line 10, *The official list, made later, shows that 272 survivors were landed at New York, viz:*

Crew—1 stewardess and 91 men; total 92.

Passengers—58 females, 118 males, and 4 infants; total 180.

Other survivors from the "S. S. Carolina" were accounted for on June 4. At 1.45 p. m. lifeboat No. 5, containing 8 women and 21 men, landed through the surf at the foot of South Carolina Avenue, Atlantic City, N. J. The same day the British steamship "Appleby" picked up from lifeboat No. 1, 9 members of the crew and 10 passengers and carried them to Lewes, Del. The first loss of life charged to enemy submarine activity off the American Atlantic coast was recorded when the survivors from lifeboat No. 1 were picked up by the steamship "Appleby," and reported that while trying to weather the rough sea that arose during the night their boat had capsized about 12.15 a. m., June 3, and it was later found that 7 passengers, the purser, and 5 members of the crew were missing and were lost.

On June 3, at 4 p. m., the Danish steamship "Bryssel" picked up the abandoned lifeboat No. 1.

Page 41, line 36, after the words "found nothing" insert *Note: The encounter of the U. S. S. "Preble" was too far north to have been with "U-151."*

Page 44, line 20, after the word "schooner" strike out "Ella Swift" and insert *Ellen A. Swift.*

Page 44, line 22, after the word "whaler" strike out "Nicholson" and insert "A. M. Nicholson."

Page 46, strike out footnote 14 and insert *The joint attack by the battleship "South Carolina" and U. S. "S. C. 234" occurred in Lat. 38° 26' N., Long. 74° 40' W. and was too far north and west to have been on "U–151." Besides Captain Ballestad says in his testimony, that from 6.20 p. m., on June 8, to 6.20 a. m., June 9, his ship followed the submarine at a slow speed, without stopping, on a course east, southeast, easterly, and they did not encounter the battleship.*

Page 50, after line 29 insert *Note: 12 lives were lost on the "Tortuguero."*

Page 55, line 18, strike out "Nauseet" and insert *Nauset.*

Page 56, line 24, strike out "Grand Island" and insert *Grand Manan Island.*

Page 56, line 29, strike out "Grand Island" and insert *Grand Manan Island.*

Page 59, in footnote 29, strike out "Elizabeth Von Bilgie" and insert *Elizabeth Van Belgie.*

Page 71, line 8, strike out "Melitia" and insert *Melita.*

Page 88, after line 6 insert *Note: There was no loss of life on the two fishing vessels, "Cruiser" and "Old Time." All reached shore in safety.*

Page 91, line 23, strike out "tampion" and insert *tompion.*

Page 94, line 13, strike out "Brazilian" and insert *American.*

Page 95, line 4, strike out words "The day after" and insert *Two days after.*

Page 96, line 44, after the word "longitude" (line 43) strike out "58°" and insert *68°.*

Page 101, after line 40 insert new paragraph, viz: *On September 7, 1918, at 8.30 a. m., the Portuguese sailing vessel "Sophia" was sunk with bombs by "U–155" in latitude 42° 51' N., longitude 45° 58' W.*

Page 105, line 38, strike out "October 19" and insert *October 18.*

Page 106, line 3, after the word November strike out the words "15 four" and insert *14 three,* line 11, after the word "Constanza" insert *Note: The British Admiralty give the name as "Constance," 199 gross tons. The vessel was salvaged,* line 33, strike out "237" and insert *239.*

Page 118, line 33, strike out "August" and insert *October.*

Page 124, line 34, strike out "August" and insert *September.*

Page 127, after line 13, insert *Note: The exact location of the sinking of the U. S. S. "San Diego" was latitude 40° 33' 15" N., longitude 73° 01' 20" W.*

Page 133, line 14, after the words Norwegian S. S. strike out "Breiford" and insert *Breifond;* also in line 16, same correction.

Page 133, after paragraph 6 insert new paragraph, viz:
Besides the three rescued by the "Breifond" five other men, including one dead, were picked up by the American steamship "Lake Felicity" and taken to Newport, R. I. The five men clung to pieces of the pilot house, on which they remained for 12 hours. One died after 9 hours of exposure. A total of 30 lives was lost, including this man.

Page 134, line 9, strike out the words "The crew of 11 men came in the inlet with the captain in one of their own boats; the balance of the crew landed on North Beach, Coast Guard Station 112," and insert in lieu thereof: *Of the crew, consisting of 29 men, the captain and 11 men came in the inlet in one of their own boats and landed at Coast Guard Station 112. Another boat with 11 men landed on North Beach and 6 men were found missing and lost.*

Page 139, table No. 1 (Vindeggen), 6th column, strike out, "73° 20' W." and insert *71° 20' W.*

Page 140, table No. 1, strike out "Notre Dame de Lagarde, F. V. 145. B. Aug. 22" and insert *Notre Dame de la Garde, F. V. 145. B. Aug. 21.*

Page 140, in Table No. 1, column 1, after "Gamo (Portuguese)" insert new line, viz: *"Sophia" (Portuguese)____do_____163 B_____Sept. 7. 42° 51' N., 43° 58' W.*

Page 157, line 27, second column, strike out "Brieford" and insert *Breifond*.

Page 160, line 51, strike out "Brazilian" and insert *American.*

Page 162, in first column, after line 33, insert: *"Sophia" Portuguese S. V_____ 101.*

CORRECTIONS CHART NO. 1

CHART TRACK OF "U-151"

May 19 (S. S. *Nyanza*). Insert sign showing vessel attacked but not sunk in latitude 38° 21' N., longitude 70° 05' W.

May 21 (S. S. *Crenella*). Change sign to indicate vessel attacked but not sunk.

June 13 (*Llanstephen Castle*). Latitude 38° 02' N., longitude 72° 47' W. Change sign to indicate vessel attacked but not sunk.

June 18 (S. S. *Dwinsk*). Latitude 38° 30' N., longitude 61° 15' W. Should have sign indicating vessel sunk.

CHART TRACK OF "U-156"

"July 23" (schooner *Robert and Richard*). 60 miles southeast of Cape Porpoise. Should be *July 22*.

August 8 (S. S. *Sydland*). Insert sign showing vessel sunk in latitude 41° 30' N., longitude 65° 22' W.

NOTE.—Sign indicating vessel sunk on August 8, on chart track of "*U-117*" should be on track of *U-156*.

August 20 (*Triumph* and fishing fleet). 52 miles southwest of Cape Canso, Nova Scotia, approximately latitude 44° 31' N., longitude 60° 30' W. Change sign to indicate vessels sunk.

"August 22" (*Notre Dame de la Garde*). Latitude 45° 32' N., longitude 58° 57' W. Should be *August 21*.

August 27 (near Cape Canso, Nova Scotia). Strike out sign indicating vessel sunk.

CHART TRACK OF "U-140"

"July 19" (U. S. S. *Harrisburg*). Latitude 45° 33' N., longitude 41° W. Should be *July 14*.

"July 19" (S. S. *Joseph Cudahy*). Latitude 41° 15' N., longitude 52° 18' W. Should be *July 18*.

July 26 (S. S. *British Major*). Approximately latitude 38° 42' N., longitude 60° 58' W. Change sign to indicate vessel attacked but not sunk.

July 30 (S. S. *Kermanshah*). Latitude 38° 24' N., longitude 68° 41' W. Change sign to indicate vessel attacked but not sunk.

August 10 (U. S. S. *Stringham*). Latitude 35° 51' N., longitude 73° 21' W. Change sign to indicate vessel attacked but not sunk.

August 13 (U. S. S. *Pastores*). Latitude 35° 30' N., longitude 69° 43' W. Change sign to indicate vessel attacked but not sunk.

"September 7" (S. S. *War Ranee*). Latitude 51° 27' N., longitude 33° 24' W. Should be *September 5*, and sign changed to indicate vessel attacked but not sunk.

CHART TRACK OF "U-117"

August 8 (S. S. *Sydland*). Latitude 41° 30' N., longitude 65° 22' W. Strike out sign indicating vessel sunk. Should be on chart track of *U-156*.

August 14 (schooner *Dorothy B. Barrett*). Latitude 38° 54' N., longitude 74° 24' W. Change sign to indicate vessel sunk.

August 15 (motor vessel *Madrugada*). Latitude 37° 50' N., longitude 74° 55' W. Change sign to indicate vessel sunk.

"August 22" (S. S. *Algeria*). Latitude 40° 30' N., longitude 68° 35' W. Should be *August 21*.

"August 25" (schooner *Bianca*). Latitude 43° 13' N., longitude 61° 05' W. Should be *August 24*.

CHART TRACK OF "U-155"

"August 28" (S. S. *Montoso*). Latitude 40° 19' N., longitude 32° 18' W. Should be *August 27*.

"September 11" (S. S. *Leixoes*). Latitude 42° 45' N., longitude 57° 37' W. Should be *September 12*, and sign indicating vessel sunk should be moved east to latitude 42° 45' N., longitude 51° 37' W.

October 17 (S. S. *Lucia*). Insert sign indicating vessel sunk in latitude 38° 05' N., longitude 50° 50' W.

CHART TRACK OF "U-152"

October 16. Strike out sign indicating vessel sunk, approximately latitude 38° 05' N., longitude 50° 50' W.

"October 18" (S. S. *Briarleaf*). Latitude 36° 05' N., longitude 49° 12' W. Should be *October 17*.

THE UNITED STATES NAVY'S FIRST U-BOAT CAPTURE.

German U-58 captured by the United States destroyers U. S. S. Fanning and U. S. S. Nicholson.

(Frontispiece.)

NAVY DEPARTMENT
OFFICE OF NAVAL RECORDS AND LIBRARY
HISTORICAL SECTION

Publication Number 1

GERMAN SUBMARINE ACTIVITIES ON THE ATLANTIC COAST OF THE UNITED STATES AND CANADA

Published under the direction of
The Hon. JOSEPHUS DANIELS, Secretary of the Navy

WASHINGTON
GOVERNMENT PRINTING OFFICE
1920

LIST OF ILLUSTRATIONS.

The United States Navy's first U-boat capture, German U-58 captured by the United States destroyers U. S. S. Fanning and U. S. S. Nicholson... Frontispiece.

	Facing page—
The Deutschland "Mercantile Submarine"	16
The Deutschland at Baltimore, Md. (Two prints)	16
The Deutschland at Baltimore, Md.	16
The Deutschland at New London, Conn.	16
The Deutschland leaving for Germany	16
German U-53 at Newport R. I. U. S. S. Birmingham in the background	16
German U-151 at sea. Taken from the deck of the American S. S. Pinar del Rio.	16
German U-151 at sea, from the Spanish passenger steamer Isabel de Bourbon.	16
The interior of a German submarine showing its instruments and high-powered engines.	32
Photographic copy of the receipt given to the master of the American schooner Hauppauge by Korvettenkapitan v. Nostitz.	32
Time fuse used on the American schooner Edna by U-151	32
Depth charge exploding	32
German submarine at sea	48
A German submarine lying near a ship which has just been boarded by the submarine's men	48
Smoke-screen defense	48
War on hospital ships	48
Receipt given to the master of the Norwegian S. S. San Jose by J. Knoeckel, Oberleutnant U-156	60
Receipt given to the master of the Swedish S. S. Sydland, by J. Knoeckel, Oberleutnant U-156	61
American steamship O. B. Jennings after her fire	80
German U-117 anchored at Washington, D. C., after the war. Used in the Victory loan campaign	80
German U-boat showing saw-teeth on the bow used for cutting nets	80
Sinking of American S. S. Frederick R. Kellogg	80
German U-155 (ex-Deutschland) as a war ship	96
Large gun mounted on U-155 (ex-Deutschland)	96
German U-155 (ex-Deutschland) after surrender anchored within the shadow of the famous Tower Bridge, London	96
U-155 (ex-Deutschland) after the war in the Thames near London	96
Survivors of the U. S. A. C. T. Lucia leaving the ship	112
Motor boat arriving alongside the U. S. S. Fairfax with a load of survivors from the U. S. A. C. T. Lucia	112
U. S. S. Ticonderoga	112
Type of U-boat which operated in American waters	112
Explosion of 450 pounds of T. N. T.	128
German and American submarines at Harwich, England	128
American tanker Herbert L. Pratt after being mined	128
Damage to the American tanker Herbert L. Pratt by mine explosion	128
U. S. S. San Diego	128
U. S. S. Minnesota	128
Damage to the U. S. S. Minnesota by mine explosion	128
Piece of the mine removed from the U. S. S. Minnesota after mine explosion	128

PREFACE.

The preparation of the data for this article has occupied the time of a large part of the personnel of the Historical Section of the Navy Department for several months.

It has been attended with great difficulties. The reports of the sightings of submarines have been without number, and great care has been exercised to try to corroborate or validate the reports, and all have been rejected which do not answer such conditions as to accuracy. It is believed to be strictly accurate with the information available at the present time.

The two charts accompanying the report, which were prepared through the kindness of the United States Hydrographic Office, are intended to show as clearly as possible the operations of the submarines. On Chart No. 1 are printed the tracks of all the operating vessels. On Chart No. 2 is shown the location of all the mine fields with the number of mines in the area covered and when and how they were removed or destroyed.

The information received as to the number of mines in each area and the reports of their destruction leave little or no doubt that the Atlantic coast is free from any danger as to mines.

C. C. MARSH,
Captain, U. S. Navy (retired),
Officer in Charge, Historical Section, Navy Department.

December 12, 1919.

GERMAN SUBMARINE ACTIVITIES ON THE ATLANTIC COAST OF THE UNITED STATES AND CANADA.

FOREWORD.

In defining in this article what should be considered as the American Atlantic coast, the meridian 40° west longitude is adopted arbitrarily to separate the submarine activities on the European coast from those on the American coast.

It is not believed necessary to go into the discussion based on opinions or surmises during the early years of the war in Europe as to whether or not an attack by the Germans would be made on the American coast. Therefore, the operations herein described are those which actually took place in the year 1918, with a description of the preliminary cruises made by the *Deutschland* and the *U-53* in the year 1916.

Of course, it must remain a matter, more or less, of conjecture as to what was actually the object of the cruises made by the *Deutschland* in 1916. Apparently they were both purely commercial voyages. The voyage of the *U-53* assumes more a character of a path-finding expedition. This vessel was a strictly combative vessel. It is interesting to note that on the arrival of this vessel at Newport, the commanding officer stated to the American submarine that he did not need or want a pilot to enter Newport, and that he wanted no supplies or provisions or materials of any kind.

In order to keep clear in the mind of the reader the dates and tracks of the several vessels, there is given here a condensed table of arrivals and departures.

Table showing arrivals and departures of German submarines off United States Atlantic coast or west of longitude 40°.

Name or number.	Left Germany.	Arrived off Atlantic coast or longitude W. 40°.	Left Atlantic coast.	Arrived Germany.
Deutschland (1st)	June 14, 1916	July 9, 1916	Aug. 1, 1916	Aug. 23, 1916.
U-53	About Sept. 20, 1916	Oct. 7, 1916	Oct. 7, 1916	Nov. 1, 1916.
Deutschland (2d)	Oct. 10, 1916	Nov. 1, 1916	Nov. 21, 1916	Dec. 10, 1916.
U-151	Apr. 14, 1918	May 15, 1918	July 1, 1918	Aug. 1, 1918.
U-156	About June 15, 1918.	July 5, 1918	Sept. 1, 1918	Struck mine in North Sea about Nov. 15, 1918; sunk.
U-140	About June 22, 1918.	July 14, 1918	....do............	Oct. 25, 1918.
U-117	July, 1918, first part	Aug. 8, 1918	....do............	In October, 1918, was towed in.
U-155 (formerly the Deutschland).	August, 1918, first part.	Sept. 7, 1918	Oct. 20, 1918	Nov. 15, 1918.
U-152	August, 1918, latter part.	Sept. 29, 1918	....do............	Do.
U-139	September, 1918, first part.	Did not get west of 43–40 N., 30–50 W.	Not on Atlantic coast.	Do.

The appended Chart No. 1 gives in detail the cruises of all these vessels. These tracks and all the data accompanying them are in accordance with all the data available at this time. It is possible that further data in the future will possibly require some corrections, but the main facts are correct.

There is, therefore, given in the following pages a brief account of the commercial cruises of the *Deutschland* and the preliminary cruise of the *U–53*, and somewhat at length, the cruises of all the submarines that operated off the American coast. The cruise of *U–139* is shown on the chart, but not referred to in the text, as she never got west of longitude 30–50 and therefore does not properly belong in the operations of the submarines off the United States Atlantic coast.

STEPS TAKEN BY THE NAVY DEPARTMENT TO PROTECT SHIPPING ALONG ATLANTIC SEABOARD.

Anticipating such attacks from German submarines, the Navy Department on February 1, 1918, appointed a special board to make recommendations as to the methods to be taken to provide for "defense against submarines in home waters." The report of the board, with certain alterations, was approved by the Chief of Naval Operations on March 6, 1918. (*Note:* Report in full of the special board, with alterations, will be found in the Appendix, page 143.) In accordance with the recommendations of this board, the following steps were taken:

1. *Submarines placed and ready to operate as soon as information received of enemy:*

   Colon.
   St. Thomas.
   Key West.
   Galveston.[1]
   Chesapeake.

   New York.
   Long Island area.
   Boston.
   Halifax.[1]

2. *Shipping:*
   (a) Shipping should be kept going with the least possible delay, at the same time taking all possible offensive measures to remove the danger.
   (b) Approach routes adopted for Atlantic seaboard for westbound ships. Now in force for New York, Delaware, Chesapeake, and being extended to whole seaboard, including Caribbean and Gulf.
   (c) Convoy lanes adopted and in force for all eastbound shipping. Aircraft escort convoys to 50-fathom curve and as far as possible beyond until dark. This escort is in addition to submarine chasers and destroyers.
   (d) Coasting trade to hug the coast, keeping within 5-fathom curve. Only smaller and less valuable ships placed in coastal service. Coastal protections to be handled by districts through which shipping passes.
   (e) Diversion of ships for entire Caribbean and Gulf coast. Shipping out of Gulf of Mexico to be routed north or south of Cuba as most expedient, depending on circumstances at time. Ships sail by day close in shore under protection patrol craft or at night by offshore diverted routes. Independent sailings to be adhered to unless situation becomes so acute as to warrant convoys.

---

[1] Not yet effective.

3. *War warnings:*
>Vested in Navy Department except such as require immediate action and are authentic. War warnings not to be given unless presumed to be authentic.

4. *District defense:*
>(a) Nets and defensive mine fields; no offensive mines.
>(b) Air patrol.
>(c) Listening stations on lightships and elsewhere. Submarine bells stopped.
>(d) Sweeping service at shipping points.
>(e) Limited escort offshore by chasers and nine destroyers retained for purpose.
>(f) Patrol craft at focal points to answer rescue calls.

5. *Intelligence Section:*
>Coast patrols have been organized and system of communications perfected to obtain information of enemy.
>
>Secret service has been expanded, particularly in Gulf and Caribbean areas, and Secret Service is in touch with British service.

6. *Wireless:*
>All route-giving officers in Europe have been instructed to warn all shipping approaching Atlantic seaboard not to use wireless for communicating instructions.

DISPATCHES FROM FORCE COMMANDER IN EUROPE.

The following dispatches from the force commander in Europe, arranged chronologically, gave the Navy Department necessary information to prepare for and meet the attacks which followed:

April 28, 1917.—With regard to submarines entering and leaving their bases, and their approximate whereabouts while operating, the Admiralty is able to maintain information that is fairly exact.

Of the thirty-four mine U-boats two for some days were not located, and the Admiralty was on the point of informing us of the probability of their being en route to the United States when their whereabouts were discovered. It is the Admiralty's belief now that at present none are likely to be sent over and that the present effort of the submarines which is successful will be kept up off the Channel entrance.

April 11, 1918 (No. 6352) (quoted in part).—The Department will be kept supplied with all information obtainable here as to the probability of hostile operations on home coast.

May 1, 1918 (7289).—Admiralty informs me that information from reliable agents states that a submarine of *Deutchland* type left Germany about nineteenth April to attack either American troop transports or ships carrying material from the States.

So far as known the Germans formed conclusions that: Nantucket Shoals and Sable Island direct to Europe.

Second: Material transports go from Newport News to a point south of Bermuda and then to Azores and thence to destination.

It is thought that the submarine is taking a northern route across Atlantic, average speed five knots.

None of new class of cruising submarines ready for service.

Admiralty experience with *Deutchland* class establishes following conclusions:

They generally operate a long distance from shore and seldom in less than one hundred fathoms.

Their single hulls are very vulnerable to depth-charge attack.

They rarely attack submerged.

There is but one known instance of attack against convoy and but two of torpedo attack against single vessels, one being unsuccessful. They attack by gun fire almost exclusively.

The most effective type to oppose them is the submarine.

They shift their operating area as soon as presence of submarine is discovered.

Admiralty requests Admiral Grant be given a copy of this cablegram.

May 15, 1918 (7289).—Information contained in this cable is given me by the British Admiralty and is necessarily somewhat paragraphed for transmission, but I have every reason to believe it is authentic. There appears to be a reasonable probability that the submarines in question may arrive off the United States coast at any time after May twentieth and that they will carry mines.

English experience indicates the favorite spot for laying mines to be the position in which merchant ships stop to pick up pilots. For instance, for Delaware Bay the pilots for large ships are picked up south of the Five Fathom Bank Light Vessel. This in our opinion is one of the most likely spots for a submarine to lay mines.

As regards information possessed by Germany on subject of antisubmarine patrol. They have from various neutral sources information that a patrol is maintained off most of the harbors and especially off Chesapeake Bay. A neutral has reported that the patrol extends as far as Cape Skerry.

It should be noted that except for mine laying, submarines of this class always work in deep water and that the Germans have laid mines in water in depths up to seventy fathoms. So far as is known there is no reason why they should not lay mines in depths up to ninety fathoms.

The foregoing completes the information furnished by British Admiralty. The following is added by me.

There are circumstances which render it highly important that nothing whatever should be given out which would lead the enemy even to surmise that we have had any advance information concerning this submarine, even in the event of our sinking her, and that such measures as are taken by the department be taken as secretly as possible and without public disclosure of the specific reasons.

I venture to remind the department in this connection that the employment of surface vessels to patrol against this submarine would probably result at best in merely driving her from one area to another, whereas the employment of submarines against her might lead to her destruction. It is suggested that having estimated her most probable areas of operation submarines be employed in a patrol as nearly stationary as may be, some of them covering the point south of Five Fathoms Bank Light Vessel, remaining submerged during the day with periscopes only showing. Of five submarines certainly destroyed in four days three were torpedoed by British submarines.

June 4, 1918—(9029).—It is practically certain that there is but one submarine on Atlantic coast, which is probably *U-151*.

June 7, 1918—(9120).—Military characteristics of *U-151* from latest Admiralty information as follows:

Length 213 feet 3 inches breadth 29 feet 2 inches surface draft 14 feet 9 inches displacement surface 1700 tons submerged 2100 tons Engine 1200 horsepower speed 11 knots and a half surface speed 8 knots submerged fuel stowage 250 tons including stowage in ballast tank, endurance surface 17,000 miles at 6 knots submerged 50 miles at 7 knots armament 2-5-9 guns two 22 pounders one machine gun six torpedo tubes 4 bow 2 stern complement 8 officers 65 men: *U-151* is converted mercantile submarine *Deutschland* type commander probably Lieutenant Commander Kophamel formerly in command of Pola submarine flotilla. In cruising last from September 10th to December 20th approximately *U-151* was out over 100 days during this period 9 steamers and 5 sailing vessels total 45,000 tons sunk by gunfire, about 400 ammunition carried for each gun, limited number of torpedoes carried—maximum of 12. Submarine may be equipped to carry and lay about 40 mines.

June 29, 1918—(357).—Second cruiser submarine at sea. At present off west coast of Ireland. Her field of operation not yet known. Can not reach longitude of Nantucket before July fifteenth. Shall keep Department informed.

July 5, 1918—(655, our 357).—Enemy cruiser submarine outward bound, reported July 4 about 45 N. 30 W. proceeding southwesterly.

July 24, 1918.—Admiralty has received reliable information indicating that *U–156* is intended to operate in Gulf of Maine but if foggy there to shift operations off Delaware.

July 26, 1918.—Admiralty report on reliable authority that harbor works, cranes, etc., at Wilmington are considered by Germans as favorable objectives for bombardment. This and other similar information is transmitted for such use as the department can make of it although apparently of not very great value.

August 1, 1918.—It is considered probable by Admiralty that a new mine-laying type submarine is on its way to American coast, and that possibly she is the one engaged by S. S. *Baron Napier* on July 26th in lat. 45–26 N. long. 32–56 W. at 0838. It is estimated this submarine can reach longitude Nantucket Lightship August 2nd. It is said that this type is a great improvement over *U–71–80*, larger than ordinary U-boats and carries following armament: One six-inch gun, one four-inch gun, two anti-aircraft guns, forty-fives. Also carries torpedoes but number of tubes unknown.

August 6, 1918.—Following cable received by British commander in chief "As submarines reported western Atlantic are at present between New York and Chesapeake Bay area, vessels from U K below speed 13 knots are being routed north of area if bound New York, south if bound Chesapeake Bay and north or south if bound Delaware Bay latter being sent by X or Z routes respectively if necessary and then hug coast. Latter case will be specified in report sent in accordance with paragraph 8 approaching routes." As the agreement with Navy Department is that after general plans meet with joint approval, we will handle the diversion routes at this end for westbound ships, this cable does not accord. It happens in this particular case to route ships direct through area of operations of the only two submarines at present on this coast. British C.-in-C. concurs in general scheme that westbound diversion better be handled from this end.

August 7, 1918.—We feel so certain that mine-laying submarine will operate in Vineyard Sound and Nantucket Sound August 10 that counter measures in mining are recommended.

August 9, 1918.—Admiralty informs that two converted mercantile type submarines will probably leave Germany middle of August for American coast. One of them will probably lay mines east of Atlantic City and Currituck. The other off St. Johns, Newfoundland, Western Bay, Newfoundland and Halifax. These submarines estimated to reach American waters about second week of September.

August 10, 1918.—Return routes of submarine now on American coast expected to be somewhat as follows: Submarine off Cape Hatteras at present by same return route as *U–151*. Submarine off Halifax at present approximately along parallel 44 north from longitude Halifax to about 50 degrees west. Mine-laying submarine after laying her mines expected to operate between Cape Race and Halifax.

September 2, 1918.—Return route of mine-laying submarine now off American coast expected somewhat as follows: Vicinity Cape Race through an approximate position 54 degrees north 27 degrees west.

September 9, 1918.—S. S. *Monmouth* reports that on September 7th she was chased in about 43.00 north 45.50 west. Should this report prove reliable submarine would be one of two converted mercantile type which were expected to sail from Germany about the middle of August and she could reach the American coast about September 15th. It is known that the other had not left Germany on September 2nd.

September 16, 1918.—*U–152* believed to be proceeding to America, appears to have been submarine which sunk Danish S. V., *Constanza* 62.30 N. 0.35 W. at 1400 September 11. She is expected to operate to southward of steamer route and lay mines east Atlantic City and southeast Currituck. It is estimated she can reach longitude Nantucket first week October.

October 3, 1918.—Not for circulation. It appears that *U–152* was in about 44 degrees north 39 degrees west, *September 30th* and is not likely therefore to reach longitude Nantucket before about October 12th. Evidently *U–159* was submarine which sunk two ships by gunfire in about 45.30 north 11.00 west October 1st and is therefore not proceeding America at present. Her commanding officer Arnauld de la Periere is firm believer in attack by gunfire.

In addition to the above dispatches the following letter from the force commander in Europe was received.

U. S. NAVAL FORCES OPERATING IN EUROPEAN WATERS,
U. S. S. "MELVILLE," FLAGSHIP,
30 Grosvenor Gardens, London, S. W., April 30, 1918.

Reference No. 01. 16416.
From: Commander, U. S. Naval Forces in European Waters.
To: Secretary of the Navy (Operations).
Subject: Areas of Operations of Enemy Submarines.
Reference: (*a*) My cable #6352 of 11 April.

1. *Submarines along Atlantic seaboard.*—Since the beginning of submarine warfare it has been possible for the enemy to send a submarine to the Atlantic seaboard to operate against allied shipping. The danger to be anticipated in such a diversion is not in the number of ships that would be sunk, but in the interruption and delays of shipping due to the presence of a submarine unless plans are ready in advance to meet such a contingency.

A more serious feature is that the department might be led to reconsider its policy of sending antisubmarine craft abroad. It is quite possible for the enemy to send one or more submarines to the Atlantic seaboard at any time. The most likely type of submarine to be used for such operations would be the cruiser submarine.

2. *Cruiser submarine.*—At the present time there are only 7 cruiser submarines completed. All of these are of the *ex-Deutschland* type, designed originally as cargo cruisers and now used to assist in the submarine campaign. Ten others of greater speed have been projected, but none have been completed, and the latest information indicates that the work on these vessels is not being pushed. This is rather to be expected owing to the small amount of damage done thus far by cruiser submarines. These submarines sink only 30,000 to 40,000 tons of shipping in a four-months' cruise.

3. Cruiser submarines now in service make only about $11\frac{1}{2}$ knots on the surface, with perhaps a maximum of 7 knots submerged. They handle poorly under water and probably can not submerge to any considerable depth. On account of their large size they are particularly vulnerable to attack by enemy submarines. It is probably for this reason that the cruiser submarine has always operated in areas well clear of antisubmarine craft. If this type of vessel proceeded to the Atlantic seaboard it would undoubtedly operate well offshore and shift its areas of operations frequently. Thus far, with one exception, which occurred a few days ago, the cruiser submarine has never attacked convoys and has never fired torpedoes in the open sea, although vessels of this type have been operating for 10 months. All attacks have been by gunfire, and as these cruiser submarines are slow, they can attack with success only small, slow, poorly armed ships.

4. If cruiser submarines are sent to the North Atlantic seaboard no great damage to shipping is to be anticipated. Nearly all shipping eastbound is in convoy and it is unlikely that any appreciable number of convoys will be sighted, and if sighted will probably not be attacked. The shipping westbound is independent, but is scattered over such a wide area that the success of the cruiser submarine would not be large, and war warnings would soon indicate areas to be avoided.

[NOTE.—Later evidence indicates two cases of attack against single ships; in one case the vessel was struck and the other missed by two torpedoes.—Wm. S. S.]

5. As there are only 7 cruiser submarines built, we are able to keep very close track of these ships. At the present time one of these vessels is operating off the west coast of Spain, en route home, two are in the vicinity of the Canaries, one is in the North Sea bound out, and three are in Germany overhauling. I have the positions of all of these cruiser submarines checked regularly, with the idea of anticipating a cruise of any of these vessels to America. These vessels are frequently in wireless communication with one another, as well as with the small submarines, and they receive messages regularly from Nauen. Their attacks against ships furnish an additional method of checking their positions, and I hope that we will be able to keep an accurate chart of all the cruiser submarines, so as to be able to warn the department considerably in advance of any probable cruise of these vessels out of European waters. At the moment the only one that might cross the ocean is the one now coming out of the North Sea, as the other three have been out too long to make a long cruise likely.

6. *Small submarines.*—There is greater danger to be anticipated from the small submarine—that is, submarines of a surface displacement not exceeding about 800 tons. These vessels can approach focal areas with a fair degree of immunity, and can attack convoys or single ships under most circumstances. The number of torpedoes carried by these vessels is small, however, not exceeding 10 or 12, and the damage by gunfire would not be serious except to slow, poorly armed ships.

7. There seems little likelihood, however, that small submarines will be sent to the Atlantic seaboard. These vessels would have to steam nearly 6,000 miles additional before arriving at their hunting ground. This would mean a strain on the crew, difficulty of supplies and fuel (although their cruising radius is sufficient), absence from wireless information, liability to engine breakdown, unfamiliarity with American coast, and so forth, all for a small result on arriving on the Atlantic seaboard.

8. The small submarines at present operating around the United Kingdom can discharge their torpedoes and start home after about 10 days' operations. In one case, *U-53*, which is considered a remarkably efficient submarine, exhausted all torpedoes after 4 days' operations in the English Channel.

9. It is certain that if the enemy transfers his submarine attack in any strength to America the submarine campaign will be quickly defeated. The enemy is having difficulty in maintaining in operation under present conditions any considerable number of small submarines. The average number around the United Kingdom at any time does not exceed about 10. The number is not constant but seems to be greater during periods of full moon.

10. *Declared zones.*—If submarines are to operate regularly on the Atlantic seaboard, it is quite probable that the enemy will make a public declaration extending the present barred zones. Public declarations were made January 31, 1917, setting limits to the barred zone and these were extended by proclamation on November 22, 1917; January 8, 1918; January 11, 1918.

The barred zone around the Azores was declared in November, 1917, but a cruiser submarine operated in the vicinity during June, July, and August, 1917. The barred zone around the Cape de Verde Islands was declared January 8, 1918, but a cruiser submarine was operating off Dakar and in the Cape de Verde Islands in October and November, 1917.

It is evident that the enemy might at any time, without warning, send a submarine to the Atlantic seaboard; but for repeated operations there he would probably declare a barred zone. The declaring of such a zone open to ruthless warfare would weaken all the arguments used to justify the declaring of zones in European waters. We know that the enemy would produce arguments if the military advantage warranted, but the advantage of operations in America should prove so small as not to justify the embarrassment in extending the barred zone.

11. *Future submarine operations.*—The enemy is working on a new type of cruiser submarine with a speed of about 17 knots and the same battery as the *Deutschland* type. It is doubtful if this type of vessel will be handy under water and it is assumed that the bulk of her work will be done by gunfire.

Convoys escorted by cruisers would have little to fear from this type of submarine; but slow vessels poorly armed would be at a disadvantage. There is some doubt, however, as to whether a convoy of vessels, even without a cruiser escort, would not make it interesting for the submarine. Altogether the type is not greatly to be feared; but it is realized that this type of vessel would have considerable advantage over the present *Deutschland* type of cruiser submarine.

12. Around the United Kingdom the small submarine seems to be committed, for the present, at least, to inshore operations.

In February of 1917 there were some 30 sinkings to the westward of the 10th meridian, extending as far as the 16th meridian; but in February of this year there were no sinkings west of the 8th meridian. In March, 1917, there were 40 sinkings west of the 10th meridian, extending as far as the 18th meridian, but in March, 1918, there were no sinkings west of the 8th meridian. In April, 1917, there were 82 sinkings west of the 10th meridian, extending to the 19th meridian, while in April, 1918, practically all of the sinkings have been east of the 8th meridian, there being only 4 sinkings west of this meridian, operations not extending beyond the 12th meridian. So far as can be ascertained the enemy are concentrating efforts on building submarines of about 550 tons surface displacement.

13. The changes of areas in which submarines operate have undoubtedly been brought about by the introduction of the convoy system. Submarines operating well to the westward have small chance of finding convoys and have the disadvantage of having to attack convoys under escort if found. By confining their operations to areas near shore submarines enjoy the advantage of always having a considerable quantity of shipping in sight, as well as of finding many opportunities either by day or night to attack ships that are not under escort or in convoy. This is necessarily so, as there is a considerable coasting trade, cross-channel trade, and numbers of ships proceeding to assembly ports, all of which sailings are either unescorted or poorly escorted, and the submarine finds many opportunities for attack without subjecting himself to the danger that he would encounter in attacking escorted convoys.

14. It is hoped during summer weather to make a wider use of aircraft and small surface craft to protect coastal waters. Whether results will be successful enough to drive the submarine farther offshore remains to be seen. Every indication at present seems to point to the submarines continuing their operations near the coast.

15. The convoy system has given us a double advantage:

(*a*) It has brought the submarine closer in shore, where more means are available for attacking it.

(*b*) It has given protection and confidence to shipping at sea and made the submarine expose himself to considerable risk of destruction in case he elects to attack a convoy.

There are many indications that the submarine does not relish the idea of attacking convoys unless the escort is a weak one or a favorable opportunity presents itself through straggling ships or otherwise. About 90 per cent of the attacks delivered by submarines are delivered against ships that are not in convoy.

16. *Department's policy.*—I fully concur in the department's present policy, namely, retaining on the Atlantic seaboard only the older and less effective destroyers, together with a number of submarine chasers and the bulk of our submarines. The submarine campaign will be defeated when we minimize the losses in European waters. If the enemy voluntarily assists us by transferring his operations to the Atlantic seaboard his defeat will come the sooner.

17. There is always the likelihood that a submarine may appear off the American coast. In the same manner, and this would be fully as embarrassing, submarines may begin operations west of the 20th meridian. The losses from all such operations must be accepted. We are certain that they will be small, and will not, for many reasons, be regularly carried on.

18. I see nothing in the submarine situation to-day to warrant any change in the present policy of the department. The situation is not as serious as it was a year ago at this time. The Allies are getting better defensive measures and are increasing offensive measures against the submarine, many of which are meeting with success. The help of the U. S. Navy has materially aided in defeating the submarine campaign. Present information indicates that we are at least holding our own with the submarine, and that submarine construction is slowing down rather than speeding up. During the first quarter of 1918 we sank 21 enemy submarines, and the best information indicates that not more than 17 new boats are commissioned. With the coming of better weather it is hoped that the situation will further improve.

19. There seems no sound reason for assuming that the enemy will transfer operations to the Atlantic seaboard, except possibly in the case of the cruiser submarines. These vessels have thus far done little damage to shipping, and it might prove good strategy to send them to our coast. In any event no great danger is to be anticipated from the present type of cruiser submarine, and adequate steps can be taken to deal with these vessels if they arrive on the Atlantic seaboard.

20. This letter was prepared prior to the dispatch of my cable No. 7289 of May 1.

THE DEUTSCHLAND.

The German submarine *Deutschland*, the first cargo-carrying U-boat, left Bremen with a cargo of chemicals and dyestuffs on June 14, 1916, and shaped her course for Heligoland, where she remained for nine days for the purpose, so her captain, Paul Koenig, stated, of throwing the enemy off the scent if by any means he should have learned what was being attempted.

The *Deutschland* was manned by a crew of 8 officers and 26 men—the captain, 3 deck officers, 4 engineer officers, 6 quartermasters, 4 electricians, 14 engineers, 1 steward and 1 cook.

Because of the danger by way of the English Channel, which was heavily netted, Capt. Koenig laid his course around the north of Scotland, and it was while he was in the North Sea that most of the submergence of the *Deutschland* (about 90 miles in all) took place. Usually the U-boat traveled on the surface, but on sighting any suspicious ship she would immediately submerge, occasionally using her periscopes. According to Capt. Koenig's account, she was submerged to the bottom and remained for several hours.

The *Deutschland* resembled the typical German U-boat, but carried no torpedo tubes or guns. Her hull was cigar-shaped, cylindrical structure, which extends from stem to stern. Inclosing the hull was a lighter false hull, which was perforated to permit the entrance and exit of water and was so shaped as to give the submarine a fairly good ship model for diving at full speed on the surface and at a lesser speed submerged. The dimensions and some of the characteristics of the *Deutschland* were as follows: Length, 213 feet 3 inches;

beam, inner hull, about 17 feet; beam, outer hull, 29 feet 2 inches; depth, about 24 feet; depth to top of conning tower, about 35 feet; draft (loaded), 16 to 17 feet; displacement, light, 1,800 tons—submerged, 2,200 tons. Speed on the surface, 12 to 14 knots per hour—submerged, $7\frac{1}{2}$ knots; fuel oil capacity, 150 tons normal, and maximum 240 tons.

At $7\frac{1}{2}$ knots per hour she could remain submerged for 8 hours; at $3\frac{1}{2}$ knots per hour, 40 hours; at $1\frac{1}{2}$ knots per hour, 96 hours. Cargo capacity, about 750 tons. The *Deutschland* was equipped with two vertical inverted, four-cycle, single-acting, nonreversible, air-starting engines of 600 horsepower each; Deisel, Krupp type; diameter of cylinders, about 17 inches; shaft, about 6 inches.

She had two periscopes of the housing type, one in the conning tower and one offset, forward of the conning tower. Her electric batteries consisted of 280 cells in two batteries of 140 cells each. There were two motors on each shaft, each motor being 300 horsepower. She was fully equipped with radio apparatus, installed in a sound-proof room. The radio set was in forward trimming station. Two hollow masts were used, height about 43 feet above the deck; length of antenna, about 160 feet. Masts were hinged and housed in recesses in starboard superstructure. They were raised by means of a special motor and drum.

The interior of the cylindrical hull was divided by four transverse bulkheads into five separate water-tight compartments. Compartment No. 1 at the bow contained the anchor cables and electric winches for handling the anchor; also general ship stores and a certain amount of cargo. Compartment No. 2 was given up entirely to cargo. Compartment No. 3, which was considerably larger than any of the others, contained the living quarters of the officers and crew. At the after end of this compartment and communicating with it was the conning tower. Compartment No. 4 was given up entirely to cargo. Compartment No. 5 contained the propelling machinery, the two heavy oil engines, and the two electric motors. The storage batteries were carried in the bottom of the boat, below the living compartment. For purposes of communication, a gangway 2 feet 6 inches wide by 6 feet high was built through each cargo compartment, thus rendering it possible for the crew to pass entirely from one end of the boat to the other. The freeboard to the main deck ran the full length of the boat and was about $5\frac{1}{2}$ to 6 feet wide.

The cockpit at the top of the conning tower was about 15 feet above the water, there being a shield in front so shaped as to throw the wind and spray upward and clear of the face of the quartermaster or other observer. The forward wireless mast carried a crow's nest for the lookout.

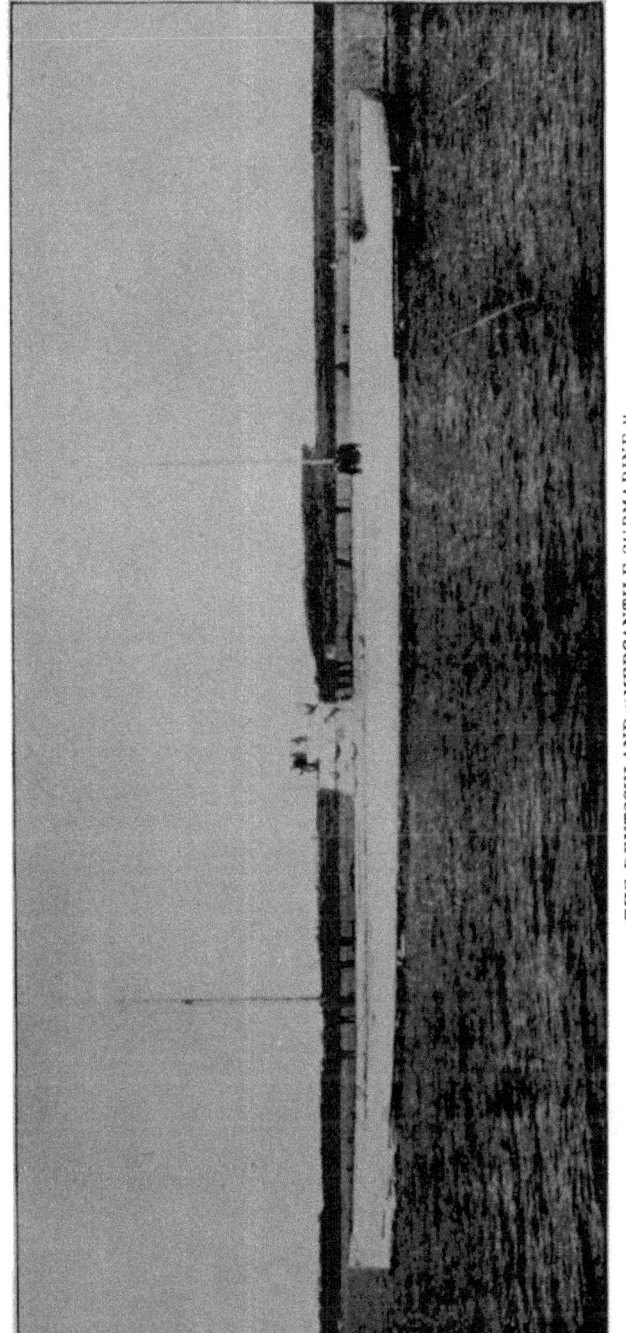

THE DEUTSCHLAND "MERCANTILE SUBMARINE."
(Page 15.)

THE DEUTSCHLAND AT BALTIMORE, MD.

(Page 17.)

THE DEUTSCHLAND AT BALTIMORE, MD.

(Page 17.)

THE DEUTSCHLAND AT NEW LONDON, CONN.
(Page 17.)

THE DEUTSCHLAND LEAVING FOR GERMANY.

(Page 17.)

GERMAN U-53 AT NEWPORT, R. I. U. S. S. BIRMINGHAM IN THE BACKGROUND.
(Page 18)

GERMAN U-151 AT SEA.

Taken from the deck of the American S. S. Pinar del Rio.

GERMAN U-151 AT SEA.
Taken from the Spanish passenger steamer Isabel de Bourbon.

The *Deutschland* made a safe passage through the North Sea, avoiding the British patrols. The rest of the trip was made principally on the surface. The weather was fine throughout. When off the Virginia Capes she submerged for a couple of hours because of two ships sighted of doubtful appearance. She passed through the Capes on July 9, 1916, at 1 o'clock a. m., and as she left Helgoland on June 23, the time of her trip was 16 days. The *Deutschland* arrived at Baltimore, Md., on Sunday, July 9, 1916. The total distance from Bremen to Baltimore by the course sailed was about 3,800 miles. Her cargo consisted of 750 tons of dyestuffs and chemicals, valued at about $1,000,000, and which was discharged at Baltimore.

The *Deutschland* remained at Baltimore 23 days and took on cargo for her return trip—a lot of crude rubber in bulk, 802,037 pounds, value $568,854.84; nickel, 6,739 bags, 3 half bags, weight 752,674 pounds, value $376,337; tin in pig, 1,785 pigs, weight 181,049 pounds, value $108,629.40. Goods were billed to Bremen and no consignee was stated.

She left Baltimore on August 1, 1916, and arrived at the mouth of the Weser River at 3 p. m., August 23, 1916. "The Berliner Tageblat," of August 24, 1918, said:

> The voyage was at the beginning stormy; later on was less rough. There was much fog on the English coast, and the North Sea was stormy. The ship proved herself an exceedingly good seagoing vessel. The engines worked perfectly, without interruption. Forty-two hundred (4,200) sea miles were covered, one hundred (100) under water.

She was made ready and reloaded with another cargo of dyestuffs and chemicals for her second voyage to the United States within a week. Her health certificate was issued by the American vice consul at Bremen on September 30, 1916. She was ready to go to sea again on October 1, 1916, but was held until October 10, 1916, for possible word concerning the *Bremen*. The last voyage to the United States covered 21 days, being somewhat retarded by hard weather. She arrived at New London, Conn., on November 1, 1916; discharged her cargo of dyestuffs and chemicals and, in addition, securities said to be to the value of 1,800,000 pounds sterling. Her return cargo was said to contain nickel and copper; 360 tons of crude nickel which had come from Sudbury, Canada, and had been purchased in 1914.

She left New London, Conn., on November 17, 1916, but half a mile from Race Rock Light in Block Island Sound, R. I., where the tide runs heavily, she rammed the American Steamship *T. A. Scott, Jr.*, gross 36 tons, which sank in about three minutes. On account of the collision the *Deutschland* had to return to New London for repairs. She again left New London on November 21, 1916. Her voyage occupied 19 days, arriving at the mouth of the Weser on December 10, 1916.

Some time after her return to Germany she was converted into warship and furnished with torpedo tubes and two 5.9-inch gu Her war activities were continued as *U-155*.

The *Deutschland* as the *U-155* left Germany about May 24, 19 and operated principally off the west coast of Spain, north of Azores, and between the Azores and the Madeira Islands; then und the command of Lieut. Commander Meusel, on a cruise which last 103 days, during which she sank 11 steamers and 8 sailing vesse with a total tonnage of 53,267 gross tons.

She attacked by gunfire the American Steamship *J. L. Luckenba* 4,920 gross tons, on June 13, 1917, at 7.15 p. m., in latitude 44° longitude 18° 05' W., but the ship escaped.

Among the sailing vessels sunk was the American schooner *Jc Twohy*, 1,019 tons gross, which was sunk by bombs placed aboa after her capture about 120 miles south of Ponta Delgada and proximately in latitude 35° 55' N., longitude 23° 20' W., on July 1917, at 6 a. m.

Also the American bark *Christiane*, 964 tons gross, was sunk bombs placed on board after her capture off the Azores and proximately in latitude 37° 40' N., and longitude 20° 40' W., August 7, 1917, at 6 p. m. She returned to Germany about S tember 4, 1917.

The *Deutschland* again left Germany about January 16, 1918 Commander Eckelmann apparently having succeeded Lieut. Co mander Meusel—on a cruise which lasted about 108 days, dur which time she sank 10 steamers and 7 sailing vessels, with a to gross tonnage of 50,926 tons, viz, 2 British steamers (armed) Italian steamers (armed), 2 Norwegian and 1 Spanish stean (unarmed), 4 British, 2 Portuguese, and 1 Spanish sailing yess From the Norwegian Steamship *Wagadesk*, which was captured a afterwards sunk, she took 45 tons of brass, which she took back Germany. During the cruise she operated between the Azores a Cape Vincent off the coast of Spain, and the entrance to the Stra of Gibraltar.

She returned to Germany about May 4, 1918.

In August, 1918, she began her famous cruise on the Americ coast.

VISIT OF THE GERMAN SUBMARINE U–53 TO NEWPOR R. I., OCTOBER 7, 1916.

On October 7, 1916, between the two visits of the German comm cial submarine *Deutschland* to the United States, the German st marine *U-53* entered the port of Newport, R. I., under the comma of Lieut. Hans Rose.

At 2 p. m. October 7 a code message was received from the U. S. submarine *D-2*, stating that a German man-of-war submarine was standing in. A few minutes later a German submarine was sighted entering the harbor of Newport. The submarine was first sighted 3 miles east of Point Judith, standing toward Newport, and the *D-2* approached and paralleled her course to convoy the German submarine while in sight of land. Upon arrival at Brenton Reef Lightship, the captain of the German submarine requested permission from *D-2* to enter port, which permission was granted by the *D-2*. The German captain stated that he did not need a pilot. The *D-2* convoyed the submarine into Newport Harbor. She was flying the German man-of-war ensign and the commission pennant and carrying two guns in a conspicuous position.

Upon approaching the anchorage the *U-53*, through the captain of the U. S. *D-2*, signaled the U. S. S. *Birmingham*, Rear Admiral Albert Gleaves commanding, requesting to be assigned to a berth. She was assigned to Berth No. 1, where she anchored at 2.15 p. m.

The commandant of the naval station, Narragansett Bay, R. I., sent his aide alongside to make the usual inquiries, but with instructions not to go on board, as no communication had yet been had with the health authorities. At 3 p. m. the commanding officer of the *U-53*, Lieut. Hans Rose, went ashore in a boat which he requested and which was furnished by the U. S. S. *Birmingham*. He called on the commandant of the Narragansett Bay Naval Station. He was in the uniform of a lieutenant in the German Navy, wearing the iron cross; and he stated, with apparent pride, that his vessel was a man-of-war armed with guns and torpedoes. He stated that he had no object in entering the port except to pay his respects; that he needed no supplies or assistance, and that he proposed to go to sea at 6 o'clock. He stated also that he left Wilhelmshaven 17 days before, touching at Heligoland.

The collector of customs located at Providence, R. I., telephoned and asked for information as to the visit of the German submarine, and when told that she intended to sail at 6 p. m., he stated that under the circumstances it not be practicable for either him or a quarantine officer to visit the ship.

Following the visit of the captain, the commandant sent his aide to return the call of the captain of the *U-53* and to request that no use be made of the radio apparatus of the vessel in port.

The submarine was boarded by the aide to the commandant, and immediately afterwards the commander of destroyer force's staff. In reply to inquiry the following information was obtained.

The vessel was the German *U-53*, Kapitan Lieut. Hans Rose in command. The *U-53* sailed from Wilhelmshaven and was 17 days out. No stores or provisions were required and that the *U-53* proposed to sail about sundown on the same day; that the trip had been made without incident, on the surface, and had passed to the northward of the Shetland Islands and along the coast of Newfoundland.

The following of interest was noted: Length above the water, about 212 feet; two Deisel Nürnberg engines, each of 1,200 horsepower; each engine had six cylinders; maximum speed, 15 knots; submerged speed, 9 to 11 knots.

The captain stated with pride that the engines were almost noiseless and made absolutely no smoke except when first starting. She had four 18-inch torpedo tubes, two in the bow and two in the stern; the tubes were charged and four spare torpedoes were visible. Each pair of tubes was in a horizontal plane. They could carry 10 torpedoes, but part of the torpedo stowage space was utilized to carry extra provisions. The torpedoes were short and they said their range was 2,000 yards. The guns were mounted on the deck, one forward and one aft. The forward gun looked to be about 4-inch and the after one about 3-inch—short and light. The muzzles were covered and water-tight. They had vertical sliding wedge breechblocks, with a gasket covering cartridge chamber water-tight. They carried a permanent sight with peephole and cross wires, and on it was a receptacle evidently to take a sighting telescope. The steel deflection and elevation scales, cap squares, etc., were considerably rusted. The guns were permanently mounted on the deck and did not fold down. A gyro compass with repeaters was installed. The control seemed to be similar to that of the American submarines. There were three periscopes, which could be raised or lowered, and the platform on which the control officer stood moved with the periscope; one was about 15 feet high above the deck and the others several feet lower. One of the periscopes led to the compartment forward of the engine room for the use of the chief engineer and the third was a periscope for aeroplanes. There was stowage space for three months' supplies of all kinds. The complement consisted of the captain, the executive and navigating officer, ordnance officer, engineer, electrical and radio officer, and crew of 33 men. The officers were in the regulation uniform, new and natty in appearance. The crew wore heavy blue woolen knit sweaters, coats and trousers of soft, thin black leather lined with thin cloth, top boots and the regular blue flat cap. They were freshly shaved or with neatly close-trimmed beard or hair, all presenting a very neat appearance.

All the electrical machinery and appliances were manufactured by the Siebert Schuman Co., except the small motor generator, taking current from storage batteries and supplying electric lights which gave excellent illumination throughout the boat, and there was no trace of foul air anywhere.

The radio sending and receiving apparatus was in a small separate room on the starboard side. The radio generator was on the port side in the engine room.

There were two antennæ—one consisted of two wires, one on each side about three-eighths of an inch in diameter, extending from the deck at the bow to the deck at the stern and up over supporting stanchions above the conning tower, with heavy porcelain insulators about 4 or 5 feet from deck at each end and from each side of the supporting stanchions. The other was an ordinary three-wire span suspended between the masts and was about 3 feet high on the starboard side. These masts were about 25 feet high and mounted outboard over the whaleback; were tapered, of smooth surface, hinged at the heel, each with a truss built out about 3 feet near the heel for leverage, to which secured, and from which led through guide sheaves along the side, a galvanized one-half inch wire rope for raising and lowering. The masts were hinged to lie along the top of the outer surface along starboard close to the vertical side plate of the superstructure. They claimed to have a receiving range of 2,000 miles.

A flush wood deck, about 10 feet wide amidships, extended the entire length. This was built of sections about 2 inches thick, each about 30 inches square and secured to the supporting steel framework by bolts. Each section had several holes about $2\frac{1}{2}$ inches by 4 inches cut through to allow passage of the water. The sides of the superstructure framework were inclosed by thin steel plates reaching nearly to the hull. The inner body of the hull was divided into six watertight compartments. They had very little beam and suggested that a large amount of available space was devoted to oil storage.

There were three main hatchways—one from the conning tower to the central station, one into the forward living space, and the other into the after living space.

Patent anchors were housed in fitted recesses in the hull just above the torpedo tubes. Electric motor-driven anchor chain winch outside the hull under the bow superstructure. There was a galvanized-wire towing hawser about $1\frac{1}{4}$ inches in diameter, shackled to the nose leading aft along the port side of the hull, stoppered on with a small wire, to the port side of the conning tower, so that the heaving line fastened to its end could be hove from the conning tower. They had a small electric galley with coppers, etc. Small room for the commanding officer amidships forward of the central; officers' room farther forward of same. Two-tier bunks about 18 inches wide for about half the crew in two other compartments. Hammocks for about half the crew. Small wash room nicely fitted and a toilet for the officers and another for the crew. The life buoys had a cork sphere, about 10 inches in diameter, attached by a long small line.

The vessel appeared very orderly and clean throughout. It was especially noticeable that no repair work whatever was in progress. All hands, except officers and men showing visitors through the boat, were on deck, where the crew were operating a small phonograph. The engineer officer said that *U–53* was built that year, 1916.

The captain stated that he would be pleased to have any officer visit his ship and would show them around. This privilege was taken advantage of by a number of officers from the destroyer force, and the aid to the commandant. All the officers who visited the ship were much impressed by the youthfulness of the personnel, their perfect physical condition, and their care-free attitude. One or two observers thought that the captain seemed serious and rather weary, but all agreed that the other officers and the crew seemed entirely happy and gave no indication that they considered themselves engaged in any undertaking involving hazard or responsibility. The freedom with which the officers and crew conversed with visitors and their willingness to show all parts of the ship was surprising. They stated that they were willing to tell all that they knew and to show all they had, this to officers and civilians alike.

The officers spoke our tongue with careful correctness, though not fluently, and answered all questions except when asked their names, which they courteously declined to give. When one officer was asked by one of the visiting officers whether he spoke English, he replied, "No; I speak American." All hands were very military in deportment, and whenever a man moved on duty he went with a run! As the boat entered and left the harbor, the crew was lined up on deck, at attention, facing vessels they passed. Upon leaving, they faced about and after passing and saluting the destroyer tender *Melville*, the officers and crew waved their caps to the last destroyer as they passed. The *U–53* got under way at 5.30 p. m. and stood out to sea. It was learned that a letter to the German Ambassador at Washington was entrusted to a newspaper representative and by him was posted.

On October 8, 1916, the day after leaving Newport, the *U–53* captured and sunk the following vessels off the coast of the United States, viz:

The British S. S. *Stephano*, 3,449 tons gross, 2½ miles E. by NE. of Nantucket Light Vessel. The *Stephano* had American passengers aboard.

The British S. S. *Strathmore*, 4,321 tons gross, 2 miles S. by E. from Nantucket Light Vessel.

The British S. S. *West Point*, 3,847 tons gross, 46 miles SE. by E. from Nantucket Light Vessel.

The Dutch S. S. *Blommersdijk*, 4,850 tons gross.

The Norwegian S. S. *Chr. Knudsen*, 4,224 tons gross.

It was thought possible that the *U-53* was accompanied by one or two other U-boats, as other U-boats marked *U-48* and *U-61* were reported. It is, however, likely that the report of three submarines was due to Capt. Rose's having his number "U-53" painted out and substituting other numbers. He did this on four separate occasions and finally came into Germany about November 1 under the number "U-61."

THE CRUISE OF THE U-151.

The *U-151* [2], a converted mercantile submarine of the *Deutschland* type, commanded by Kapitan Van Nostitiz und Janckendorf, sailed from Kiel on April 14, 1918. Although her route to the American Atlantic coast is not definitely known, it is probable that she followed the more or less recognized path later taken by other enemy cruiser submarines to and from America.[3] The *U-151* was first located early in May, when the office of Naval Operations, Washington, D. C., received the following message from Kingston, Jamaica:

U. S. steamer engaged enemy submarine 2 May, 1918, lat. 46° N., long. 28° W.[4]

The position indicated by this message was a point about 400 miles north of the Azores.

On May 15, 1918, the British steamer *Huntress*, 4,997 gross tons, bound for Hampton Roads, reported that she had escaped a torpedo attack made by an enemy submarine in latitude 34° 28' N., longitude 56° 09' W.[5]

These reports were considered authentic. All section bases were ordered to be on the alert, and the following message was broadcasted by the Navy Department on May 16, 1918:

Most secret.—From information gained by contact with enemy submarine, one may be encountered anywhere west of 40 degrees west. No lights should be carried, except as may be necessary to avoid collision and paravanes should be used when practicable and feasible. Acknowledge, Commander in Chief Atlantic Fleet, Commander Cruiser Force, Commander Patrol Squadron, Flag *San Domingo*, Governor Virgin Islands, Commandants 1st to 8th, inclusive, and 15th Naval Districts. 13016.OPNAV.

The first definite information of the activity of the German raider off the American coast was received by radio on May 19 at 12.14 p. m. The Atlantic City radio intercepted an S O S from the American steamship *Nyanza*, 6,213 gross tons, advising that she was being gunned and giving her position as latitude 38° 21' N., longitude 70°

---

[2] The Germans classified their submarines in three general groups: The U or ocean-going type, the UB, or coastal type, and the UC, or mine-laying type. The classification UD was made by the British Ad. miralty to designate the converted mercantile submarines, the *Deutschland* type, from others of the U class-

[3] This in spite of the fact that the crew of the *U-151* stated to prisoners that her route had been via the Danish West Indies, a Mexican port, and then up the Atlantic coast to her field of operations.

[4] The identity of this vessel has not been established.

[5] This position is about 1,000 miles east of Cape Hatteras.

W., or about 300 miles off the Maryland coast. That the submarine was proceeding westward into the waters of the fourth naval district was indicated by information received on May 20 from the master of the *J. C. Donnell*, who, upon his arrival at Lewes, Del., on that day, reported that his ship's radio had intercepted a message from the American steamship *Jonancy*, 3,289 gross tons, on May 19, saying that she was being gunned and giving her position as 150 miles east of Winter Quarter Shoals. On May 21, at 11.15 a. m., the Canadian steamer *Montcalm* relayed a message to Cape May radio station from the British steamship *Crenella*, 7,082 gross tons, stating that a submarine had been sighted in latitude 37° 50′ N., longitude 73° 50′ W., a point about 80 miles off the Maryland coast. Six shots were fired at the *Crenella* by the submarine, but no hits were registered. At 1 p. m. on the same day the *Montcalm* reported that the *Crenella* had escaped.

The information that merchant vessels had reported a German submarine proceeding toward the coast was immediately disseminated to the section bases, to the forces afloat, and to the commanders of the coast defenses. In addition to the regular patrols, detachments of sub-chasers were established and ordered, whenever practicable, to proceed to the positions given in S O S messages.

Subsequent information indicated that as the submarine approached the American coast she picked as her prey sailing vessels not likely to have means of communication by radio, and in attempting further to conceal her presence in the vicinity took as prisoners the crews of the first three vessels she attacked, the *Hattie Dunn*, the *Hauppauge*, and the *Edna*.

On May 26, 1918, the *Edna*, an unarmed American schooner of 325 gross tons, owned by C. A. Small, Machias, Me., was found abandoned near Winter Quarter Shoals Lightship. She was taken in tow by the Clyde Line steamer *Mohawk*. The schooner's towing bitts carried away and she was abandoned by the *Mohawk*; later she was picked up by the tug *Arabian* and towed to Philadelphia, arriving May 29. An investigation made by the aide for information, fourth naval district, disclosed the presence of two holes, 20 to 30 inches in diameter, in the vessel's hold just above the turn of the bilge, evidencing an external explosion.[6] A time fuse was found, the extreme end of which had been shattered by an explosion. Thus, the naval authorities received the first visual evidence of the work of an enemy raider off the coast.

In interviews with the survivors of the *Edna*, who had been held as prisoners aboard the submarine until June 2, it was learned that the damage to the *Edna* had been inflicted by the enemy in an attempt to sink her, and that the vessels, *Hattie Dunn* and *Hauppauge*, had

---

[6] See the story of Capt. Gilmore, of the *Edna*, p. 27.

been sunk earlier on the same day, May 25. At the same time definite information was gained concerning the identity and military characteristics of the submersible. Although there were no identifying marks, letters, or numbers on the hull, M. H. Sanders, mate of the *Hauppauge*, stated that he saw the letter and figures "U-151" at the foot of several bunks and on the blankets aboard the submarine; T. L. Winsborg saw the letter and figures on the hammocks and on the machine guns; other survivors noticed that tools, furniture, and equipment were similarly marked. These facts, together with a comparison of the photograph of the submarine known to have sunk the first ships, with photographs and silhouettes of submarines obtained from official sources, proved conclusively that the raider operating off the American coast was the *U-151* of the *Deutschland* type. The description of the submarine as given by Capt. Gilmore of the *Edna* and Mate Sanders of the schooner *Hauppauge*, and by other survivors, was most complete. This description, together with the information gained from official sources, furnished the basis for the dissemination, on June 7, to all naval forces of the following data concerning the *U-151*:

Identity, *U-151*, *Deutschland* type of converted mercantile submarine, complement; 8 officers and 65 enlisted men; length, 213 feet 3 inches; breadth, 29 feet 2 inches; surface draft, 14 feet 9 inches; displacement (surface), 1,700 tons; displacement (submerged), 2,100 tons; engine, 1,200 H. P.; speed (surface), $11\frac{1}{2}$ knots; speed (submerged), 8 knots; fuel storage, 250 tons, including storage of ballast tank; endurance (surface), 17,000 miles at 6 knots; endurance (submerged), 50 miles at 7 knots; armament, two 6-inch guns, two 22-pounders, one machine gun, six torpedo tubes—four in bow and two in stern; ammunition capacity, 400 rounds per each gun; maximum number torpedoes, 12; many time fuse bombs; equipped to carry and lay 40 mines; a two-kilowatt wireless set, and a portable set which could be rigged up in a few hours on a captured merchant vessel to be used as a decoy or as a mother ship. Submarines "U-converted mercantile type" are especially fitted with submarine cable-cutting devices.

That the *U-151* carried a cable-cutting device is apparently borne out by the statements of Capt. Sweeney, of the *Hauppauge*, and of Capt. Holbrook, of the *Hattie Dunn*, describing a mysterious device on the deck of the submarine. Along the center line of the ship's deck, fore and aft, there were two stanchions about 70 feet apart, around each of which a coil of 48 turns of $\frac{3}{8}$-inch wire rope was taken. On one end of this rope, which was covered only with a coat of heavy grease, there was an eye splice, and at the other end there was a cable attached to some instruments and appliances hidden and carried in sets abreast of and on each side of the conning tower. Capt. Holbrook stated that on one occasion when the prisoners were below deck they noticed that the submarine gave a sudden lurch and listed on beam end. He was unable to state the cause of the lurch. As far as he could make out, the submarine was at the time, May 28, off New York Harbor. It is possible that this lurch may have been caused by the submarine's grappling with or cutting cables leading from New York. As a matter of fact, one cable to Europe and one to Central America were cut 60 miles southeast of Sandy Hook, on May 28, 1918. This device had disappeared when the prisoners came on deck on the morning of May 30.

The statements of survivors also furnished details concerning the procedure and the methods employed by the *U-151* in her attack upon vessels. The first sinking by the *U-151* off the American coast occurred when the *Hattie Dunn*, an unarmed American schooner of 435 gross tons, was attacked off Winter Quarter Shoals at 10.10 a. m. on May 25. Capt. C. E. Holbrook, master of the *Hattie Dunn*, tells the following story:

> The *Hattie Dunn* sailed from New York on May 23, 1918, en route for Charleston, S. C., in ballast. On Saturday, May 25, about 10.10 a. m., when about 15 to 25 miles off Winter Quarter Lightship, I heard a cannon go off; I looked and saw a boat, but thought it was an American. That boat fired once; I started my ship full speed to the westward. He fired again, and finally came alongside and said:
> "Do you want me to kill you?"
> I told him I thought his was an American boat. He told me to give him the papers, and get some foodstuff. He then wanted me to get into his small boat, but I was anxious to get ashore, so I immediately got into one of my own boats and shoved off. He halted me because he did not want me to get ashore. He then put a man into my boat so that I would come back to the submarine. An officer and other men from the German submarine then boarded the schooner and after placing bombs about her ordered the crew of the *Hattie Dunn* to row to the submarine, which we did. The schooner was sent to the bottom by the explosion of the bombs in latitude 37° 24' N., longitude 75° 05' W. The second officer in command aboard the submarine gave me a receipt for my ship.
> There were no casualities. The weather was fine and clear, the sea was calm.
> We kept aboard the submarine until the morning of June 2. While we were aboard, the second officer and others of the submarine crew wrote some letters and gave them to me to mail. I told them I would not mail the letters if there was anything in them detrimental to my country. I handed them to the first naval officer I came to.

A few minutes later the *U-151* made another attack in the same vicinity, which culminated in the sinking of the *Hauppauge*, an unarmed American schooner of 1,446 gross tons, owned and operated by R. Lawrence Smith, New York. Capt. Sweeney, master of the *Hauppauge*, gave the following information:

> We left Portland, Me., on Friday, May 17, 1918, en route for Norfolk, Va., in ballast. The voyage was uneventful until the morning of Saturday, May 25, when at about 10.15 a. m. we sighted what appeared to be a submarine standing to the westward about 5 miles distant. We immediately heard a shot and the remark was passed by one of the men that firing was going on somewhere. A few minutes later we heard another shot and then a third one. We tacked ship and headed in about northwest for the shore. This brought us broadside to the German submarine, who immediately fired a shot which landed about 225 feet away. We kept going at a speed of about 4 or 5 knots, and a second shot was fired, which passed through the ship's side about 5 feet above the water; a third shot passed through the vessel's wake about 75 feet astern.

The shots were fired in sequence of about four or five minutes. We stopped the schooner in latitude 37° 27′ N., longitude 75° 09′ W. and shortly after the submarine came close to us. An officer aboard the submarine called to us:

"Leave your ship immediately."

The submarine then pulled away from the ship, 50 feet or more, and ordered us to come alongside. We obeyed and went aboard. The commanding officer asked me for the ship's papers, and when I told him they were on the ship he replied:

"Well, we have to have the papers."

A copy of the receipt for the *Hattie Dunn* and photostatic copy of that for the *Hauppauge* are on file and are practically the same in effect. The receipt for the *Hauppauge* reads as follows:

PROTOKOLL.

Am 25 ten Mai 1918, 11 Uhr 10 Min. Vormittags ist auf 37° 27′ N. und 75° 09′ W. der amerikanische 4 Mast Schooner *Hauppauge* L T Q H von S. M. Unterseeboot vernichtet worden.

Aug See, den 25 ten Mai 1918.

Der Kommandant,

v. NOSTITZ,
Korvettenkapitän.

Then they took me back to the schooner for the papers; they also took three bombs with them which they placed aboard the *Hauppauge.* We had just returned to the submarine when the bombs exploded and the *Hauppauge* sank at 11.30 a. m.[7]

There were no casualties. The weather was fine and clear; the sea was calm.

Upon boarding the submarine we found the crew of the *Hattie Dunn* sunk a short while before. We were retained as prisoners until the morning of June 2, when we were placed in boats with the survivors of two sunken vessels—the *Isabel Wiley* and *Winneconne.*

The sea had scarcely closed over the sinking hull of the *Hauppauge,* before the submarine cast about for new prey, and early in the afternoon she made the attack upon the schooner *Edna,* in latitude 37° 30′ N. and longitude 74° 52′ W. In describing the attack on his vessel, Capt. C. W. Gilmore, master of the *Edna,* said:

We cleared Philadelphia on the 17th of May and sailed from Delaware Breakwater on May 24 en route to Santiago, Cuba, with a cargo of case oil. About half past 1 on May 25 we heard a gun fired and a little later a shell struck in the water about a half a mile from us. We had heard firing inshore about an hour or so before. About a minute after the first shot there came another shot which fell about 50 feet away. I then ran up the American ensign; he had run up a German flag. He was standing about 4 or 5 miles northwest. I hauled down the jibs and hove to. The submarine then came toward us towing a yawl boat belonging to one of the schooners he had sunk before; finally he came alongside. Two German officers and four men came over the *Edna's* railing; they shook hands with us and greeted us just the same as they would have done men on one of their own naval vessels. They ordered us to lower our boat and gave us 10 minutes to abandon ship, saying that they were going to blow her up. They asked me where I was from, where I was bound, and what my cargo consisted of. The officer in charge took me into the cabin and said he wanted me to come below and that he wanted my papers. When we got below he said to me:

---

[7] The *Hauppauge* was later towed to port and salvaged. The schooner turned over and floated bottom up.

"Now, don't get excited; if you want to change your clothes and get everything of value to you, we are going to be around here an hour."

He took possession of all my official papers, which I had encased in one envelope. When I came from below I noticed that they had placed some little black tubes about 10 inches long and one-half inch in diameter, which looked like sticks of dynamite and which were tied to ropes extended over the side of the vessel abreast of the main hatch.

Twenty minutes after the German officer and his crew had boarded the schooner, and after I had had time to have everything of value placed in the lifeboat, he ordered us to proceed over to the submarine, and laughingly said:

"You will find some of your friends over there."

Upon being ordered below I found Capt. Sweeney of the *Hauppauge* and Capt. Holbrook of the *Hattie Dunn*, who said they and their crews had just been taken aboard the submarine.

The explosion of the bombs aboard the *Edna* occurred at 2 p. m. in latitude 37° 30′ N., longitude 74° 52′ W. The submarine immediately quit the spot, leaving the *Edna* in apparently a sinking condition. She did not sink, I understand, but was towed into Philadelphia.

There were no casualties. The weather was fine and clear; the sea was calm.

Upon the arrival of the crew of the *Edna* there was a total of 23 prisoners aboard the submarine. The description of what occurred on the submarine as given by M. H. Saunders, mate of the *Hauppauge*, is as follows:

Shortly after the sinking of the *Hauppauge* we were ordered below. We then heard two shots fired, but nothing else to indicate that another vessel was being attacked. The next we knew was when the captain and crew of the schooner *Edna* appeared below decks about 2.20 p. m.

About 2.30 p. m. the submarine started on a course to the eastward, moving at a speed of about 7 or 8 knots an hour. She remained on the surface until about 4.30 p. m., when a steamer was sighted and the submarine submerged. She remained submerged for about one hour and a half, moving all the time at about 4 knots an hour. Coming to the surface about 6 p. m., the submarine maintained a speed about the same as earlier in the afternoon. At this time all the prisoners were allowed on deck for about an hour.

During the night the submarine submerged several times but again came to the surface. On the morning of Sunday, May 26, we were again allowed on deck, and it appeared that the submarine was heading westward, as indicated by the bearing of the sun. At 11 a. m. a steamer was sighted and the submarine immediately submerged, allowing the steamer to pass over her. Upon being questioned, the crew said that the vessel sighted was a Norwegian steamer bound inshore. After remaining submerged about two hours the submarine rose again, but the prisoners were not allowed on deck until later in the afternoon, when they were given liberty for an hour or more. During the night the submarine spent part of her time running submerged.

Upon coming to the surface on Monday morning, May 27, some of the crew, in referring to the sub chasers they had seen, asked:

"What are the little kite boats?"

They also remarked that there was a big traffic along the coast, and wanted to know where the tugs with "boxes" were bound. They were told that these boxes were barges used along the coast. The day's occurrences were a repetition of Sunday's—periods of running submerged and running on the surface. Late in the afternoon, while we were on deck it was quite chilly. I noticed the smell coming from fishing fields and said:

"This seems like Nantucket here."
Kohler, a sublieutenant, replied:
"You ain't far from there."

During the night the submarine remained submerged most of the time and apparently was headed back to the westward. On Tuesday, May 28, there was a fog all day and the U-boat ran on the top of the water at about her usual speed, blowing her whistle all the time.[8]

On Tuesday evening at 8 o'clock a light was sighted and the submarine went down all night. That evening the commanding officer said he thought he would put us ashore next morning.

On Wednesday, May 29, the submarine came to the surface and we were allowed on deck, but were not permitted to approach the apparatus that resembled a cable-cutting device. At 2.30 p. m. we sighted another steamer and immediately submerged, allowing the vessel—they said it was a Norwegian steamer, inbound—to pass over us.

When we came on deck the following morning, the coils of wire had disappeared. During the day they had torpedoes up, overhauling them and trying the pins, wheels, and other machinery of the torpedoes. They even had the crew of the *Hauppauge* to help get the torpedoes up and to put them back below again. Thursday night was rough and foggy; the submarine stayed below all night.

The next morning, May 31, the submarine came up, but the day was foggy. Another inbound Norwegian steamer was sighted and the submarine submerged as usual. In the afternoon the submarine rose to the surface again; the prisoners were kept below deck. At this time the commanding officer remarked:

"If I run across a small vessel, I will sacrifice it to put you on board it."

During the afternoon the submarine was on the surface from time to time, but every time she sighted anything she would submerge. At one time a steamer came so close to us that the vibration of the propellers could be heard distinctly.

On Saturday, June 1, the submarine cruised all day, watching for a suitable vessel; during the evening several ships were sighted but no attacks were made

It was on this day that the United States battleships *Ohio*, *New Hampshire*, and *Louisiana* reported the sighting of a submarine. The three vessels had been at target practice off Hampton Roads and had reassembled previous to returning to their base when the periscope of a submarine appeared. The war diary of the *New Hampshire* gives the following in regard to the encounter:

All ships being stopped, this ship forced ahead and around bow of the leading ship (*Louisiana*). At this moment, 11.10 a. m., *Ohio* signaled submarine alarm, and all ships went ahead at full speed, separated, and acted in accordance with doctrine. The commanding officer and a number of others sighted a periscope showing twice, bearing to the northward and westward and apparently standing toward this ship and between *Louisiana* and *Ohio*. A few moments later numerous observers, including the commanding officer, sighted a torpedo wake coming down from the northward and eastward across the bow of the *Louisiana* and toward the port quarter of this ship. A few moments later a number of observers saw a periscope to the southward and eastward of this ship and a torpedo wake crossing the stern of this ship. All ships proceeded independently to westward at full speed. *Ohio* having dropped target, making rapid and radical changes of course as prescribed, the *New Hampshire* and *Ohio* firing upon all suspicious objects.

[8] On this date the Cape May radio station received a message from the American steamer *Adelhei!* reporting that she had sighted a submarine in latitude 36° 45' N. and longitude 73° 38' W.

This report is supported by the war diary of the *Ohio:*

A disturbance in the water, bearing from this ship 270°, distant about 1,200 yards, was observed, and on careful examination it appeared to be a wake of a submarine. Three observers, two of them officers, reported positively that they observed a periscope in this wake. The signals indicating submarine were made to ships present, the target was cut adrift, fire was opened with torpedo battery, and maximum speed was obtained as soon as possible. The ship was gradually brought around to a heading toward Buoy 2CB, distant about 12 miles, and we returned to port zigzagging. In all twenty-one 6-inch service projectiles were fired. Firing was heard from the *New Hampshire* and possibly from one other vessel. The low visibility prevented an accurate determination of this point. The tug was directed to pick up the target. Two submarine chasers investigated the locality about where the *Ohio's* first 6-inch projectiles fell, which was near the locality in which the wake appeared. After considering these facts, the commander in chief was informed by radio of the occurrence.

In speaking of life and conditions aboard the submarine, Saunders said:

The food was good. In the morning we had rolls and fresh butter. The butter was fine. The bread was black and came in loaves about 3 feet long. We had cognac nearly all the time.

They had three graphophones on board. The members of the crew were cheerful and joked with us, especially after indulging in cognac. They were apparently young fellows and frequently talked of their mothers. The crew expressed great surprise when Capt. Sweeney told them we had shipped 2,000,000 men overseas and had 10,000,000 more as reserves.

None of the Germans would give us any information as to the number of submarines over here. We were told that the *U-151* left Kiel on April 14, 1918; the bread wrappers bore the stamp of April 9. The commanding officer said he expected to remain out about eight weeks.

At 5.30 a. m., June 2,[9] word was passed to prisoners by an officer, who said:

"Get ready, there's a sailing vessel alongside we are going to put you aboard of."

All the 21 men were ordered upon deck. A little later the schooner *Isabel B. Wiley* and the steamship *Winneconne* were sighted. Instead of putting us aboard either of those vessels, they sank them and transferred us to the four boats—one from the *Wiley* and three from the *Winneconne*—with the survivors.[10]

In describing the incidents in connection with the sinking of the *Isabel B. Wiley*, an unarmed American schooner of 776 gross tons owned by the Atlas Shipping Corporation, which occurred off the Jersey coast, Capt. Thom I. Thomassen, master, stated the following facts:

We sailed from Princess Bay anchorage at 3 o'clock p. m. on June 1, passed out by Sandy Hook at 4 p. m. en route for Newport News, Va., to load coal for Montevideo.

---

[9] The tug *Anson M. Bangs* sent an allo from 1 mile east of Five Fathom Bank light at 10.30 a. m. on this date. The presence of the *U-151* in that place at that time is impossible, but it is not unlikely that an American submarine was sighted.

[10] The *U-151* planted a number of mines on the American coast. Actual dates and exact locations must remain somewhat uncertain, in spite of the fact that the German charts delivered to the American naval authorities after the signing of the armistice show the general location of the mine fields. However, since it is certain that no enemy submarine other than the *U-151* visited the American coast until July, 1918, the sinking of the *Herbert L. Pratt* and the numerous sightings of mines reported during the month of June may be ascribed to the activities of the *151*. Moreover, the date of the mining of the *Pratt*, June 3, 1918, proves that at least a part of these operations were completed before the survivors of the *Hattie Dunn*, the *Hauppauge*, and the *Edna* were released from capitivity.

At 7.50 a. m., June 2, I came on deck and noticed off the port quarter a suspicious-looking object about 1,200 yards away. The craft was heading toward my ship, and as it approached I noticed it had two flags and a small German naval ensign. When about 1,000 yards off the submarine fired a shot and the shot fell about 100 yards off the vessel. I then went below and got an American ensign, came on deck, and hoisted it. Then I hove my vessel to and hauled down the jibs. The weather was hazy and the sea calm. As the submarine approached us, another ship appeared ahead of us and the submarine fired a shot at her.

In the meantime I ordered the steward to get some provisions to put in the lifeboat and directed the engineer to get some oil and gas for the engine. Without waiting orders from the German commander the entire crew got into the lifeboat and we pulled off about 100 yards, waiting for the submarine to return from the steamship *Winneconne*. The *Winneconne* was stopped and the crew got into three boats; the submarine then came toward us and ordered my lifeboat alongside. I asked him what he wanted, and he said that he desired to put some men in my lifeboat whom he had on the submarine. He put 11 men from the submarine on my boat; that made 19 men on board my lifeboat. He ordered the boats from the *Winneconne* to come alongside and distributed 12 men from the submarine on the three lifeboats. All four lifeboats—one from my vessel and three from the *Winneconne*—were told to shove off.

The submarine commander launched a boat from the submarine and sent three or four men with bombs to the S. S. *Winneconne*. Shortly after these men returned to the submarine, and after they arrived the bombs on the *Winneconne* exploded. In the meantime the *Wiley* had drifted some distance away. The submarine then headed toward the *Wiley*. When they got near the *Wiley* they put a small boat overboard with some men in her. They went aboard and hauled down the American ensign.

We observed in the meantime several trips between the *Wiley* and the submarine by the sailors in the small boat from the submarine; apparently they were taking provisions from the *Wiley*.

Before shoving off from the submarine I informed the captain that I did not have sufficient water to take care of the extra men, and he gave me a large keg of water.

I did not see the *Wiley* blown up, but about one hour afterwards I heard three distinct explosions. When bombed the *Wiley* was in 39° 10′ north latitude and 73° 7′ west longitude.

I consulted with those in the other three lifeboats and concluded that, as I had the only power lifeboat, it would be best for me to make for shore as soon as possible, with a view of hailing some ship and have them advise the location of the other three lifeboats and to send them help. I instructed the other three lifeboats to remain where they were. At 5.30 my boat sighted the Ward Line steamer *Mexico*. They picked us up and sent a wireless to Washington that three lifeboats, holding 50 men, were in the position I indicated. At about 7.30 Monday morning, the S. S. *Mexico*, which was heading south, stopped the *Santiago* bound north, and all who were in my lifeboat were transferred to the S. S. *Santiago* and taken to New York, where we arrived Tuesday, June 4, at 12 o'clock.

Capt. Waldemar Knudsen, master of the *Winneconne*, described how his vessel, an unarmed American steamship of 1,869 gross tons, owned by the American Trans-Atlantic Co., was sunk after appearing upon the scene while the submarine was overhauling the *Isabel B. Wiley*:

We cleared Newport News, Va., on Saturday, June 1, en route to Providence with a cargo of 1,819 tons of coal. I came on the bridge at 7.30 a. m. Sunday and heard that the third mate and chief officer had seen a schooner and a dark object which they thought was an American patrol boat lying alongside the schooner. At 8.10 a shot was fired and we tried to make for shore. At 8.12 they fired another shot and a shell burst about 200 or 300 yards ahead; the *Winneconne* hoved to in latitude 39° 26′ N., longitude 72° 50′ W. The submarine came closer ready for action and then launched a small boat. An officer and two men came on board and gave orders to leave the ship immediately, as they were going to sink her. I asked him how long they were going to give us, and he said he would give us one-half an hour. He asked me where the chronometer was, and I told him it was my private property, and he said I could take it. He took the ship's log, ship's register, and ship's papers. We launched the two boats and the crew got in. The chief mate and I were still on board and were under the impression that we were to go aboard the schooner, but he told us to launch the small boat and go alongside the submarine, which we did. He placed four bombs on our ship, one on the fore deck, one on the aft deck, one in No. 1 hatch, and one in No. 3 hatch.

I asked him what was the reason he came over and sank our vessel, and he said he was sorry to do it, but war was war and that England was to blame. He said that he had been in that game for four years and had been over here 10 days and this was the first steamer he had sunk, but he had sunk three or four schooners.

When he went off to the submarine we went alongside and some sailors from blown-up schooners came off the submarine into our boats. I asked the officer to give us a tow and he said:

"What do think this is, a passenger boat?"

About 15 minutes after we left the ship we heard three explosions, and the ship sank about 9.12.

Then we pulled for dear life to the westward. We were rowing all day and all night until 7.40 in the morning, when we were picked up by the S. S. *San Saba*, about 25 miles southeast of Barnegat.

The submarine was about 230 feet long and 30 or 40 feet wide. She was armed with two 6-inch guns, one forward and one aft. I saw the figures on the stern, which were covered with rust and paint which read, "151."

The chief officer, H. Wasch, of the S. S. *Winneconne*, gave the following information concerning certain incidents that occurred while the German officer was on board:

When the submarine officer boarded the bridge, the captain, the third mate, and myself were on the bridge, and the German officer said:

"Good morning, fine weather to-day. You men take to your boats, you had better get your boats ready."

The captain asked, "What are you going to do?"

"Well,)" replied the officer, "I got to sink you. War is war, and I can not help it."

We got the boats ready, and the officer ordered me to the wheel, and said "Starboard" to me. He then looked on the wheel teller and asked: "Is this ship set for starboard?"

"Yes," I replied. He said "All right," and gave half speed ahead for about two or three minutes or so; stopped again, then slow speed for a little while; then he signaled to his own commander and ordered the engines of my ship reversed; then he stopped the ship for good. We lowered the boats; the crew took two lifeboats, the captain and I took the other. Finally he said:

"Hurry now. I can not wait any longer. I gave you enough time."

So we left the ship and proceeded to the submarine. All the prisoners on the submarine boarded our boats and then we left the submarine.

About 11.30 we heard two shots fired; about 12.30 we heard two shots again, at intervals of 5 to 8 seconds; about 4 o'clock eight shots were fired at intervals of 15

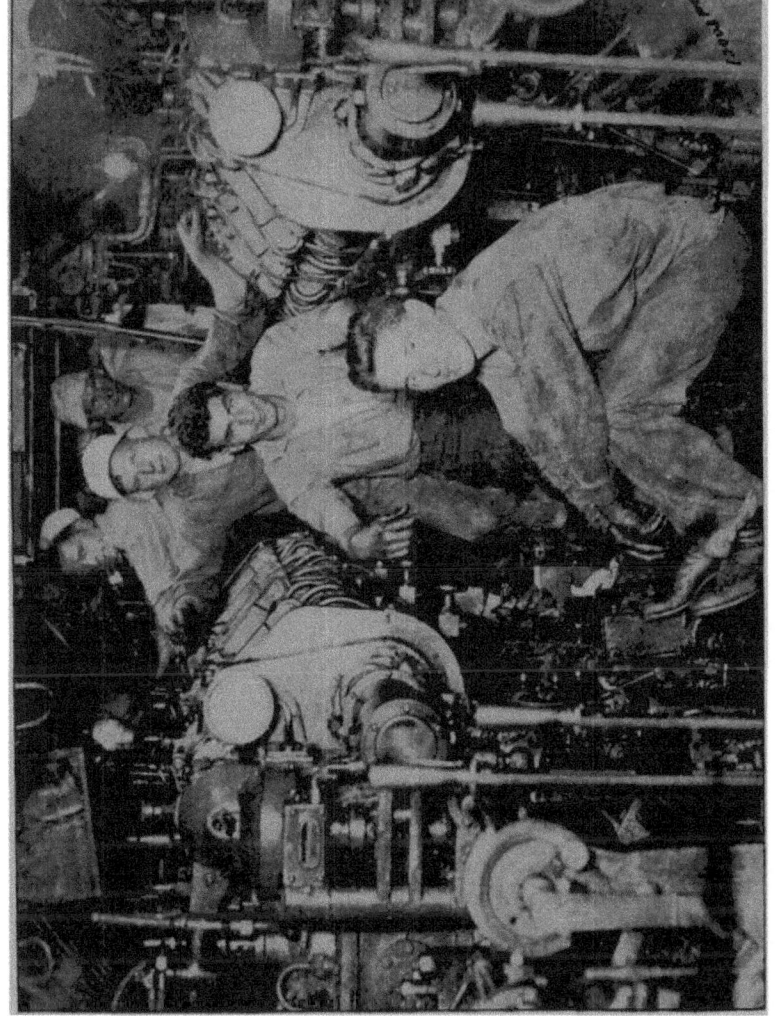

INTERIOR OF A GERMAN SUBMARINE.
Showing its instruments and high-powered engines.

PHOTOGRAPHIC COPY OF THE RECEIPT GIVEN TO THE MASTER OF THE AMERICAN SCHOONER HAUPPAUGE BY KORVETTENKAPITAN V. NOSTITZ.

(Page 27.)

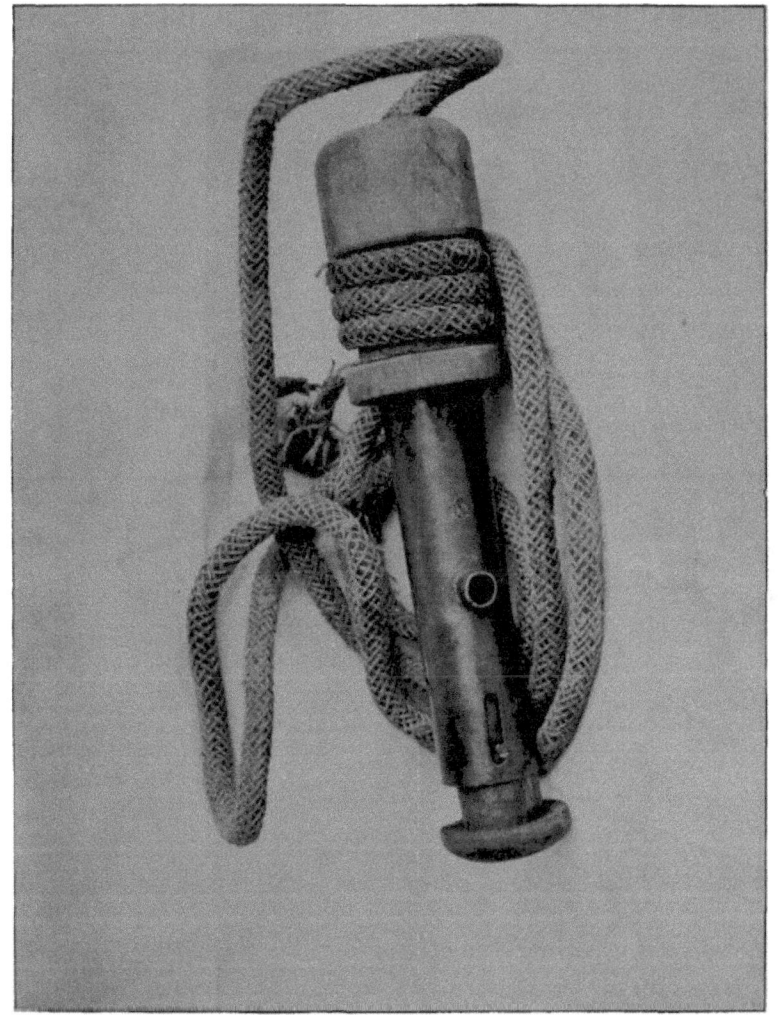

TIME FUSE USED ON THE AMERICAN SCHOONER EDNA BY U-151.

(Page 27.)

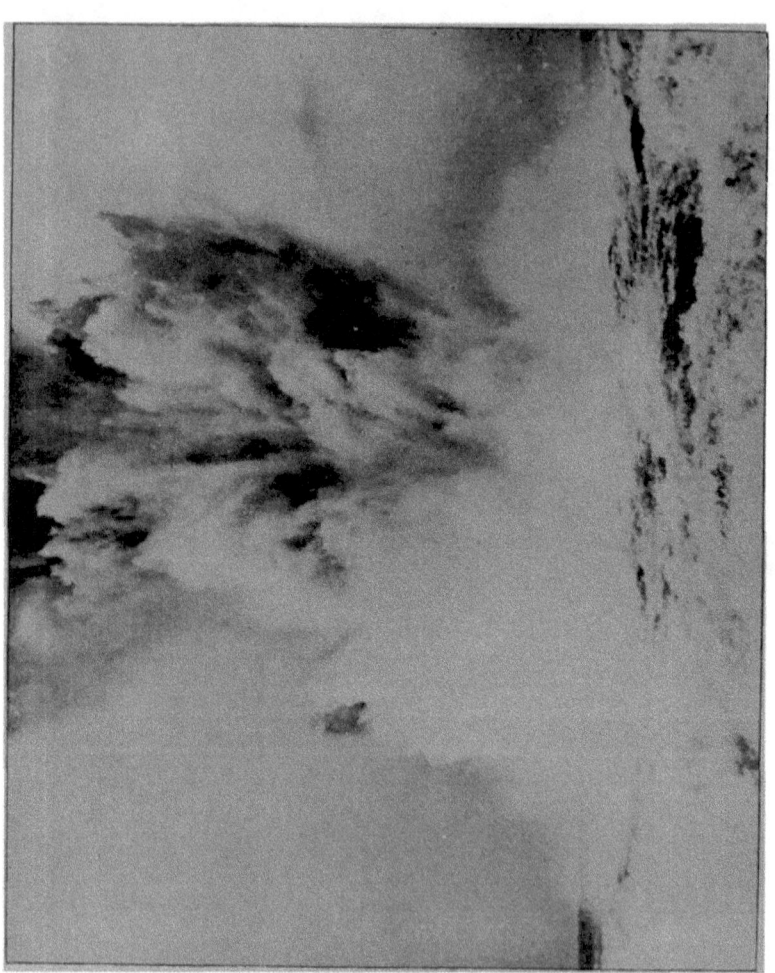

DEPTH CHARGE EXPLODING.

seconds; at 7 o'clock five shots were heard; at 7.12 two shots were fired; at 7 16 wo shots were heard.

At 7.40 the next morning we were picked up by the S. S. *San Saba*.

The first shots heard by the survivors of the *Winneconne* were those fired across the bows of the *Jacob M. Haskell*, an unarmed American schooner of 1,778 gross tons. Capt. W. H. Davis, master of the *Jacob M. Haskell*, made the following statement concerning the destruction of his vessel:

On Sunday, June 2, about noon, in a calm sea, the schooner *Jacob M. Haskell*, with a cargo of coal, proceeding under sail from Norfolk, Va., to Boston, Mass., at about 3 miles an hour, and about 50 miles east by south of Barnegat Light, was fired upon by having a solid shot sent across her bows. A few minutes later a second shot was fired across the ship's bows and the approaching submarine displayed the international signal "Abandon Ship." We made arrangements to abandon, and dropping the boats into the water prepared to take the crew off. While we were doing this, a rowboat containing one officer and six heavily armed seamen rowed alongside. The men came aboard the schooner and the officer demanded the ship's papers, log book, and crew list, which were delivered. The captain then directed men to hurry and get the crew off. During this time, the bombing party had placed four bombs over the ship's side—two forward, one on each side, and two aft, one on either side. The bombs were about 6 inches in diameter and 14 inches in length. They were hung so that the bombs themselves rested about 2 feet under the surface of the water and alongside of the schooner's hull. The men went about their work in a business-like manner; the officer was so polite that he almost got on our nerves. Each seaman was armed with two automatic revolvers and a long vicious-looking knife.

According to Gustave Nelson, a seaman aboard the *Jacob M. Haskell*, after the officer had posted his men they stood grinning while he demanded the ship's papers. The officer then hauled down the American flag and wrapped it in paper. Just before the ship was abandoned, the cook remarked:

"You had better take the food we have on board before you sink the ship."

The officer snapped back: "We don't want your food; we have plenty food of our own. We don't want your lives either; we want your ships. Now get away from here; you have three minutes before the ship goes down."

Upon leaving the ship,

the statement of Capt. Davis continues,

we were allowed to take our valuables, the chronometer, the sextant, and some sailing charts. As we were shoving off, an officer on the deck of the submarine hailed us and demanded the ship's papers. When told that the papers had been turned over to the boarding officer, and he ordered us to proceed on our way. A few minutes later the *Haskell* was blown up and disappeared with all sails set. As we were starting on our way, the boarding officer called out:

"Good luck. The New Jersey coast is just 40 miles away. Better go there."

The submarine proceeded slowly on her way almost due east. Later we heard firing coming from the general direction in which the submarine had proceeded.

We were finally picked up by the American coastwise steamer *Grecian*.

After moving eastward for a short time the *U-151* changed her course to the southwest and bore down upon and subsequently sank *the Edward H. Cole*, an unarmed American schooner of 1,791 gross tons, owned by Edward H. Cole Co., Boston. The following account summarizes the statement of H. G. Newcombe, master of the schooner, concerning the sinking of his vessel:

We sailed from Norfolk, Va., on May 30, for Portland, Me., with a cargo of 2,516 tons of coal. I might not have been on the regular steamship course, as I had to follow God's good winds. At 3.10 in the afternoon of June 2, when about 50 miles southeast of Barnegat Light, we sighted a boat on the starboard bow about 2,000 yards away. She circled around and came aft on the port quarter. When she came pretty close I put the glasses on her and saw it was a German flag she was flying. She came up then about 150 feet off us and told us to clear away the boats, as they were going to sink us, which we did. An officer and some of the men lowered a boat from the submarine and came on board and demanded the ship's papers and took them, and while in the cabin he told me we had seven and one-half minutes to clear His men had already placed bombs on the ship, two on each side, and I believe there were others. He told me to get some clothes and supplies, but we were too busy getting the boats cleared to do it; we had no water or compass in the boat. I went down into the cabin and got a few papers, licenses, barometer, etc., and showed them to the officer and asked if it was all right. He said, "Sure, go ahead." We got into the boat and pulled away, and about 16 minutes after we left, the ship sank.

About an hour after this we were about 4 miles away from the submarine, which had not moved, when the steamer hove in sight. The submarine opened fire, firing five shots. The steamer turned around and headed in the opposite way and stopped. About 15 minutes later we heard an explosion, such as we heard on the *Cole*. I suppose they did the same thing to that as they did to ours.

Then we rowed away, hearing several reports later from this submarine. We were picked up by the American steamship *Bristol* about 8 p. m. While we were boarding the *Bristol* we heard this submarine still firing off to the south, I judge about 12 miles distant.

A few minutes after we got on board, another submarine appeared under the *Bristol's* starboard quarter about 500 yards away. I did not see much of the submarine and did not pay much attention to it. We saw much driftwood. We arrived in New York at 5.37 a. m., June 3.

The steamer that the survivors of the *Edward H. Cole* saw attacked by the submarine just after their own vessel had been sunk, was the *Texel*, an unarmed American steamship of 3,210 gross tons, owned and operated by the United Shipping States Board. In telling how his vessel was attacked by gunfire and sunk by bombs, Capt. K. B. Lowry, gave the following information:

We sailed from Ponce, P. R., on May 27 en route to New York with a cargo of sugar.

On Sunday June 2, at 4.21 p. m., the first intimation we had of submarines operating in the vicinity was when a solid shot was fired, passing over the vessel forward of the funnel and ricochetting about 200 yards to port. I immediately went up to navigating bridge and proceeded to maneuver the vessel in a manner to elude the enemy as prescribed by the United States Navy Department. At this time the vessel was in latitude 38° 58′ N., longitude 73° 13′ W. The submarine was directly on the starboard beam; I immediately ordered the helm hard starboard, as to bring the aggressor directly over the stern. When the vessel had assumed this position I steadied and ordered all possible speed. The vessel at the time of the attack was running at her maximum speed. A second shot was fired when the vessel had assumed her new position. This shell was of the shrapnel variety and exploded on the water to the starboard of the vessel. The first and second shots were fired at a range of approximately 2,000 yards. After the second shot I discovered another submarine directly ahead who was coming to the surface with his conning tower clear; a hatch opened and an officer stepped out.

After I stopped he submerged and disappeared. He was afloat about 10 or 15 minutes. He tried to intercept me after I changed my course. As far as I could see, it was the same kind of conning tower and had three periscopes.

In this predicament with one submarine astern who had my range to a degree of disconcerting nicety and another ahead at a distance of about 1,500 yards, further attempt to escape or to disconcert the enemy seemed not only useless but an act unnecessarily exposing the crew to injury or loss of life. At this time I stopped the engines and hove to; soon after this the submarine that had fired the previous shots opened fire again, firing two shots in quick succession, the first hitting the working boat on the starboard side under the bridge, carrying it away and shattering the starboard wing of the upper bridge; the next shot passed over the bridge at a height of about 10 feet and struck the water about 100 yards forward of the bow and exploded.

During this time the first firing submarine drew steadily nearer, encircling the vessel twice, and shaping a course so as to come up under our stern; he arrived alongside at 4.46 p. m. An officer boarded the vessel with three seamen and an underlieutenant. He asked me for any and all papers that the vessel might have. I told him that being in the coastwise trade that we carried no Navy Instructions or codes, and that in view of the fact that the vessel had been formerly of Dutch nationality we carried no register—the Navy Instructions had been thrown overboard previous to this time. After leaving the ship all the vessel's papers were in my boat in charge of the second officer. I destroyed the register, manifest, and articles as he headed toward our boat, rather than let them fall into his hands.

After I had concluded my business with the German, I watched (with the permission of the lieutenant) the placing of the bombs. Lieut. Kohler said: "I know how to do this, I have been in the business four years."

I asked him where his home was and he replied:

"My home is in Germany, that's all I can tell you."

Three bombs were set at the base of each mast; bombs were also set in the engine and fireroom, but as to the numbers I can not say. When all the bombs were set, the lieutenant ordered me to leave as they would explode in 10 minutes. As he proceeded to leave, I did as ordered.

The submarine, the one that sank the vessel, came to within 20 feet of the ship. I had a good chance to see the commanding officer. He was about 5 feet 8 inches; probably weighed about 200 pounds, stocky build; he had light hair, wore a mustache and Van Dyke beard; he was about 40 years of age and wore a Navy uniform with long overcoat. His rank was indicated by two gold stripes on his sleeve, slightly above his wrist. He spoke English.

One of our boats was jammed between the submarine and the ship, and the captain of the submarine, shouted down:

"You dunder head, why don't you get out of there? I'll break your boat up!"

I asked Kohler, "What are you going to do when we get in the boats? Are you going to shell us?"

"We don't bother you at all;" replied Kohler. "Get away."

My boat left the ship at 5.10 p. m. and the explosion took place at 5.18 p. m. After the explosion the vessel settled rapidly by the stern and listed to the starboard, sinking at 5.21 p. m.

As soon as she was out of sight we shaped our course for Absecon and pulled away. The submarine set his course about true ESE. and disappeared in the haze running on the surface. At 6.20 p. m. we again heard four shots, which probably signified that he had encountered another victim, and again, at 7.20 p. m., a repetition of the shooting was heard from this time until we reached the coast. We saw no vessel. We reached Absecon Light and beached our boats at Atlantic City on June 3, where we were met by the Coast Guards of Station 123, and arrangements were made for accommodations for the night. All the crew of 36 men were saved.

The reported sighting of a second submarine, off the bow of the *Texel*, was the first indication that possibly two enemy raiders were present in American waters and were acting in company. The belief was materially heightened for the time by the report of Capt. Walter M. Hart of the American steamship *Bristol*, in which he told how he picked up the survivors of the *Edward H. Cole* and later sighted a submarine on the afternoon of June 2:

The *Bristol* left Boston on June 1, en route to Norfolk, Va., in ballast. On June 2, about 8 p. m. we sighted a lifeboat with 11 men, crew of American schooner *Edward H. Cole*, schooner having been sunk by submarine at 3.30 p. m. about 50 miles southeast of Barnegat Light. The crew of the *Edward H. Cole* was picked up.

At about 8.20 p. m., when about 38 miles southeast of Barnegat Buoy, bearing 120° true, we sighted a submarine about 5,000 yards off the starboard quarter, heading directly toward the ship. By traveling at maximum speed of 12 knots, we managed to outdistance him and arrived at New York at 5.37 a. m., June 3.

The submarine appeared to be about 200 feet long and to be armed with two rifles, which appeared to be either 5 or 6 inch.

Taking into consideration the possible mission of the enemy submarine campaign in American waters, the Navy Department at this time expressed its views as follows:

From the character of these enemy operations, the enemy's mission is estimated to be primarily political, with the object of causing us to inaugurate such an offensive campaign as to prevent us placing our naval forces where they will operate to best military advantage. If this estimate of the enemy's primary mission is correct, it is reasonable to expect the enemy submarines to shift their base of operations frequently, both to gain added victims and also to create the impression that more submarines are on this coast than are really here.

Later developments failed to disclose the presence of more than one submarine operating off the coast at this time, and proved beyond a reasonable doubt that the *U-151* continued to operate alone.

The firing heard about 6 p. m. by survivors of vessels sunk earlier in the day was that employed by the *U-151* in attacking the *Carolina*, an unarmed American steamship of 5,093 gross tons owned and operated by the New York & Porto Rico Steamship Co. The following facts concerning the sinking of the *Carolina* were given by Capt. Barber, master of the vessel:

We left San Juan, P. R., May 29 at 5 p. m., en route to New York with 218 passengers, a crew of 117, and a cargo of sugar.

About 5.55 p. m., Sunday night, ship's time, I got the wireless S O S saying the *Isabel B. Wiley* had been attacked by a submarine and giving her position 39° 10′ N., 73° 07′ W. I immediately ordered all lights closed down on my ship; I ordered the chief engineer to open her up all he possibly could and steered due west by the compass. My position at 6 o'clock by dead reckoning was 38° 57′ N., 73° 06′ W., so that I figured that I was about 13 miles south of where the *Isabel B. Wiley* was.

I just got my vessel steadied on the new course and scanned the horizon to find the submarine, when I saw the conning tower and two guns on my starboard quarter distant 2 miles. Although the weather was quite hazy at the time, I could make out the outline plainly. She seemed to be rising in the water.

Shortly after, about 6 p. m., she fired, the shell falling astern of my ship about 100 yards. The second shot went overhead and landed straight ahead about one-half ship's length, the third shot landing quite close to amidships on the starboard side.

I had already ordered the chief wireless operator to send out a wireless S O S that we were being attacked by gunfire from a German submarine. After the second shot I stopped my ship, ported my helm, and brought her broadside onto the submarine. I hoisted the signals "I am all stopped," and the American ensign.

Realizing the uselessness of trying to escape, not having the necessary speed, I at the time gave the wireless operator orders to send the foregoing dead reckoning position broadcast, but thinking that if I sent it out he would possibly shell the ship, and having many women and children aboard the ship, I recalled the order. Later the chief wireless operator informed me that the submarine had wirelessed under low power the message: "If you don't use wireless I won't shoot." Our ceasing to use the wireless, I presume, was the reason for his stopping firing.

After the third shot was fired, the submarine bore down on my starboard bow and when he got nearer I saw he was flying the signal "A. B.," abandon ship as quickly as possible. I had already ordered a boat full out and now I ordered all hands to leave the ship. The women and children were put into the boats first and the men entered after the boats were lowered. After I had seen everyone off the ship into the boats, and after I had destroyed all the secret and confidential papers, I, myself, got into the chief officer's boat, this being the only boat left alongside. Upon clearing the ship's side, about 6.30 p. m., I was ordered by the submarine commander, both in English and by signals with the hand, to make for shore.

I collected all the boats near me and moored them head and stern one to the other. Being eventually joined by all the boats except the motor lifeboat and lifeboat No. 5, we pulled to the westward and out of the line of gunfire as much as we possibly could.

When the boats were clear, the submarine then ranged alongside the ship on the port side at what seemed a short distance off and at 7.15 fired one shell into No. 2 hold, lower port, as near as I could judge. She then fired another shell into the wireless room and another into the vicinity of my own room behind the pilot house. The submarine proceeded around the ship's bow and seemed to watch her sink from there. The Germans did not board the steamer as far as I could see.

The ship remained steady about 20 minutes then listed to port, gradually sinking on her port side, and finally sank at 7.55 p. m. with the ensign and signals flying. Great clouds of fire and steam arose as she went down.

By this time I had eight made fast in line. The boat I was in was in the lead; I steered a course to the best of my ability somewhere near west. During the night I heard other firing and presumed that the submarine was attacking some other ship.

We had light and variable airs and fairly smooth seas until about 12 a. m. when we encountered a heavy rain and lightning. I ordered the boats to put heads to seas, riding to sea, anchored until the squalls passed. Then we resumed our voyage to the westward, attached in the same manner as before. We kept this formation until daylight when I ordered the boats cut adrift to make rowing easier.

At 11 a. m. June 3, I sighted a schooner standing to the northward and sent the second officer's boat to intercept her. We saw her haul down her jibs and heave to. I ordered all the boats to proceed to the schooner, which proved to be the *Eva B.*

Douglas. Capt. G. Launo, master of the schooner, and his wife and daughter received us with fine courtesy and placed all their supplies and stores at our disposal.

After struggling with light and variable winds, the schooner finally anchored off Barnegat Inlet, about 11 a. m., Tuesday, June 3. I sent my chief officer ashore with a message to the owners of my vessel telling them where we were and requiring assistance. In the meantime the U. S. S. P. 507 appeared from the south and her captain, Ensign J. A. Fasset, U. S. N. R. F. offered his services to help out in any way we saw fit. S. P. 507 stood by and towed us to New York, arriving at 4 a. m., June 4.

There were about 160 passengers, as near as I could judge, and 94 of the crew on board the *Eva B. Douglas.*

Other survivors from the *Carolina* were accounted for on June 4. The first naval district reported that 19 people had been picked up and brought to Vineyard Haven; at 1.45 p. m., lifeboat No. 5 containing 5 women and 25 men, landed through the surf at Atlantic City, N. J., and the same day, the British steamship *Appleby* picked up 18 survivors at sea and carried them to Lewes, Del.

All the men and women aboard the *Carolina,* however, did not reach safety. The first loss of life charged to enemy submarine activity off the American Atlantic coast was recorded when one of the lifeboats containing 8 passengers and 5 members of the crew of the *Carolina* was capsized about 12.15 a. m., June 3, while attempting to weather the rough seas that arose during the night. At 4 p. m. the same day, when about 60 miles east of Cape May, N. J., the Danish steamship *Bryssel* picked up a lone motor dory swamped and abandoned, belonging to the S. S. *Carolina,* which told the mute story of how its occupants had perished.[11]

When the day of June 2 was done, the *U–151* had registered nine successful attacks upon unarmed vessels within 75 miles of the coast and before the dawn of June 3, had been charged with the loss of 13 lives.

It thus became apparent that the enemy raider was intent upon wreaking her harvest, if possible, from the unarmed and unprotected vessels in close proximity to the coast. In anticipation of this fact, Admiral W. S. Benson, the chief of Naval operations, on February 6, 1918, had appointed a special Planning Board to study the situation and to formulate a plan for the defense of the coast and the control and protection of merchant shipping. The plan prepared by the board was approved March 6, 1918. (See Appendix, page 143.)

Following the approval of this plan the department forwarded on March 28, 1918, to the commandants of Atlantic coast naval districts a general plan for coastwise shipping, and directed commandants to prepare detailed recommendations for each district. (See Appendix, page 152.) This general plan placed the control of coastwise shipping in the hands of the district commandants, and in order to avoid misunderstandings as to jurisdiction, district boundaries were extended to

---

[11] Nine passengers and four of the crew of the *Carolina* were lost; two were women, one a passenger, and the other the stewardess of the ship.

seaward and sharply defined and the location of the office having jurisdiction over each area was given.

This was followed on May 4 by a circular letter to all shipowners and masters containing the general plan itself and giving instructions as to the procedure to be followed in case it became necessary for the Navy to assume control of shipping. (See Appendix, page 153.) A letter was also sent on May 8 to commandants informing them that upon the receipt of the dispatch "Assume control of coastwise shipping," they were immediately to put into effect the general plans previously prepared. They were further instructed that prior to the receipt of this dispatch they should assure themselves that all the routing preliminaries and requirements of coastwise shipping and the military and commercial requirements on shore were fully developed and well understood by the various parties interested. (See Appendix, page 155.)

On May 12, 1918, another letter was issued to commandants advising that war warnings for coastwise shipping would be sent out only from the office of Naval Operations upon receipt of information from the naval districts and other sources.

On the morning of June 3, therefore, the office of Naval Operations sent the following dispatch to district commandants:

Assume control of coastwise shipping and handle traffic in accordance therewith.

A little later in the morning of June 3 Naval Operations sent out the following message:

Unmistakable evidence enemy submarine immediately off coast between Cape Hatteras and Block Island. Vessels not properly convoyed advised to make port until further directed.

On the same day, June 3, a Coastwise Routing Office was organized at Washington, D. C., and became a part of the office of Naval Operations.

Thereafter, Navy control of coastwise shipping became an actual fact, and through the Routing Office the work of protecting shipping became centralized and proceeded along the following general plan:

1. In all cases the control of shipping within a district will be in the hands of the district commandant. In order that the proper coordination may be obtained along the whole coast, this control will follow a general doctrine, and the commandant of each district will be informed of the control of those districts adjacent to his own.

2. The best practice is to have coastwise shipping to proceed by day hugging the shore and keeping within the 5-fathom curve or as near it as practicable. Also, since it is the policy of the Shipping Committee charged with such work, to allocate the smallest and least valuable ships to the coasting trade, it, as a matter of expediency, should be the policy to protect such shipping by means within the districts through which coastwise shipping passes.

3. When it is found expedient to route coastwise shipping by night, it should proceed independently, being routed with due regard to the war warnings received concerning the location of enemy submarines.

General instructions were also laid down to cover the routing of shipping within the districts and of coastwise shipping passing through the district.

In the case of providing escorts for convoys passing through successive districts, the commandant of the district in which the convoy was made up routed it and provided an escort for it through his district and arranged with the adjacent district for relief of the escort upon the convoy's arrival within the latter's jurisdiction, and each successive district in turn arranged for the relief of its escort. Thus, convoys proceeding south in the third naval district were escorted by vessels of that district to the vicinity of Barnegat Light, where the escorting craft were relieved by vessels of the fourth naval district, which acted as escort to the convoy until reaching the vicinity of Winter Quarter Shoals, where in turn the escort duty was assumed by craft attached to the fifth naval district, and so on along the coast.

This same practice prevailed in the case of northbound convoys. All arrangements were made through the Communication Service, the details of the convoy, the facts relating to the rendezvous, and other matters of a confidential nature being transmitted in code.

Routing offices were established later in every Atlantic port wherein coastwise shipping was likely to originate, at Halifax, in West Indian ports, and on the station ship at Tampico, Mexico. These offices were controlled from the District Routing Office at the district headquarters. They were kept well supplied with the latest information as to routes to be issued, and dangers to be avoided. Masters of coastwise vessels were required to call at these offices before leaving port and to receive written instructions which were carefully explained to them. These instructions specified the routes to be followed, and areas to be avoided; they also included latest war warnings, war-warning schedules, and the location of the speaking stations with the signals that would be displayed at each. Masters were instructed to turn in their routing instructions at the port of arrival and submit to the routing officer a report of delays at speaking stations.

In order that no vessel should leave port without proper instructions, guard ships at harbor entrances were required to turn back any ship not possessing them.

It soon developed that masters were willing to report to routing officers for instructions and little difficulty was encountered in securing their compliance with this requirement.

If vessels after leaving port failed to follow their instructions, it was found that a report of the fact to the owners resulted in orders being issued to masters to comply strictly with instructions received from the Navy.

Routing officers in each port were able to communicate with the shipping interests through the customs officials, the Maritime Exchange, and the pilot associations. This close cooperation mutually benefited all organizations concerned.

The speaking stations were established at points along the coast in order to expedite the flow of coastwise shipping from one district to another, to provide a means for communicating with vessels not equipped with radio, to call vessels into harbor if necessary, and to divert vessels which might be proceeding into danger. These stations were manned by Navy personnel and were equipped with gear for day and night signaling according to a simple code of distance signals.

Vessels were instructed to speak to all stations along their route, but they were not to be delayed. Sand Key and Jupiter Stations were called reporting stations. All vessels passing out of the Gulf coastwisebound were required to speak to Sand Key; all vessels northbound through Old Bahama Passage were required to speak to Jupiter. These stations proved valuable in diverting vessels for their owners when it was desired to change a vessel's destination after she had sailed.

The successful consummation of convoying activity according to the general scheme laid down necessitated a considerable fleet of escorting vessels, usually subchasers, of fair speed and armament, and meant that the work of these small ships was to be one of incessant activity.

The fact that no convoy was attacked off the American coast indicated clearly that the presence of these small men-of-war meant security to the very essential cargoes, both of men and the material transported up and down the coast.

On the morning of June 3, the day that plans for the protection of coastwise shipping were being evolved, the U. S. S. *Preble* reported that she was engaging an enemy submarine in latitude 39° 31′ N., longitude 73° 31′ W. The U. S. S. *Henley* was immediately dispatched to the position indicated, and at 1 p. m. reported that she had searched the vicinity in which the U. S. S. *Preble* had made contact, but had found nothing.

Though the American tanker *Herbert L. Pratt*, 7,145 gross tons, was mined and sunk at 3.35 p. m., June 3, 2½ miles off Overfalls Lightship, as the result of the mining activity of the *U–151* in that vicinity, it was not until 6 p. m. that the submarine registered her first sinking for the day by attack, when she overhauled the *Sam. C. Mengel*, an unarmed schooner of 915 tons gross, owned by C. C. Mengel & Bros., Louisville, Ky., and sunk her by bombs placed aboard in 38° 08′ N., 73° 35′ W.

John W. Wilkins, the first officer of the *Mengel* stated that he overheard a conversation between the boarding officer and Capt. Hans T. Hansen in which the officer said his name was Kohler; that the submarine had been out six weeks and had sunk 17,000 tons, three schooners and three steamers, off the coast. According to Wilkins, when the crew of the schooner left their ship the boarding officer shook hands with them and said, "Send Wilson out here and we will finish him in 10 minntes. Wilson is the only one prolonging the war."

Early next morning the submarine attacked by gunfire and finally sank with bombs the *Edward R. Baird, jr.*, an unarmed American schooner of 279 gross tons, owned by D. J. Fooks, Laurel, Del. Her location was off the coast of Maryland. Approximately 37° 35′ N., 74° W.

They placed bombs on the schooner, one on each side, suspended from the rigging. It was about 7.30 a. m. sun time (8.30 a. m. Navy time) when we shoved off from the schooner. They shoved off and went after and fired at a steamer which appeared on the scene. When they shoved off after the steamer they were towing their dory astern the submarine. The bombs went off five minutes after we left the schooner. The weather was fine and clear; the sea was calm.

While the submarine was chasing the steamer mentioned above, the U. S. S. *Hull*, a coast torpedo vessel, hove in sight; the submarine immediately abandoned the chase and submerged. The *Hull* then picked up the survivors of the *Edward R. Baird* at about 8.20 a. m., three quarters of an hour after their ship had been sunk.

The destroyer had intercepted an attack upon the French tanker *Radioleine* and later sent in the following message which was received at Norfolk at 11.30 a. m.

From: U. S. S. *Hull*.

To: Commandant Fifth Naval District.

Rush intercepted attack enemy submarine on steamer *Radioleine* lat. 37° 38′ N. long. 73° 42′ W. 9.30 a. m. Took on board crew of Schooner *Edward Baird* bombed and sinking 11304.

The commanding officer, R. S. Haggart, U. S. S. *Hull*, made the following report concerning the attack upon the *Radioleine:*

At 8.30 a. m., June 4, 1918, while this vessel was proceeding to station in accordance with radio orders from the commandant, fifth naval district, making 15 knots speed, course 61° true, latitude 37° 15′ N., longitude 74° W., sound of firing was heard nearly ahead. Full speed was put on at once and shortly after S O S signal was received from the steamship *Radioleine* and the steamer which appeared to be firing was seen on the horizon about one point on starboard bow; headed for the submarine and sounded general quarters; noted steamer to be headed in our direction zigzagging and firing her stern gun. Splashes from enemy shells were seen falling near steamer between her and this vessel. Firing ceased when we were about 400 yards from steamer. No sight of enemy was seen. The steamer proved to be the French steamship *Radioleine*, which in passing headed toward Hampton Roads at full speed; she signaled, "Large enemy cruiser fired on sailing ship, then on us." We proceeded in the direction of the sailing vessel dead ahead about 3 miles distant. We sighted an object in water and headed for same; it proved to be a dory containing crew of American schooner *Edward R. Baird, Jr.* They reported their ship fired upon and bombed by German submarine and boarding officer had forced them to abandon ship.

We searched the vicinity for submarine, but found nothing. We went close aport the schooner, which was still afloat, to determine if she could be saved. The executive officer of this vessel (U. S. S. *Hull*) went on board with crew of schooner and found decks awash and holds full of water from bomb holes inside; the vessel was floating, due to the cargo of lumber. A device believed to be a German percussion fuse igniter was found on board and is forwarded herewith. We took the crew of the schooner on board once more and circled in the vicinity searching for the enemy. We sighted full-rigged ship *Doon* and warned her out of the danger area. We remained in the vicinity until 1 p. m., when we proceeded toward station."

The master of the French tanker *Radioleine* in reporting the attack on his vessel said that on June 4, at 7.10 a. m., in latitude 37° 10′ N., longitude 74° W., they were attacked by a German submarine which chased them for an hour, at the end of which time the American torpedo boat *Hull* appeared in answer to S O S calls of the *Radioleine*, and the submarine gave up the chase. A number of shots were fired by the submarine and the *Radioleine* returned the fire. The *Radioleine* finally exhausted her supply of ammunition.

After abandoning the chase of the *Radioleine* about 8.30 a. m., the submarine continued her route southward and about 4.15 p. m. when in latitude 37° 12′ N., longitude 73° 55′ W., made an attack upon and subsequently sank the Norwegian steamship *Eidsvold*, an unarmed vessel of 1,570 tons, chartered by the United Fruit Co. Capt. J. Johnson, master of the *Eidsvold*, told how his vessel was overhauled and sunk by the submarine:

On June the 4th, at 4.15 p. m. in latitude 37° 12′ N. and longitude 73° 55′ W., a submarine appeared off the starboard bow about 500 yards. She fired one shot over the steamer; we then stopped our engines. He signaled me to send a boat over to the submarine; one of the mates, three seamen, and I took the ship's papers over to the submarine and boarded her. I told him we were bound from Guantanamo, Cuba, to New York with a cargo of sugar. When he heard that it was sugar for New York he said that he was sorry that he had to sink the ship.

I then asked him for a reasonable length of time to get into the lifeboats, as I had my wife on board. He stated that he would give me as much time as it would take to get into the boats. I then returned to my ship and at 5 p. m. the boats got clear of the ship.[12]

They then fired three shots into the starboard side, then turned around and fired three shots into the port side, all shots taking effect at the water line. My ship disappeared at 5.20 p. m.

The submarine remained in view till dusk. She seemed to follow us slowly waiting for some vessel to come along and try to pick us up, when she would become easy prey for the submarine.

When about 40 miles south of where she had sunk the *Eidsvold*, the submarine registered her next sinking at 9 a. m. on June 5,

---

[12] The boats of the *Eidsvold* were picked up next day by the Morgan Line steamer *Proteus*, after having been at sea 22 hours.

when she torpedoed, without warning, the *Harpathian* an unarmed British steamship of 4,588 tons gross, en route from London to Newport News in ballast. The master of the *Harpathian* supplied the following information to the commander, Newport News, Division Transport Force:

> The *Harpathian* was sunk without warning by a torpedo from an enemy submarine at 9.30 a. m. June 5, Cape Henry bearing N. 70 W. (true) 90 miles.[13] The ship was torpedoed in latitude 36° 30′ N., 75° W.; sank in about seven minutes. All hands were saved. One member of the crew, a Chinaman, was struck between the eyes by a piece of the torpedo that sunk the ship. The captain did not see the submarine till after the ship was hit, and only a few of the crew saw the torpedo before it struck.
>
> The crew got away in the boats. The submarine commander called the boats alongside and asked if all were saved and if any were sick; he also asked if they had food and water. The Chinaman was given treatment aboard the submarine and was then returned aboard the lifeboat. The submarine commander gave each boat a bucket of water and asked the captain of the vessel if he had sent a wireless and on being told that there had been no time, gave the boats the course to the nearest land.

The crew of the *Harpathian* was picked up by the British steamer *Potomac* on June 6, at 10.30 p. m.

At 3 p. m., June 5, the American schooner *Ella Swift* sighted the submarine in latitude 36° 30′ N. and longitude 73° 40′ W.; less than an hour later the American whaler *Nicholson* was halted at the same spot. The master of the whaler urged the submarine officers to spare his ship saying that it would ruin him financially if the vessel was destroyed. After a brief conference the submarine officers informed him that he might proceed and ordered him away from the vicinity.

The same day the *U-151* sank the Norwegian steamer *Vinland*, 1,143 gross tons, in latitude 36° 32′ N. and longitude 73° 58′ W.

> The *Vinland* sailed from Guantanamo for New York with a cargo of sugar. On June 5 at 6 p. m. a German submarine sent a shot over the ship which landed 300 yards on the other side. The submarine was about 3½ miles away and one point abaft the port beam. I went aboard the submarine and they told me to get the boats ready as quickly as possible. I went back to my ship and told every man to get as many clothes as he could. About the same time one German officer and four or five men came aboard. They took two bags of sugar. After that they placed a bomb on the outside about 2 feet below the water line. It was cylindrical in shape and pointed at both ends and they dropped it down with a piece of rope. The attitude of the Germans while aboard was very nice; they said they were going to give us as much time as they could and it was 20 minutes after they came aboard before we left the ship.
>
> One of the men struck a match and lighted the fuse it being a fuse bomb and it exploded in about five minutes.
>
> When first sighted about 4 miles away the submarine looked like an ordinary tramp steamer.

---

[13] Evidence of the difficulty which the Navy Department experienced in keeping correctly informed of the submarine situation is shown by the fact that two submarine chasers reported the probable sinking of a submarine late in the morning of June 5. It was found by a comparison of distances that the *U-151*, the only enemy submarine on the coast at the time, would have been obliged to cruise 100 knots in two hours to have been in the position given the object fired upon by the chasers.

On June 6, at 10 a. m., the British S. S. *Mantella* reported a submarine in latitude 36° 2′ N., longitude 73° 41′ W.

On the same day at 2 p. m. the American steamship *Cacique* reported sighting a submarine in latitude 31° 5′ N., longtitude 75° 35 W. This position, however, was too far south and too far west at the time to have been that of an enemy submarine.

On June 7, Coast Guard Station No. 115 reported that a submarine had been sighted in latitude 39° 41′ N., longitude 74° 5′ W. On the same date the British S. S. *Huntsend* reported an oil patch in latitude 39° 45′ N., longitude 73° 42′ W. These positions were also too far north to have had any connection with the enemy submarine, which, even on this date, was still operating further south as shown by the fact that on June 8, at 5.30 a. m., in latitude 36° 25′ N., longtitude 74° 20′ W., the submarine captured the Norwegian S. S. *Vindeggen*, a vessel of 3,179 gross tons owned by Jens Folkmans hailing from Skien, Norway, and after transferring part of her cargo of copper to the submarine, sank the steamship on June 10, at 11.07 a. m., in latitude 36° 25′ N., longtitude 73° 20′ W.

The statement of Edward Ballestad, master of the *Vindeggen*, covers the story of his experience with the submarine:

The steamship *Vindeggen* left Chile May 31 bound for New York to discharge a cargo of wool, copper, and salted skins. Everything went all right until June 8, ·5.30 a.m. in 36° 25′ N., 74° 20′ W., when a submarine immediately came to the surface in easterly direction about three-quarters mile off. The submarine fired two shots and hoisted signals to stop immediately. We lowered the port-side boat and it went over to the submarine with the ships papers. During the work of lowering the starboard boat some Chinamen jumped into it and it capsized and one of the Chinamen was drowned. At 7.30 a. m. we sighted another steamer and the submarine proceeded down to the eastward and ordered us to follow. At 11.30 the submarine came back to us. It was the intention of the submarine to sink the ship right away but when they found out we had copper they decided to bring it over to the submarine.

At 9 a. m. on the 9th they commenced bringing copper to the submarine and they continued until 8 p. m. Next day they began work again at 5 in the morning and continued until 11. Then the submarine commander gave orders that the ship should be sunk and said he would tow us to port. They planted bombs and in seven minutes the ship disappeared. The submarine then proceeded westward with the boats in tow. At 6.30 p. m. another steamer was sighted and the captain of the submarine gave us orders to cast off the ropes and sail in a westerly direction. He went for the steamer and sank her; he was back in half an hour. The submarine picked us up again and towed us till 8.30 p. m., when they sighted another steamer and cast us off again and submerged.

They did not say how many tons of copper they took from my ship, I should say about 70 or 80; they estimated the value at about 1,000,000 marks. One of the officers told me that off Cape Henry they dived in water so shallow that when he got to bottom he was about the water line. He said he could easily sink a battleship, but had orders not to sink it that day. He called all the officers to look through the periscope and see what a fine target that ship would make.

The first steamship that appeared on the scene about two hours after the *Vindeggen* had been captured was the *Pinar del Rio*, an

American steamship of 2,504 tons gross, en route to Boston from Cuba with a cargo of 25,000 bags of sugar. The crew of the steamer took to the boats at once and the submarine coming within 100 feet of the ship sank her with gunfire in latitude 36° 16′ W., longitude 73° 50′ W., at 8.15 a. m., June 8, 1918.

Early in the morning of June 9 the U. S. S. Battleship *South Carolina*,[14] with the U. S. S. C. *No. 234*, sighted and fired upon a periscope, S. C. *No. 234* dropping depth bombs in the neighborhood of Cape Henry, and on the afternoon of the next day the *Henrick Lund*, a Norwegian vessel, of 4,322 gross tons, was overhauled and sunk by the *U–151*,[15] in latitude 36° 30′ N., longitude 71° 29′ W.

On June 10, at 6.40 p. m., the Coast Guard Station No. 82 reported sighting a periscope bound east. At 7.22 p. m. on the same date the U. S. S. *L–5* reported a submarine running awash 2 miles distant in latitude 37° 32′ N., longitude 73° 49′ W. At 9.22 p. m. the U. S. S. *L–5* reported that the submarine fired a torpedo which crossed the bow of the U. S. S. *L–5* at 10 yards distant. On June 10 when in latitude 39° 15′ N., longitude 74° 15′ W., the steamship *Sodral* sighted a submarine and at the same time saw an American ship on the starboard bow turn her guns on the object and fired three shots, one of which fell close to the object. The object disappeared; seven minutes later the same steamer fired five more shots. A submarine was reported by a fishing boat and an aeroplane on June 10, 9 miles' northeast of Winter Quarter Shoals. On the same date the Coast Guard Station No. 83 sighted what appeared to be a periscope 2½ miles southeast of Fire Island. It will be seen that all these positions indicated are at points too far north to have any connection with the *U–151*, which was still operating farther south in latitude about 36° 30′ N.

The whereabouts of the *U–151* during the two days that followed the sinking of the *Hendrik Lund* must remain an open question. There were numerous reports of sightings, but none of these can be accepted as authentic.[16] On the morning of June 13, however, the British steamer *Llanstephan Castle* encountered the raider which gave up the chase of that vessel to attack the *Keemun*, another British ship which appeared nearer at hand. Capt. Chope of the *Llanstephan Castle* reported his escape to the aid for information at New York as follows:

June 13, 5.15 p. m., latitude 38° 02′ N., longitude 72° 47′ W., 76 meridian time, I sighted strange looking craft on my starboard beam, which was taken to be, by my officers and myself, a destroyer of the British "T" type. She was steaming with us

---

[14] The *South Carolina* is probably the vessel referred to in the conversation of the submarine officer with the captain of the *Vindeggen*.

[15] The steamer spoken of by Capt. Ballestad in the latter part of his narrative.

[16] Among the sightings reported were the following: *Mapleleaf*, 39° 30′ N., 68° W.; *Author*, 30° 10′ N., 78° 20′ W.; *Randwijk*, 39° 05′ N., 74° 37′ W.

about 10 miles off, closing in on the ship. When it was noted that the submarine was closing in my vessel turned away, so as to keep the submarine astern. He did not follow us, however, for about five minutes, and changed his course to the westward. He again started for us after another five minutes, and then he changed his course to the eastward. I noted two big guns on the submarine, one forward and one aft. She had a rounded stern and a raised bow, and two periscopes which looked like a funnel at that distance. My gunner reported to me, after looking at her through his sight, that she had removed two clows from her fore deck since we had first sighted her. When we had the submarine astern of us the S. S. *Keemun* appeared on our port bow. I hoisted the "B" flag, with a ball underneath and the proper signal, "North."

The *Keemun* apparently did not see our signal, as she did not answer it. Therefore I sent out an "allo" message, giving the ship's position. The *Keemun* at that time was astern of us, about 5 miles distant. The Marconi officer on the ship at this time reported that he had picked up a message that the *Keemun* was being shelled. I noted three shots fall near the *Keemun*. The *Keemun* returned the submarine's fire. The submarine was about 300 feet long.

The report of the Master of the *Keemun*, Thomas Collister, supplements that of Capt. Chope, and tells of the final escape of his ship:

On the evening of June 13th at 6.50 p. m. after receiving a wireless message from the steamship *Llanstephan Castle* stating that a submarine was in latitude 38° 02′ N. longitude 72° 47′ W., we sighted a submarine while in latitude 37° 51′ N. and longitude 70° 50′ W. The submarine was about 7 miles from my vessel. It was not submerged and was making about 12 knots, about the same speed my vessel was running. Ten shells were fired by the submarine. My vessel opened fire at 7,000 yards and at 11,000 yards the last shot was fired. After our last shot was fired the submarine apparently came to a standstill.

On the next day the Norwegian bark *Samoa*, of 1,138 tons gross, owned by Jacobsen & Thon, Norway, bound from Walfich Bay, South Africa, for Perth Amboy, N. J., with a cargo of wool and copper ore, was overhauled in latitude 37° 30′ N., 72° 10′ W. by an enemy submarine and subsequently sunk by gunfire at 8 a. m.

The following gives the summary of a statement made by Harold Grostock concerning the sinking of the *Samoa:*

I do not know the exact latitude, but the captain of the German submarine told us we were 200 miles off the Virginia coast. We sighted her about 5 a. m. while she was cruising around us on the surface until about 6 a. m., when she came within 100 yards of us.

She gave us 15 minutes to leave the ship. She fired a shot across our bow to stop; then she gave us the signal to get into lifeboats.

After we had gotten into the lifeboats she went around on the west side and put three shots into our vessel; the *Samoa* sank on the third shot.

The captain of the *Samoa* asked the commander of the submarine what latitude and longitude we were in and the submarine gave him a paper which stated that the Norwegian bark *Samoa* was sunk in latitude 37° 30′ N., longitude 72° 10′ W.

All members of the crew got away safely; none were taken aboard the submarine. There was no number on the hull of the submarine. She had a wireless and sent a wireless message asking assistance for us. She sailed off, going southwest.

The crew of the *Samoa* were picked up by the schooner *George W. Truitt, Jr.*, at 4 p. m. on June 15, and later were transferred to the

Paul Jones and subsequently landed at Norfolk by boat. The weather was fine and clear. There were no casualties.

On the afternoon of June 14, at 5 o'clock, when in latitude 38° 02' N., 71° 40' W., the enemy submarine accounted for her next vessel when she attacked and sank by gunfire the *Kringsjaa*, a Norwegian bark of 1,750 gross tons, owned by Knudsen & Christiansund, Norway, which left Buenos Aires on April 25, 1918, en route to New York with a cargo of flaxseed.

The captain of the *Kringsjaa* requested the submarine officers to give his boats a tow toward land. To this Lieut. Kohler replied that that was impossible; that they had other business, and that the submarine was bound north. He then told Capt. Gunwald Magnusdel that he was 150 miles from the coast and to steer a course west by north in order to reach the coast as soon as possible. He then said, "I will report that you have been sunk, by wireless, in order that you may be rescued." Capt. Magnusdel of the bark then heard the wireless of the submarine cracking.[17]

On June 15 at 7.30 p. m. the British S. S. *City of Calcutta* sent in an "allo" advising that she had sighted a submarine in latitude 39° 08' N., longitude 66° 18' W.

After the sinking of the *Kringsjaa* on June 14, the *U–151* began her homeward journey. The fact that the *City of Calcutta* sighted a submarine in latitude 39° 08' N., longitude 66° 18' W. on June 15 indicates that on that date submarine was well on her homeward way and was not sighted by the British steamship *Aras* on June 15, or by the *Princess Matoika* on June 16, or the U. S. S. *Mexican* on June 17, as was reported at the time. The assumption is further substantiated by the fact that on June 18, at 9.20 a. m., the British steamship *Dwinsk*, 8,173 gross tons, commanded by Lieut. Commander H. Nelson, R. N. R., was torpedoed, and subsequently sunk by gunfire about two hours later in latitude 38° 30' N., longitude 61° 15' W.

About two and one-half hours after the *Dwinsk* had been abandoned the U. S. S. *Von Steuben* appeared on the scene and bore down on the lifeboats. She suddenly stopped, however, avoiding a torpedo and opened fire on a periscope, firing 19 shots and dropping depth charges.

On June 19 the American steamship *Advance* reported the sighting of what appeared to be a submarine at 4.15 p. m. in latitude 38° 32' N., longitude 71° 12' W., and on June 20, U. S. S. *Prairie* reported a submarine and the sighting of what appeared to be a torpedo passing astern in latitude 33° 56' N., longitude 68° 25' W.

It was most probable that the objects sighted by the crew of the steamship *Advance* or the U. S. S. *Prairie* were not enemy submarines,

---

[17] The crew of the *Kringsjaa* was picked up by the U. S. destroyer *Patterson*, after having been at sea for 42 hours.

GERMAN SUBMARINE AT SEA.

A GERMAN SUBMARINE LYING NEAR A SHIP WHICH HAS JUST BEEN BOARDED BY THE SUBMARINE'S MEN.

SMOKE-SCREEN DEFENSE.

WAR ON HOSPITAL SHIPS.

since on June 22, when in latitude 39° 30′ N., longitude 53° 40′ W., the *U–151* attacked and sank the Belgian transport *Chillier* at 12.30 p. m.

The *Chillier*, a vessel of 2,966 gross tons, was bound for New York in ballast. She was armed with "an old French 90-mm. gun, which could be loaded with powder and cartridges," and with this antiquated piece she fired several ineffective shots at the submarine before she surrendered. The day after the *Chillier* had been abandoned one of her lifeboats with six members of the crew aboard foundered and all were lost.

On the morning of June 23 the raider scored another success, the victim being the Norwegian steamer *Augvald*, a vessel of 3,406 gross tons. The following account of the attack is given by Alfred Pedersen the chief engineer of the merchant ship:

On Sunday morning about 9 o'clock in latitude 38° 30′ N., longitude 53° 42′ W., the submarine made its attack by gunfire. When we first saw the submarine she was about 4 miles away. We stopped the engines. She came abeam of us and began to fire again. Nothing struck us till about 11 o'clock. We abandoned ship about 9.30 before the shots began to strike the vessel. At about 11 o'clock the submarine fired 25 or 30 shots into the vessel. We had only two lifeboats. We had grub, water, and everything in the boat I was in, but we lost it all and the mate, too, when the boat capsized. The first time she capsized we lost our compass. There were 14 men in the boat when she left the ship; after she had capsized the third time there were only 11 left. We saw many steamers, but none of them would pick us up. We were not picked up until July 4. The only thing we had to eat after the boat capsized on June 25 was small bits of seaweed and little fish we caught in the seaweed. We had plenty of rain water for a while, but later we had to use salt water.

The *Augvald* was the last victim of the memorable cruise of the *U–151*. The raider did not cease her efforts to add to the list of her victims, however, and the last part of her homeward cruise was marked by unsuccessful attacks and running engagements with American and British vessels.

On June 25 at 7 a. m. the British steamship *Glenlee*, 4,915 tons gross, was shelled by submarine in latitude 40° N., longitude 49° W. The *Glenlee* was saved by her own guns. There were no casualties. On the same day at 7 p. m. the U. S. S. *Dochra*, 4,309 gross tons, reported being shelled by a submarine in latitude 40° 25′ N., longitude 47° 29′ W. The *Dochra* also escaped.

Two days later the U. S. S. *Lake Forest*, 4,100 tons displacement, a Naval Overseas Transportation Service vessel, at 6 a. m. sighted the *U–151* in latitude 41° 12′ N., and longitude 44° 03′ W., and was shelled, returning fire in a battle which lasted till 7.25 a. m., when the submarine disappeared. The submarine fired 60 shots and the ship 24 rounds.

On June 28 the U. S. A. C. T. *McClellan* reported a submarine at 4.55 a. m. in latitude 42° 15′ N., longitude 41° 19′ W. This submarine was also reported at 8 a. m. by U. S. S. *Minneapolis*, giving the position 42° 17′ N., 41° 22′ W.

On July 2 U. S. S. *Lake Erie* sighted the submarine in latitude 40° 12′ N., longitude 33° 55′ W. Three days later at 1.50 a. m. the radio station at Bar Harbor intercepted an S O S from a ship whose name is not given, advising that she was being chased in latitude 45° 40′ N., longitude 25° 30′ W. On the next day the British steamship *Nevassa*, 9,071 tons gross, reported that she was being chased by an enemy submarine in latitude 49° 06′ N., longitude 26° 51′ W.

After the attack on the *Nevasa* the *U-151* passed from the scene of submarine activities and no more is heard of her until the surrender at Harwich after the signing of the armistice. According to the reports to the British Admiralty she reached her base early in August and remained there until the war came to an end.

Although the cruise of the *U-151* was not successful in drawing home any of the naval vessels of the United States operating in foreign waters, it must be admitted that the raider fulfilled the expectations of the German high command in her rôle as a commerce destroyer, sinking 22 vessels, the aggregate tonnage of which exceeded 52,000 gross tons.

THE CRUISE OF U-156.

The *U-156*, another submarine of the converted mercantile cruiser type left her base at Kiel for American waters on or about June 15, 1918 under the command of Kapitanleutnant von Oldenburg. After making her way across the North Sea and around the Shetland Islands she engaged in her first offensive on the 26th, when she torpedoed and sank the British steamer *Tortuguero*, 4,175 gross tons, in latitude 55° 50′ N., longitude 15° 30′ W.

The next encounter [18] of her voyage took place late in the afternoon of July 5 when she attacked the U. S. S. *Lake Bridge*, 1,984 gross tons, bound from Lamlash, Scotland, for Hampton Roads, in latitude 43° 35′ N., longitude 43° 50′ W. The submarine had disguised herself as a steamer and it was not until she housed her false funnel, headed directly for the American vessel at high speed and opened fire at 10,000 yards that her enemy character was recognized. The *Lake Bridge* at once returned the fire and a running fight was carried on for some time, both vessels attempting to conceal their positions by the use of smoke screens. The *Lake Bridge* finally outdistanced her pursuer and escaped without injury, although one of the shells from the submarine exploded so close aboard that pieces of it were thrown on the decks of the American ship.

---

[18] The U. S. S. *Susquehanna* reported an attack on July 2 while in latitude 41 N., longitude 41 W.

Two days later the *U-156* sank the Norwegian bark *Marosa*, 1,987 gross tons, in latitude 40° N., and longitude 50° 35′ W. The vessel, which was proceeding from Newport News to Montevideo with a cargo of 3,171 tons of coal, received her first warning of the presence of the submarine when a shot was fired across her bow. She hove to; the crew took to the lifeboats and rowed to the submarine where the ship's papers were examined and the officers questioned regarding the precautions taken to protect the American coast, the location of American war vessels, and the feelings of the American people in regard to the war.

From the report of Andreas A. Nyhus, captain of the *Marosa*, to the American Naval Intelligence officers, at Halifax:

The hour and day of attack was 4.30 p. m., 7 July, 1918. The position was latitude 40 north longitude 50.35 west, the *Marosa* being on a true NE. course, close hauled on the starboard tack, a good latitude having been observed at noon and a good p. m. line of position obtained at 2. She carried a coal cargo of bituminous, 3,171 tons. The first intimation that a submarine was in the vicinity was a shrapnel shot striking the water close to the *Marosa*. The submarine was seen on the surface dead in the water, three points on the port bow of the vessel about 3 miles off. The *Marosa* then backed her main and mizzen yards. This movement made the submarine bear broad on the vessel's starboard bow. The submarine then fired another shot, which went over the ship, and struck the water close to, splinters from the shrapnel shell flying back on board. The *Marosa* then lowered her two lifeboats. All the ship's company, including the captain, left the ship and rowed toward the submarine. The small sculling boat was the only other boat left on board. It took the boats an hour or so to pull up to the submarine. The mate's boat got alongside first. When the captain of the *Marosa* got alongside in the boat he was in, he was ordered on board the submarine and told to bring the ship's papers and log book. The second officer of the submarine interrogated him as to the present and previous voyages of his vessel. The captain of the submarine was not seen on deck during the entire time the submarine was in sight. The second officer and one sailor did all the interrogating in broken English. The ship's papers and log book were kept by the submarine, and the crew list and all the passports of the crew and the captain's pocketbook, which contained about $40 in American currency, was returned to him. The submarine then took the boats in tow back to the ship and ordered the *Marosa's* crew to lower the remaining sculling boat and bring it back to the submarine. The submarine's crew then made several trips in this boat carrying a bag which they handled carefully in the first trip, and which I took to be bombs. They searched the vessel sending a man aloft on the mizzen with a pair of binoculars as a lookout and took off the hatches. They then left the ship. My men were then permitted to go on board and take everything they wanted. We took provisions, oilskins, and plenty of water. We left our ship the second time about 6 p. m. and pulled off and stood by. They did not sink the ship as long as we could see nor were any explosions heard. They were still using our small boat to transfer what I believed were provisions. At 7 p. m. having a fair wind we set sail in our two boats and left the vicinity. It came on dark about 8.30 p. m. I did not see them sink my ship but saw the same submarine, which was painted dark gray and black and had two long guns about not less than 6 inches, sink a three-masted full rigged sailing vessel the next day about noon. The next day was misty. We shaped our course for her, she was not under command, all courses were made fast, and everything else clewed up except lower topsails. I did not hear an explosion, but as the submarine passed the boats about a mile off, heading true west, no boats from this vessel were seen, and as we could obtain no assistance from this sinking vessel we headed on a course NW. by W. magnetic. The condition of the weather on July 7 was light southeasterly breeze, clear, and it blew up during the night with heavy rain squalls. There was no loss of life or injury to any one. The vessel was not armed. Not one of the survivors saw my vessel actually sink, nor did we see the full rigged vessel I sighted the next day actually sink. The exact position of the second vessel, I am unable to give. All my efforts were bent on getting away from the vicinity.

The following is a statement of S. E. Holte, chief officer of the Norwegian bark *Marosa*, as received from the United States Naval Intelligence officer of Halifax, Nova Scotia:

We had a latitude at dinner time of 39° 54′ N. and longitude 50° 56′ W. About 5 p. m., local apparent time, after sailing 25 miles ENE. (true) from the noon position, I was lying in bed when I heard a shot. I immediately came out and went up on the poop deck and saw a submarine lying about 3 miles to our windward on the starboard side. I ordered all hands on deck right away. We lowered down the top-gallant sails, brailed up the mainsail, braced back the main and mizzen yards, and I ordered one-half the crew to hoist out the lifeboats. They were swung out. The steward and cook got provisions into the boats about five minutes after the first shots. When we were not quite finished they fired another shot, which landed about 15 yards from the starboard lifeboat, and pieces of shrapnel flew close to the vessel.

The submarine then bore down on our vessel until they were one-half mile off, when they let us go, and five German sailors armed with revolvers came on board my boat. On going alongside, they told us that they would give us 20 minutes to get our oilskins. We put more provisions into our boat and our oilskins. Then they asked me if the gig up forward was any good, and I told them yes; they then ordered me to put her into the water, which I did. As we had all we could get, we pulled away, laying off half a mile from our vessel in our boats until darkness set in. All we could see of what the submarine's crew was doing was hoisting articles in the gig by the starboard davit. The last we saw of them was when they pulled from our ship to the submarine and they were still using the gig. The kind of stores they took, I do not know, but they were carrying bombs with them or some apparatus with long white lanyards on them. The German sailors, who boarded the ship went through the cabin, and the rest of the ship. They stationed a man on the mizzen royal yard as a lookout with large powerful binoculars, and they also tore all the hatches off.

Description of the submarine.—About 200 feet long, one conning tower, two masts for wireless (small stumps), large guns, about 8-inch, white square with red cross on it about 4 inches square on conning tower, exactly like the Red Cross. Two patent anchors forward, all rusty. Two periscopes, one of them telescopic. Amidships, fore and aft, were life rails. Hull painted gray and black. Guns and everything else painted in the same way. Deck about $\frac{1}{2}$ inch thick. Had big holes about $1\frac{1}{2}$ feet in diameter around the stern. As we came up to the submarine they asked us if there was any one else on board, and we told them no. They unloaded their guns, using a wooden rammer about 10 feet long to eject the shells from the guns. Two men, having long wires leading below deck with ear pieces on their heads, walked about on the deck all the time. There were about a half dozen officers, who wore powerful binoculars and carried revolvers. We did not see any mines on her, just ammunition for the guns—ammunition fixed—brass case. The second officer of the German submarine spoke English and several of the crew spoke Norwegian. The skipper of the submarine was a tall man, with black beard and mustache—not very stout—sort of thin. The crew were all young men and two of them wore on their hats "II Flotilla." One of the crew of the German submarine in Scandanavian told one of the crew of the *Marosa* to take plenty of clothing and provisions, as they were a long way from home.

About 9 p. m., after dark, we proceeded on our course NW. by W. and lost sight of the vessel. They gave us no course, but told my captain to steer to westward and some one on board the submarine shouted, "Good trip and God bless you, you are 800 miles from land." We then steered NW. by W. to gain north of the Gulf Stream.

About 4 p. m. the next day we sighted a full-rigged sailing ship with only the lower topsails on her. Everything else was lowered down. The mainsail was brailed up, foresail and cross jack were furled. We bore down on it to within 2½ miles. She looked suspicious, so we waited a while to see what it was. We waited there for a while and then started, keeping on our course for about a quarter of an hour. Suddenly the ship disappeared and we could not have been more than 3 miles off at the time when we saw the same submarined. Just as we were looking they saw us and steered NW. by W. magnetic. At night we saw some lights, whether they were the lights from the submarine or the lights flashing from the boats of the full-rigged ship, I do not know. The lights were not flare-ups, they were flashes, caused either by signal or motions of the seaway. Heavy rain, squalls, a very rough sea, and a westerly wind had set in by this time.

The next day we saw nothing, and the day after that we saw nothing. The next morning there was a light southwesterly breeze, and we sighted the barque *Sorkness*, home port, Farhsund, Norway, and we pulled up to that ship. They picked us up, took our boats on board, and carried us 200 miles toward the Nova Scotia shore. On the same day we sighted the schooner *Linda*, from Liverpool, and the captain of my vessel went over and asked them if they would take us to Nova Scotia. He said he could take the captain and a couple of men, but not all. The captain then came back and Capt. Daniels of the barque *Sorkness* said he would take us closer to the Nova Scotia shore.

We shoved off again in our two boats, loading up with provisions again, and during the next two days we saw several fishing vessels from Newfoundland. We held our course and kept the boats together so that they would not get lost in the fog. A large British man-of-war came up to within 10 yards of us and nearly ran us down. They saw us and altered their course. She was using her siren constantly. Our boats got mixed up with the propeller wash. They never answered our signals and at the time one could not see more than 200 feet ahead on account of the fog. We landed on the night of the 16th, at 11 p. m., at Cranberry Island.

The second officer of the submarine told me that they had to sink the ship, as she was chartered by an American firm.

The vessel which the captain and first officer of the *Marosa* saw sunk on July 8 was the Norwegian schooner *Manx King*, 1,729 gross tons, bound from New York to Rio de Janeiro with general cargo, and was sunk in approximately latitude 40° north, longitude 52° west. The captain of the *Manx King* protested against the seizure of his vessel, pointing out that she was of neutral register, but the submarine officer insisted that the type of cargo carried (oil, cotton, barbed wire, sheet iron, and shoes) was contraband and that the vessel must be destroyed. As in the case of the *Marosa* the crew of the merchant vessel was given ample time to provision the boats while the Germans were removing supplies to the submarine and searching for other prey from the main gallant yard. They then placed bombs in the hatches of the ship, using the victims' flag lines for the purpose,[19] and after advising the Norwegian captain "to sail

---

[19] These bombs were described as being 18 inches in length and 3 to 4 inches in diameter, with small plugs resembling "the binding posts of an electric battery" on top.

in a westerly direction, saying that he would be sure to be picked up by a passing ship," ordered the lifeboats to get underway. The crew of the *Manx King* did not see their vessel sink, as she disappeared in the fog after they had gone 2 miles.

After the sinking of the *Manx King* nothing was learned of the whereabouts of the *U–156* [20] until an allo was sent out on the 17th by the U. S. S. *Harrisburg*, giving her position as latitude 40° 10' N., longitude 68° 55' W. The submarine, which was lying on the surface, made no effort to attack, and after remaining in view for 10 minutes submerged at a distance of about 10,000 yards from the *Harrisburg*.[21]

Four days after she was sighted by the *Harrisburg* the raider raised a storm of excitement along the seaboard by attacking the tug *Perth Amboy*, 435 gross tons, and her tow of four barges in sight of the Massachusetts coast and within a few miles of the Chatham naval air station. The war diary of the first naval district gives a graphic account of the attack:

A German submarine attacked the tug *Perth Amboy* of the Lehigh Valley R. R., and her four barges, 3 miles off Orleans, on the southeastern elbow of Cape Cod, Mass., at 10.30 a. m. to-day. The one-sided battle lasted one hour and one-half. The tug was burned to the water's edge by shell fire, while the barges *Lansford* and *No. 766*, *No. 403*, and *No. 740* were sunk by gunfire. The barges were bound from Gloucester, Mass., for New York, N. Y., and only one was loaded, her cargo consisting of stone. Of the 41 persons, including 3 women and 5 children on board, 3 men were wounded.

The attack was witnessed by large crowds of natives and summer visitors, who had flocked to the cape for the week end, seeking relief from the hot wave. All accounts agreed that the submarine's shooting was very bad. Her torpedo work was no better. According to Capt. Ainsleigh of the *Lansford*, the U-boat launched three torpedoes at the tug and all went wild. This is not believed to be true.

The attack occurred only a few miles from the naval air station at Chatham. Four hydroplanes attacked the raider with bombs. The depth bombs dropped did not explode. The fire was returned, keeping the planes high. Finally, the U-boat submerged and was last observed heading south.

To-night the tug was still afloat, and it is thought she can be saved. The net result of the raid was the sinking of barges valued in the aggregate at $90,000 and the serious damaging of a tug valued at $100,000, and the expenditure of some ammunition.

The appearance of the raider so near the treacherous shoals and tide rips of the cape and her subsequent actions caused amazement to the thousands of eyewitnesses rather than consternation. The natives of the cape could not understand why she should waste torpedoes and shells on barges running to a coal port.

A fog bank lying 4 miles offshore hid the U-boat from her approaching victims. The *Perth Amboy*, steaming leisurely through the calm summer sea, was unaware of the presence of danger until a deckhand sighted a streak in the water shooting by the stern.

---

[20] The U. S. S. *Kroonland* reported firing upon a submarine on the 10th when in latitude 36° 28' N., longitude 62° 32' W.

[21] It is supposed that the time between the sinking of the *Manx King* and the sighting by the *Harrisburg* was occupied in the sowing of mines, one of which sank the U. S. S. *San Diego*. (See page 126.)

Before he realized that it was a torpedo, two other missiles sped by, wide of their mark. He shouted a warning. At the same time there was a flash from the fog and a shell crashed through the wheelhouse. A fragment of the flying steel took off the hand of a sailor as he grasped the spokes of the steering wheel. In quick succession came other shots, some of which went wide and some of which struck home.

Capt. J. P. Tapley, of the *Perth Amboy*, who was in his cabin at the time, ran out on the deck just as the submarine loomed out of the fog bank, her deck gun flashing out its storm of steel. The bombardment set the tug on fire, and the German then turned his attention to the helpless barges.

Shrapnel bursting over the *Lansford*, second in the tow, struck down Charles Ainsleigh, master of the barge. The shooting of the enemy was amazingly bad. For more than an hour the blazing tug and the drifting barges were under fire before the enemy succeeded in getting enough shots to sink them. In the meantime, the submarine crept nearer until her range was only a few hundred yards. This at length proved sufficient, and the barges disappeared beneath the surface one by one until only the stern of the *Lansford* was visible. The tug was a burning hulk.

The crews, with the three women, the five children who were aboard and the wounded, rowed ashore, landing in Nauseet Harbor, Cape Cod, Mass. (Coast Guard Station No. 40), while naval hydroairplanes came out, located the U-boat in the haze, and engaged her.

Some of the summer residents grew uneasy when they saw how wild the German gunners were shooting and feared stray shells would hit their cottages. Many of these residents went to cottages which had substantial cellars and watched the firing there, ready to seek shelter should the German try his markmanship on shore targets. Some residents reported shells falling on shore.[22]

On July 22, 1918, the day following the attack on the *Perth Amboy*, the *U-156* sank the American fishing schooner *Robert and Richard* 60 miles southeast of Cape Porpoise, in latitude 42° 42′ N., longitude 68° 23′ W. The submarine fired her first and only shot at a distance of 2 miles. The schooner hove to and the submarine approached. A German officer ordered one of the fishermen's dories alongside, and with two sailors boarded the schooner. On the way to the *Robert and Richard* the German officer seemed willing to talk: "He said he had a big house in the States. I asked him what he was going to do with us, and he said he was not going to do anything, and when we got ashore he wanted us to tell the authorities that we

---

[22] A thrilling story of how the Boston fishing boat *Rose*, on a seining trip, was fired upon several times by a German submarine off Orleans, Cape Cod, Mass., being missed by only 10 feet, together with her flight for safety, was told to-night upon her arrival in Provincetown by Capt. Marsi Schuill. The captain and his crew of seven witnessed the attack on the tug *Perth Amboy* and the four barges. The captain said:

"We were about 5 miles off Orleans at 10.30 this morning, and the sea was as calm as a mirror. About 2 miles ahead of us the tug and her tow of four barges was steaming lazily along. Suddenly we heard the report of a big gun. We looked toward the tug and her tow and were startled to see a submarine break water.

"She looked like a big whale, with the water sparkling in the sunlight as it rolled off her sides. Then we saw the flash of a gun on the U-boat and saw the shell strike the pilot house of the tug. A few minutes later we saw fire break out and the crew running toward the stern. Then the U-boat turned her attention to the barges. We then saw one of the deck guns on the U-boat swung around toward us and there was a flash. A shell came skipping along the water. I ordered full speed ahead. and the *Rosie* jumped ahead through the brine, making us feel a little bit more comfortable. The Germans must have fired as many as five shots at us, the nearest coming within 10 feet of our stern but we were traveling pretty fast and when the submarine crew saw their shots were falling short they gave up. A few minutes later we saw a naval patrol boat tearing toward the submarine, but we didn't stop."—*War Diary of the First Naval District.*

do not do anything to those on the vessels we sink. He said 'You think too much of what Wilson tells you.' They acted as though they had plenty of time. They only brought one bomb aboard and they carried this in a canvas bag. This they swung underneath the ship by the use of a sounding lead. They started on the stern end of the ship and pulled it up to about midships." [23]

In this instance the submarine crew removed nothing from their victim other than the flag and the ship's papers.

On the 23d and the 27th sightings were reported by the American S. S. *Temple E. Dorr* and by the British S. S. *Gymeric*. The *Dorr* was 8 miles east of Fire Island at the time, while the *Gymeric* was in latitude 38° 27′ N. and longitude 70° 42′ W. In the latter case it was reported that two submarines were seen and in the former the object was far away when sighted; it is doubtful, therefore, that the *U-156* was seen in either case, although it is possible that American submarines, which were operating in the vicinity at the time, might have been sighted.[24]

The next victim of the *U-156* was the Biritsh motor schooner *Dornfontein*, which was sunk August 2 in latitude 44° 17′ N. and longitude 67° W.

The war diary of the first naval district furnishes a good account of the sinking:

The little cloud of smoke rising to-day from the hulk of the British schooner *Dornfontein*, 7 miles south of Grand Island, at the entrance of the Bay of Fundy, marked the scene of the most recent German submarine attack on the Atlantic coast.

The schooner, lumber laden, from St. Johns, New Brunswick, for a port south, was overtaken just before noon yesterday by a German submarine, her crew driven into their dories, and the vessel robbed and burned. After rowing three hours the men reached Grand Island.

The fact that the submarine ventured so close to the shoals and shallows of the Bay of Fundy, as did the one which sank four coal barges in the dangerous waters close to Orleans, on Cape Cod, Mass., two weeks ago, led shipping men to believe that it was the same German craft. This belief was substantiated by the fact that the second officer of the submarine which sank the *Robert and Richard* told Capt. Wharton of that schooner that he had maintained a summer home on the Maine coast for 25 years prior to the war. It is believed that no navigating officer of a submarine would venture so close inshore unless he was very familiar with the details of the coast line.

The schooner was just getting into open sea, 25 miles off Briar Island, the westernmost point of Nova Scotia, when the submarine rose from the water and fired two shots across her bow. The schooner quickly came to and a few minutes later was boarded by a party of Germans who left the submarine in a small boat.

The Germans wasted no torpedoes, shells, or bombs, but set the vessel afire. Every stitch of available clothing owned by the crew, together with a six-months' stock of

---

[23] Testimony of Capt. Robert A. Wharton before American Naval Intelligence officers.

[24] It appears likely that on this day the *U-156* was operating in the vicinity of Barnegat Inlet. At 9.30 a. m., the 27th, the *Florence Olson* reported a sighting off Barnegat Light. At 5.03 in the afternoon the U. S. S. *Colhoun* reported an attack in latitude 38° 35′ N. longitude 70° 40′ W. A little over an hour later the British S. S. *Melitia* reported an attack in latitude 38° 36′ longitude 70° 20′ W

provisions, was taken off by the German raiding party. The officers and crew of the schooner made the best of their time while in contact with the Germans and brought in the best account of the vessel and her crew that had been obtained up to date. Part of their report is as follows: "The submarine was the *U-156*, and the crew numbered 73. Their ages would run from 20 to 35. They were well clad and appeared to be in good health and condition. The men stated that the only thing they suffered from was a lack of vegetables. The captain of the submarine was a stout man, apparently about 32 years of age and about 5 feet 7 inches tall, and the crew were pretty much the same type of men. The captain spoke only broken English, while the second lieutenant spoke English fluently. Nearly all the crew spoke English."

Many false statements were made to the Englishmen by the submarine crew, but these were mixed with truths that aided the navy men in tracing the activities of the vessel.[25]

Following the destruction of the *Dornfontein*, the U-boat turned its attention to the fishing fleet operating in the vicinity of Seal Island, Nova Scotia. On August 3 the American schooners *Muriel*, 120 gross tons, *Sydney B. Atwood*, 100 gross tons, *Annie Perry*, 116 gross tons, and the American motor schooner *Rob Roy*, 112 gross tons, were destroyed by bombs. The affidavit of the master of the *Muriel* before the American consul at Yarmouth, Nova Scotia, is as, follows:

The affiant, Eldridge Nickerson, states that he is a naturalized American citizen living at Everett, Mass.; that he was the master of the fishing schooner *Muriel*, belonging to the Atlantic Maritime Co., of Boston, Mass.; that the said schooner's gross tonnage is 120 and net tonnage 83; that the said schooner sailed from Gloucester on August 2, 1918, bound for Browns Bank, intending to call at Pubnico, Nova Scotia; that about 11 o'clock of August 3, 1918, when the said schooner was about 45 miles W. by N. of Seal Island, Nova Scotia, a submarine was sighted about 4 miles to the south; that the said schooner's position was about the same when abandoned and sunk; that the said schooner's course at the time was due east, sailing at a speed of 10 knots, and that no flag was flying; that the submarine was steaming on the surface at about 10 miles an hour, headed NE. and flying three German flags; that he attempted to escape and was drawing slightly away from the submarine when the latter fired two shots, one across said schooner's bow and one across said stern; that he immediately hove to and waited for the submarine's approach; that the commander of the submarine ordered the crew of the said schooner into their four boats and to come alongside of the submarine; that the submarine's commander then went aboard the said schooner with some of his own seamen and took away the said schooner's American flag, the ship's papers, and some of her provisions, such as eggs, and then tied a bomb to said schooner's sounding lead, placing it under said schooner's stern, and that about a quarter of an hour after noon he fired off said bomb by means of a time fuse; that the said schooner sank in about two minutes, going down by the head; that the submarine remained on the surface and steamed away to SE. at a speed of about 6 miles an hour; that the submarine's commander wore a uniform

---

[25] Some of the statements made by the Germans to the crew of the *Dornfontein* were: That prior to entering the Bay of Fundy the submarine had waited 3 miles off Portland, Me., but as no shipping appeared they had proceeded to the Bay of Fundy.

That they had been operating off the American coast for six months.

That they had sunk the *San Diego*.

That there were two larger submarines and one the same size operating on the American coast.

Tell Wilson that in six months there would be 200 submarines operating on the American Atlantic and Pacific coasts and against Japan.

which looked old and worn and that the sailors wore rough civilian clothes; that the submarine's commander looked about 40 years of age, was of medium height and thick set, being of a dark complexion, and wore a beard and mustache; that about 20 of the submarine's crew appeared on deck; that the commander of the submarine asked him from what port he came and where he was bound, and tonnage of the said schooner, and demanded said schooner's papers and flag; that the said questions were asked in English; that after the submarine steamed away the four boats rowed for the Nova Scotia coast, arriving at Yarmouth on the morning of August 4, 1918; that as the weather was good the crew did not suffer from cold, but suffered a little from hunger, owing to the fact that the said schooner's bread placed in the dories was soaked with water at the time the said schooner was sunk and was not fit to eat.

The *Atwood* was the next victim, followed at 2.30 p. m. by the *Perry*. The *Rob Roy* was sunk at 6 p. m. A statement of a member of the crew of the *Annie Perry* tells of their capture and treatment by the Germans:

Mr. Charles H. Swain states that they left Boston, Friday noon, August 2, 1918, and that on Saturday about 2.30 p. m. they sighted a boat about 5 miles due north. They did not know it was a submarine till it was about 4 miles away. The submarine then fired a shot across the bow when about 3 miles away and they hove to. Mr. Swain states that they saw the *Rob Roy* sunk. The crew then put off in four dories with 19 men. They were 35 miles from land off the Nova Scotia coast, W. half south from Seal Island. The sub came close to dory and the officer of the sub called for the captain to go aboard. Our captain and four men went aboard. The German captain was a young man, German, about 23 years old. He said, "Don't be afraid, we won't hurt you, but we're going to sink your ship." He further stated that we were fortunate to be near land, and told us that he sank one ship 400 miles from land, and that he was the man who had sunk the *San Diego*. He said that he had supplies to remain out three months. The sub crew consisted of 60 or 70 men and about 30 or 35 were on deck. The submarine was battleship gray and had two large guns fore and aft. The submarine was clean. They took all the supplies from our ship and the sub captain gave the crew in dory brandy and cigarettes. The sub captain then asked for newspapers.

On the 4th the *Nelson A.*, a Canadian schooner, was captured and sunk by bombs and the day following the Canadian schooners *Agnes B. Holland* and *Gladys M. Hollett*[26] were disposed of in the same manner. The sinkings of the 5th took place 15 miles off Lehave Banks, about 50 miles SE. by S. of the locality in which the attacks of the two previous days were made.[27] The *Gladys M. Hollett* was later towed to port.

At 11.40 this same morning the Canadian tanker *Luz Blanca*, a vessel of 4,868 gross tons, which had cleared the port of Halifax bound for Tampico, Mexico, five hours before, was struck by either

---

[26] These two fishing vessels were formerly reported as *Agnes B. Halliard* and *Gladys Frehaleit*. The British Admiralty give the names as above.

[27] The rumor that one of the officers of the submarine was well acquainted in the United States recurred continually. Fishermen claim to have identified the commander of the German submarine that has been sinking fishing boats as a skilled navigator, formerly in the fisheries service of the United States. Two men from different schooners that were sunk claimed to have recognized a former acquaintance, who has changed little except that he has grown a beard since they last saw him. Shipping men are satisfied that one of the officers of the submarine had an exact knowledge, as he operated the most dangerous waters in safety. The suspected man is said to know these waters, from Wood's Hole, Mass., to Nova Scotia, as well as anyone who has ever sailed them.—*From Diary of the First Naval District.*

a torpedo or a mine. She put about with the intention of returning to Halifax to repair the damage caused by the explosion. At 2 o'clock in the afternoon the *U–156* appeared between 4 and 5 miles off her port quarter and opened fire. The *Luz Blanca* carried one 12-pounder aft, and although the explosion in the morning had tilted the gun deck, making it impossible to use the gun to the best advantage, its crew returned the fire of the enemy. The submarine quickly found that she outranged the *Luz Blanca* and therefore kept at a safe distance, firing in all 30 shots. Meanwhile the tanker, which at the beginning of the engagement had been making 12 knots an hour in spite of her injuries, suddenly stopped. The master was of the opinion that one of the shells from the submarine which struck just astern of the vessel destroyed the propeller. The shells of the submarine now began to strike home, two men were killed and several others wounded aboard the tanker, and at 3.15 the vessel, afire in several places, was abandoned by her crew. The submarine continued to shell the burning hulk which, when last seen by her crew, was settling rapidly, in latitude 43° 48′ N., longitude 63° 40′ W.[28]

On August 8 [29] the *U–156* overhauled the Swedish S. S. *Sydland*, a vessel of 3,031 gross tons, in latitude 41° 30′ N., longitude 65° 22′ W. This vessel, which had before the present trip been engaged in Norwegian-American trade, had been chartered by the Allied Governments for use as a Belgian relief ship and was proceeding from Bagen, Norway, to Hampton Roads to receive her orders and her cargo. The statement of Capt. Alexandre N. Larson, master of the *Sydland*, was summarized as follows by the aid for information at New York:

On August 8, at 2.30 p. m., the captain and chief officer were standing on the deck, and first knew of the presence of the submarine when they heard the report of a gun and saw the splash of a shell about 20 fathoms in front of the *Sydland*. The captain then stopped his vessel, although he did not see the submarine. About 2.33 p. m. another shot was heard and a shell landed about 10 fathoms amidships. A short time afterwards the submarine appeared apparently 6 or 7 miles astern of the ship, about ESE. from the vessel and was at the time heading SW. by W. ½ W.

The submarine was next observed signaling, International Code "A F," which meant "Bring your papers on board." Orders were at once given by the captain to put out a small boat to the submarine. The captain himself, with three of his crew, first mate, boatswain, and one sailor, put off for the submarine, which at that time appeared within 2 miles of the *Sydland*. The captain gave his papers to a member of the crew, who in turn gave them to the prize officer of the submarine. The captain stated that the submarine appeared to be about 300 feet long. The submarine had two guns, one forward and one aft. The guns appeared to be about 5.9. No other guns were observed.

---

[28] Newspaper reports that the boats of the *Luz Blanca* were shelled are not borne out by the statements of the crew.

[29] On August 7 the Belgian relief steamer *Elizabeth von Belgie* was halted in latitude 42° 15′ N., longitude 64° 17′ W. Her papers were examined and her officers questioned by the Germans. She succeeded in establishing her character to their satisfaction and was allowed to continue her voyage.

When the captain came alongside of the submarine there appeared to be about 40 men of the crew standing on deck. They appeared to be men between 30 and 40 years of age. The prize officer was the only officer seen by the captain. He was a short man, brown eyes, and dark hair, clean shaven, and had about three or four days' growth of beard. He looked like a Spaniard, and had on a brown leather coat with a blue cap. The captain talked to the prize officer, first in German, which he spoke slightly, and afterwards in English.

The prize officer and six men of the submarine got into the boat and rowed back to the *Sydland* with the captain, and asked if he had any license from the German Government to show that the *Sydland* was a Belgian relief ship. As the captain could not produce the necessary German papers, the prize officer returned to the submarine and at 4.10 p. m. came back to the *Sydland* with papers from the commanding officer of the submarine stating that the *Sydland* must be sunk. Orders were given to the crew of the *Sydland* to man the boats, and at 4.25 p. m. they abandoned the ship. Between 2.30 p. m. and 4 p. m. the submarine had moved, and at the time the ship was abandoned she was lying about a ship's length on the starboard side of the *Sydland*. Capt. Larson protested against leaving his ship, and demanded a paper from the prize officer showing for what reason he was about to sink the vessel. After a little conversation he gave the captain a document, copy of which was obtained by this office.

After the vessel was abandoned the boats rowed about five or six ship's lengths from the submarine and one of the boats went alongside of the submarine to obtain the proper course to steer for land. The course was furnished to the man in the boat, and the crew of the submarine were very insolent. The boats started to row away, steering on a course due west. As they were rowing away, the captain noticed that a number of the men from the submarine were making for the *Sydland*. The last seen of the submarine was about 5 p. m., as the weather grew foggy and it was impossible to see after that time. When last seen the submarine was alongside the *Sydland*.

At 8 o'clock p. m., August 8, while the crew of the *Sydland* was still rowing, three or four explosions were heard, three loud and one very slight, which it was thought to be explosions of bombs on the *Sydland*. At the time that the prize officer returned to the *Sydland*, about 4.10 p. m., he brought three bombs on board the *Sydland*. These bombs were round and appeared to be about 12-inch and were painted gray.

One of the members of the crew of the submarine told the second officer of the *Sydland* that he had been chief officer on board one of the Hamburg-American Line vessels, that he was married in New York, and that although he was qualified to be an officer in the German Naval Reserve he had to take the place of a seaman on a submarine because he was married in New York and had a brother in the United States Navy.

The sinking of the S. S. *Sydland* has previously been charged to *U–117*, but a comparison of the receipt given to Capt. Larsen for his ship and that given to Capt. Hans Thorbyonsen for his ship (the *San Jose*, which is known to have been sunk by the *U–156*) proves conclusively that the loss of the *Sydland* should be charged to the account of the *U–156*. Further evidence develops in the fact that while the *U–156* was busy with the *Sydland*, the U. S. S. *Tingey* sighted another submarine, without doubt the *U–117*, 5 miles southeast of Sable Island.

A photographic copy and a translation of the two receipts are as follows:

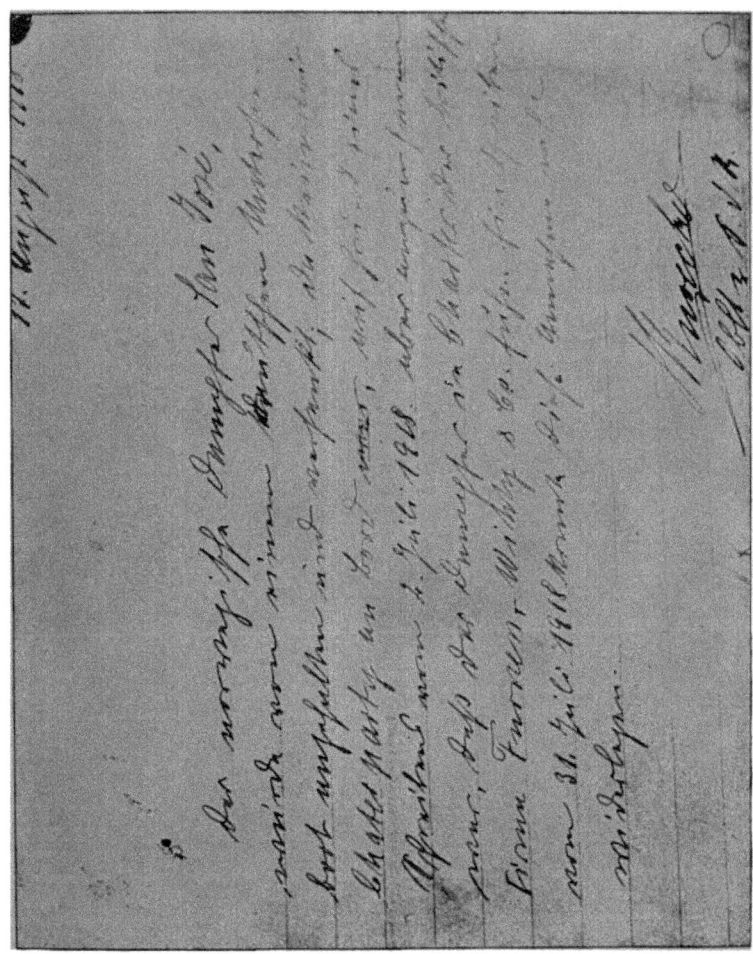

RECEIPT GIVEN TO THE MASTER OF THE NORWEGIAN S. S. SAN JOSE BY J. KNOECKEL, OBERLEUTNANT, U-156

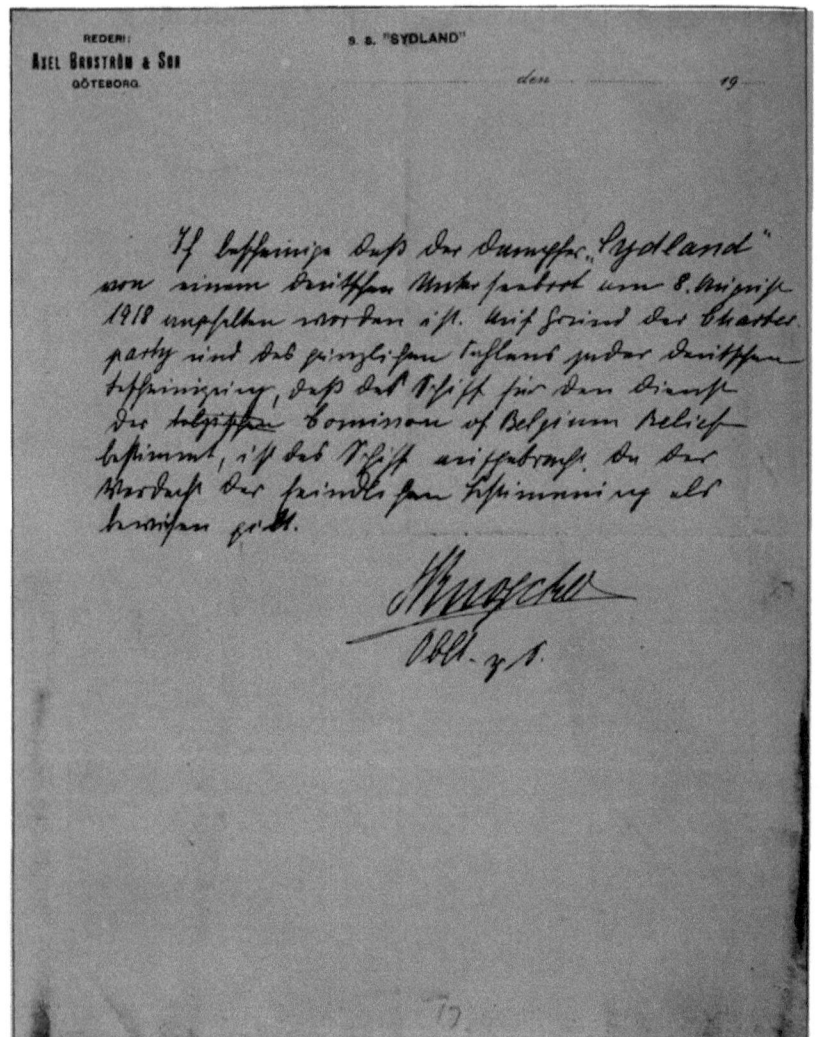

RECEIPT GIVEN TO THE MASTER OF THE SWEDISH S. S. SYDLAND
BY J. KNOECKEL, OBERLEUTNANT, U-156.

17. AUGUST, 1918.

Der norwegische Dampfer *San Jose* wurde von einem Deutschen Unterseeboot angehalten und versenkt: da keinerlei Charter party an Bord, auf Grund eines Schreibens vom 2. Juli 1918 aber anzunehmen war, dass der Dampfer in Charter der Britischen Firma Furness-Wihty & Co. (Furness Withy & Co.) fuhr. Ein Schreiben vom 31. Juli 1918 konnte diese Annahme nicht wiederlegen.

J. KNOECKEL, *Oblt. z. S. d. R.*

AUGUST 17, 1918.

The Norwegian steamer *San Jose* was stopped by a German submarine and sunk, as there was no charter party on board, but it was to be concluded on account of a communication of July 2, 1918, that the steamer ran under the charter of the British firm Furness-Withy & Co. A communication of July 31, 1918, could not contradict this assumption.

J. KNOECKEL, *Lieutenant.*

Rederi: S. S. "SYDLAND,"
Axel Broström & Co. ....den....19..
Göteborg.

Ich bescheinige dass der Dampfer Sydland von einem Deutschen Unterseeboot am 8. August 1918 angehalten worden ist. Auf Grund der Charter party und des gänzlichen Fehlens jeder Deutschen Bescheinigung, dass das Schiff für den Dienst der Commission of Belgian Relief bestimmt, ist das Schiff aufgebracht, da der Verdacht der feindlichen Bestimmung als bewiesen gilt.

J. KNOECKEL, *Oblt. z. S.*

Ship owners: S. S. "SYDLAND,"
Axel Broström & Co. ....the....19..
Göteborg.

I certify that the steamer *Sydland* was stopped by a German submarine on August 8, 1918. The ship is captured as the suspicion of the hostile intentions is considered proved by reason of the charter party and the complete lack of any German certificate that the ship is intended for the service of the Commission of Belgian Relief.

J. KNOECKEL, *Lieutenant.*

On August 11 the British S. S. *Pennistone*, 4,139 gross tons, was torpedoed and sunk about 1 mile astern of latitude 39° 50′ N., longitude 67° 25′ W.; and on the same day the *Herman Winter*,[30] 2,625 gross tons, an American steamship, was attacked in latitude 40° 45′ N. and longitude 67° 10′ W.

David Evans, the master of the *Pennistone*, was taken aboard the submarine when his vessel was destroyed and remained a prisoner for six days. He tells an interesting story of the loss of his ship and of his subsequent captivity.

The *Pennistone* left New York on the 9th of August in convoy. There were 18 all told in the convoy at the time I was torpedoed and we were the last ship in the right wing of the column. Our escort was at the head of the formation with one cruiser. At time of attack, we were about 3 miles behind convoy in latitude 39° 46′, longitude 67° 30′. The weather conditions were fair, with a moderate sea.

The first indication we had of the attack was when we were struck about 10 a. m., August 11. We were hit on the starboard side, engine room. The signal man told me that he saw the torpedo about 15 feet away. I know we did not strike a mine. We started to sink. The explosion smashed one lifeboat, so we got out in two small

---

[30] The *Herman Winter* was reported as sunk at the time of the attack, but this report proved to be false.

boats. We sent out an S O S after we had been hit. Our speed was 8 knots. The speed of the convoy was 8½ or 9. We had fallen behind during the night from 4 o'clock till morning (up to time we were hit). We were driving along as hard as we could to get up to them. The cruiser came back about 8 o'clock and warned us for keeping behind. We were not zigzagging.

It took us five or ten minutes to get away in the small boats. There were 41 in our crew. One of our engineers was killed and a fireman. There were only 39 in the boats when I counted them. We rowed away from the ship. The submarine did not come to the surface. The ship went down almost to her decks and then she hung. The wireless officer, third engineer, and three gunners, signalman, and one fireman were in our boat when I saw she was hanging. I was going to go aboard her, but when we were about 20 yards from ship the submarine came up alongside of us. She came up broadside. She came toward us, we went alongside, and I went on board. They asked for the captain and I said I was the captain, although I was not in uniform. When I was in the submarine, they kept the boat alongside and the boarding officer and two men went on board and went on the boat. They went to my room and took some clothing and shoes. I was sent down below immediately when I went on the submarine, but was not covered by guns. They took bombs on board our boat. It took the boarding officer about ten minutes to bomb our boat and sink her. I did not see her sink or hear the explosion; they just told me that she had sunk. I did not destroy the confidential publications before they got on board. I did not have my plans on board. I had Instructions for Ship Masters, Ocean Code, Marconi Code, and Radio Code. I don't know whether the radio operator destroyed them. They were eft on the ship as far as I know.

I was aboard the submarine from noon on Sunday to noon on Saturday—six days. I was rescued by a Norwegian steamer. As soon as the crew of the submarine saw smoke on the horizon I was sent below. I was about an hour and a half below when the commander sent for me to come on deck. He said he was going to sink the Norwegian boat and that I was entitled to go with the crew of the Norwegian steamer in the lifeboats or stay on the submarine. I chose the lifeboats. The boats came alongside of the submarine with Norwegian crew in it and I went on board the boat. The crew of the submarine gave me provisions for three or four days. They told us how to make the beach and told us we were 84 miles from Cape Sable. The *Derbyshire* picked us up at half past 2, August 18. We had been in the open boats from half past 1 till half past 2—25 hours.

The crew of the submarine told me it was 200 feet long. The breadth was about 25 or 30 feet, I should say. It had two guns, one forward and one aft; the forward gun was about 20 feet from conning tower, the after gun 25 to 30 feet. Both guns were of same size and caliber, 15 centimeters or 5.9. The barrel was about 10 feet long. The ammunition was kept under deck almost amidships, just aft of the conning tower. There was a tube from the deck down to the locker where the ammunition was kept and a small derrick fitted under the conning tower to go over these tubes. They had cases to put the shells in and heave them up. They hoisted the supply up through the tube to the gun. It was fixed ammunition in big brass cases, somewhere about 2 feet long. Judging by the looks of the shells, they would weigh about 50 or 60 pounds. The shell was about 6 inches and had a brass cap on the end of it. I saw them using them on Friday afternoon. At that time they fired on an American oil tanker, but they did not get it, as she was too fast for them. Whenever anything was doing I was sent below, that is, as soon as smoke was seen on the horizon; at all other times I was allowed roam of the deck. She had a smooth deck as far as I know, except the hatches. She had one anchor on the starboard side, just flush of the water. They told me she was of the same class as the *Deutschland*. Her bow sloped away gradually into the water. The conning tower was rounded and had three steps going up on after end. The conning tower was of iron. She had a screen and a periscope coming up from conning tower right in the middle. She had two periscopes—one on starboard side of conning tower, the other in the conning tower. She had two wires running from conning tower aft, fastened to a stanchion on the conning tower on the starboard side. They ran aft to same place. These wires were for wireless (radio wires); she had no wire from forward to conning tower. She had two masts for wireless that she could raise up. They were about 30 feet high. She used to put them up sometimes. There were two wires on these. There was about 120 feet space between these poles. They lay right on deck and were made of thin steels. The poles were 6 or 8 inches in diameter. The wires were always fastened to poles. It took three men to raise the poles up. They had guide wires for them and the guide wires fastened on the after pole. The poles braced each other. The two of them came up forward. They were lying down aft. There was a guiding wire from the forward one of the deck. All they did was to connect the wires on them onto the other wireless. They made the connection on the conning tower. The deck was sloped. About three feet from the curve up to the top of the rail there was a platform. There were three holes in the curve-like steps. I, when boarding submarine, jumped right from boat to curve. The submarine was painted gray (old paint). They told me she had been out for two months. There was no name or number on submarine, neither were the names on caps the same. One of the caps had the name "Porsen," another the German words meaning "Under the sea boat."

While on the submarine, I was quartered along with the sailors and firemen. There were about 40 men in the one room. We slept on wooden lockers. They gave me a kit the same as a man-of-war is given, with a hammock and a thin mattress. There were 77 men on board. There were five on watch always. Some of the crew were active service men, others were Reserves. The skipper was an active service man, but I could not say as to his rank. I do not know the names of any of the officers. The discipline on board was very lax. There was disagreement between officers and sailors and firemen. Captain did not mix much with crew, except to pass time of day.

I noticed her torpedo tubes back of forward end. She had just one tube on port side and the only time I saw that, they were just finishing putting a torpedo in after the one they used on me. Then the place was closed up. I don't know whether the submarine carried mines. There were iron doors at the torpedo locker.

There was no machinery in the crew's quarters. There were some stores underneath the deck. There were iron shutters and underneath were little compartments. I saw them getting stores up one day. The second compartment was about 35 to 40 feet long. I was not in the first compartment. After crew's quarters there was an alleyway to the right forward hatch. There were some rooms there on the right where some of the petty officers used to live. After that came the officers' mess rooms and the officers' and commanders' rooms. On the left of the alleyway there was nothing. Alleyway ran along the left side of craft, not amidship. I was not in the officers' mess rooms. The officers had separate staterooms. There were three or four on each side, occupying a space of about 50 or 60 feet to a place called the "Central," where the controlling valves were. The conning tower rose right above the central quarters. There were two decks—one into lower part of conning tower and the second in the top of the conning tower. We went on deck through forward hatch by way of an iron ladder. There was just one flight to main deck. The air in the submarine was very foul; they did not seem to have many ventilators. There was one ventilator on forward deck that opened right into hold. I only saw that open up once, and as soon as the alarm was given a man was ordered to take that down. Just aft of the central compartment was where the munition lockers were. The munition lockers were on both sides. Aft of munition lockers there were rooms for the engineers and the galley was in the after end of the engine room. I never was in the engine room. The farthest aft I ever got was to engineers' quarters. The place seemed to be full of engines. I could not say how many engines there were. There were engines on the starboard side and engines on the other side and engines in the middle. There seemed to be no longitudinal in engine room. There was a horizontal wheel controlling the periscope. The glass of the periscope was not more than an inch in diameter, so far as I could see. There were some figures on the line of vision in periscope. These figures were on horizontal line.

The captain of the submarine was a man about 5 feet 7 inches. He was about 30 years, German appearing, and weighed about 170 pounds. He was fair, had a fresh complexion and blue eyes, light eyebrows, medium nose. He was of very military appearance. He spoke English, but not very well. The man next in command was thinner than the captain. He was about 35 years old, weighed about 150 pounds, and was about the same height as the captain. They looked healthy and were tan. The second commander had a little mustache. He also was fair. I would recognize these men if I were to see them again. The first officer was the best English-speaking man. The boarding officer had whiskers, weighed about 140 pounds, was about 5 feet 6 inches. He spoke very little English. Boarding officer was about 30 or 35 years old.

The officers wore American dungarees and had on their caps, indicating commissioned officers. The ages of the crew ranged between 20 and 30 years. All were young men. The crew was very contented. We had tea and coffee, bread and butter and marmalade, all tin stuff. There was a little sugar, but not much. Crew got very little sugar, and butter was not very good. Everything was canned, even the bread. The bread was dark and was made up in tins.

Several of the crew spoke English and some of them had been sailing on the Hamburg-American Line and on the North German Lloyd Line. The war was never mentioned. We did not discuss the sinking of ships and they never asked me for any information whatsoever. They treated me fairly well, and never jeered or insulted me. The submarine had been out two months and was supposed to stay another month. The submarine ran on the surface all the time and they did not submerge from Sunday till Thursday afternoon. We just ran along slowly, and two or three nights we just lay to. We never sighted anything from Sunday till Thursday afternoon. We were probably somewhere around the entrance of New York. After that we started north, then south again. We did not sight land at all. I spent most of my time on deck. The speed on the surface was about 12. They fired about 40 shots after an American oil tanker from the forward gun, as I stated above, but she got away. The first I knew of the oil tanker was when I was ordered below, then I felt the vibration of the shots. The guns appeared to be far too heavy for the ship. The oil tanker made smoke like a fog and got away. That was Friday afternoon. The next thing attacked was the Norwegian *San Jose*, which they sank. They sank her with bombs, but did not torpedo her. We saw one explosion from out lifeboat about 5 o'clock, and we had left at half past 1. At about 6 we could see nothing.

From the 11th until the 16th, when the British steamer *Lackawanna* was gunned, the movements of the *U-156* are not definitely known. At 3.20 that afternoon when the *Lackawanna* was in latitude 40° 45' N., longitude 64° 40' W., the officer on watch sighted a periscope about 2,000 yards away. Shortly after two torpedoes were fired from the submarine, the first passing about 20 feet astern and the second being diverted by gunfire. After this failure the submarine opened fire with her bow gun, closing up to 1,200 yards and holding her position in spite of the effort of the merchantman to put on speed and escape. The submarine fired rapidly and badly, as none of the 40 shells took effect. The *Lackawanna* returned the fire and her twentieth shot was observed to take effect on the bow of the submarine, which submerged very soon afterwards, while the steamer made the best of the opportunity to escape.

On the following day the Norwegian steamer, *San Jose*, 1,586 gross tons, in ballast from Bergen to New York, sighted the *U-156* emerging from the water in latitude 42° 10′ N., longitude 64° 42′ W. The submarine opened fire as soon as she was on the surface and the steamer at once hove to and stopped her engines. Acting upon orders from the raider the master of the *San Jose* rowed to the submarine, took a prize officer and crew into his small boat, and returned to his ship. The prize officer examined the papers of the steamer and despite the protests of her captain decided that she must be sunk. Capt. David Evans, of the *Penistone*, was placed in boat with the master of the *San Jose*, who was given a receipt for his vessel signed by "Knoeckel, Oberleutnant zur See," informed the best direction to make sail, and ordered to leave the vicinity. The crew of the *San Jose* saw their ship settling in the water as they pulled away but did not hear the explosion of the bombs which sank her. The boats of the *San Jose* were picked up almost immediately by the British S. S. *Derbyshire* which was so near at the time of the sinking of the *San Jose* that they heard the explosion of the bombs aboard her.

After this sinking the submarine made her way to the northward, where, on August 20, she made a new attack on the fishing fleet. The results of this fresh outburst of *"schrecklichkeit"* was the sinking of 11 fishing vessels, only one of which registered above 160 gross tons.

The method used in this attack was entirely new, the first step being the capture of the 239-ton Canadian steam trawler *Triumph* and the arming of the prize as a raider. The story of the seizure as told by the crew of the trawler is as follows:

At 12.10 p. m., August 20, 1918, ship's time, approximately 60 miles S. by W. off Canso, Nova Scotia, the captain and crew of the *Triumph* sighted the conning tower of a submarine, coming out of the water astern, 1½ to 2 miles away.

Five minutes later a shot was fired, landing in the water over port side about amidships. Engines were stopped, lifeboats manned, and hasty preparations were made to shove off, taking practically no belongings except a box of biscuits for each boat.

After putting off, the submarine came up to within 50 yards of the trawler and Capt. G. Myhre proceeded for the side of the submarine in a dingy with the ship's papers and articles, while the other boats laid by. The commander of the submarine took the papers from the captain and ordered him aboard. He then ordered another one of the lifeboats to come alongside. The 11 men in this boat were ordered aboard the sub.

The Germans then put armament into the lifeboat and proceeded with two of the *Triumph* crew to board the ship. The armament taken aboard consisted of the following:

(a) Either one or two 3-pounders, not assembled, including base and all.

(b) Approximately 25 high-explosive bombs, about 1 to 1½ feet in height and 6 to 9 inches in breadth, with time attachment visible.

(c) A large sea bag, the contents of which were not visible or possible to learn, it being about twice the size the Navy regulation sea bag.

[To face page 67.]

TABLE V.—WEIGHTS OF FULL CHARGES AND PROJECTILES FOR B.L. AND Q.F. ORDNANCE.

B.L. Ordnance.	Mark.	Full charges. Powder.		Full charges. Cordite.		Weight of Projectile.	Nature of Projectiles used with B.L. and Q.F.
		lbs.	Size.	lbs.	oz.	lbs.	
Guns.							
12-pr. (6 cwt.)	L	..	5	..	$12\frac{7}{16}$	$12\frac{1}{2}$	*Armour-Piercing Shot*, of steel, are used with 6-inch B.L. guns and upwards, and with 4-inch Q.F. and above.
15-pr.	L	..	5	..	$15\frac{3}{4}$	$14\frac{1}{16}$	
30-pr.	L	..	10	2	6	30	
4-inch (jointed)	II. to VI.	12 S.P.	5	3	1	25	*Pallister Shot* are used up with 4 to 16·25-inch B.L. guns, and with 4 and 6-inch Q.F.
4-inch	II. to V.	$15\frac{3}{4}$ S.P.	$7\frac{1}{2}$	4	$7\frac{1}{4}$	25	
5-inch	L	25 S.P.	..	..	..	50	
80-pr.	III. to VI.	48 E.X.E.	20	14	12	80	*Case Shot*, with 12-pr. to 13·5-inch B.L., and the 5-inch B.L. howitzer.
6-inch	III.	36 E.X.E.	..	..	..	100	
,,	V.	45 Prism¹ black	..	..	..	100	*Pallister Shell* are used with 4 to 16·25-inch B.L. guns, except the 80-pr., a base fuze being used.
8-inch	III.	104 Prism¹ brown	20	28	12	210	
,,	IV., VI.	118 Prism¹ brown	20	32	10	210	
,,	VII., VII.A.	90 Prism¹ black	20	22	..	180	
9·2-inch	I., II.	140 Prism¹ brown	30	42	..	380	*Pointed Common Shell*, with 4 to 16·25-inch B.L. guns, except the 80-pr., and with 12-pr. Q.F. guns and above. They are of cast steel, made with a point, and have a base fuze hole.
,,	III. to VII.	164 Prism¹ brown	30	53	8	380	
,,	VIII.	..	40	63	..	380	
,,	IX.	..	..	..	..	..	
10-inch	I. to IV.	252 Prism¹ brown	30	76	..	500	*Common Shell*, of cast iron and of cast or forged steel and filled with powder, are used with all B.L. guns and howitzers, and with Q.F. guns.
12-inch	I. to VII.	295 Prism¹ brown	30	88	8	714	
,,	VIII.	..	50	167	8	850	
13·5-inch	I. to IV.	630 S.B.C.	..	..	..	1250	
16·25-inch	L	960 S.B.C.	..	..	..	1800	
Howitzers:							*Common Shell, filled with lyddite*, of forged steel, are used with 6 and 9·2-inch B.L. guns and with howitzers, also with 4 to 6-inch Q.F. guns.
5-inch	L	..	$3\frac{3}{4}$	..	$11\frac{7}{16}$	50	
5·4-inch	L	..	$3\frac{3}{4}$	..	$13\frac{1}{2}$	60	
6-inch (25 cwt.)	L	..	$3\frac{3}{4}$	2	1	$118\frac{3}{4}$	
,, (30 cwt.)	L	..	5	1	12	$118\frac{3}{4}$	*Shrapnel Shell*, of cast iron, cast and forged steel, are used with all B.L. and Q.F. guns, and B.L. howitzers.
Q.F. Guns:							
3-pr. Nordenfelt and Hotchkiss	..	$1\frac{1}{4}$ Q.F.¹	5	..	$6\frac{3}{4}$	$3\frac{5}{16}$	
6-pr. ,,	..	$1\frac{11}{16}$ Q.F.¹	5	..	$7\frac{1}{2}$	6	*Double Shell*, with 80-pr. B.L. guns.
12-pr. (8 cwt.)	L	..	10	..	$13\frac{3}{4}$	$12\frac{1}{2}$	
,, (12 cwt.)	L	..	15	1	15	$12\frac{1}{2}$	*Star Shell*, with 12 and 15-pr. B.L. guns, and with howitzers.
4-inch	I. to III.	..	15	3	9	25	
4·7-inch	I. to IV.	12 S.P.	20	5	7	45	
6-inch	I. to III.	$29\frac{1}{2}$ E.X.E.	30	13	4	100	*Ring Shell*, with 4-inch B.L. guns.

On getting nearer, I made out that the vessel was the schooner *A. Piatt Andrew* of Gloucester, and I was going up alongside her to speak to the captain when the beam trawler approached us under full steam. I could see that it was the trawler *Triumph* of Halifax, as we had fished alongside of him on our last trip and I knew the captain of her quite well. I did not mistrust anything out of the way until they got within 150 yards of us, when they stopped their vessel and the captain, through a megaphone, ordered us to heave our vessel to. I thought the captain was joking with us and kept on toward the *A. Piatt Andrew*, and the first thing we knew four shots were fired across our bow from rifles. We brought our vessel up in the wind and the beam trawler came up alongside of us and I then saw that she was manned by a German crew and had a German flag at her masthead. The captain ordered me to come aboard of his vessel with our papers, so I took one of my dories and with one of the crew rowed alongside of him and the German gave me quite a calling down for not stopping my vessel sooner and said that if we expected him to do the right thing, we would have to do the right thing by him. He then ordered three of his men to come in the dory with me and they brought a bomb along. The bomb was a small round thing and they had it in a bag and hung it under the stern with a line. They took one of our other dories and after touching off the fuse, returned to the beam trawler. The bomb exploded shortly after they left and the vessel went down stern first, the topmast being the last thing to disappear. In the meantime, we had forgotten all about the *A. Piatt Andrew*, but shortly before they blew up my vessel, we heard a muffled explosion and saw the *A. Piatt Andrew* go down. All of this happened in about one half or three quarters of an hour and the vessel went down about 3.30 in the afternoon. We were then about 55 miles south half east from Canso so the crew and myself started in our dories and rowed toward land. A small fishing boat picked us up off Canso and took us into Matthews & Scott's wharf, arriving there at about 9 o'clock in the morning of August 21. I telegraphed home the loss of my vessel and got in communication with the American consul who sent us home to Gloucester. I arrived home Sunday, August 25.

Only one of the schooners, the *Uda A. Saunders*, was sunk by the submarine.

The submarine came up on our bow and came right alongside, her decks awash. She was about 280 feet long, with guns fore and aft. I was practically alone on the vessel, all but three of the crew being out in the boats from half mile to a mile away. The Huns hailed us and ordered a dory alongside. I sent two men out to her in a dory and three of the raider's crew came aboard. "Don't be afraid," said the one who appeared to be in command. "We are going to sink your vessel. I will give you 10 minutes to gather up food and water enough to last you until you get ashore." One of the Boches set about storing bombs below and soon after we left the *Uda A.*, I heard a muffled explosion, the two masts broke off short, she seemed to crumple in the center and immediately went under. We had enough food and water, but the men in the other dories had only their working clothes and we who were on board had only the barest necessities. The Hun commander took all my papers and the flag. We set out for the nearest shore and rowed 18 hours before landing. We had 700 quintals of fish and 7 casks of oil.[31]

On the 21st the *Triumph*, accompanied by the *U–156*, stopped the French fishing schooner *Notre Dame de la Garde*, 145 tons gross, in latitude 45° 32' N., longitude 58° 57' W., and sank her with bombs, giving the crew scant time to take to the boats. (The vessel had aboard at the time 640,000 pounds of fish.)

---

[31] Story of Capt. Publicover of the *Uda A. Saunders*, Gloucester Times, August 20, 1918.

After sinking the *Notre Dame de la Garde* the submarine again disappeared for three days, resuming her activities on August 25 by the sinking of the small British S. S. *Eric*, 583 gross tons. The following account of the sinking of this ship is taken from the report made by British communication officers to the Admiralty.

The unarmed British steamer *Eric*, 610 tons gross, carrying a crew of 18 all told, owned by James Speir, Ltd., of St. Johns, Newfoundland, and under charter of the Government of Newfoundland, was sunk by a German submarine on August 25, 1918.

The *Eric*, 610 gross tons, left St. Johns, Newfoundland, on August 23, 1918, for Sydney, Nova Scotia; she was in ballast and was to make the voyage without any intermediate stops. The master of the *Eric* was Capt. W. Lane, of 43 Longsail Street, St. Johns, Newfoundland.

About 1.30 a. m., on August 25, 1918, the *Eric* was about 70 miles NW. by W. from Galantry Light, St. Pierre. She was proceeding straight on her course; was not zigzagging. The *Eric* was entirely darkened, but there was a nearly full moon, giving a fair degree of visibility. There was no land in sight, St. Pierre, about 70 miles distant, being the nearest land.

The first intimation that the crew of the *Eric* had of the presence of a submarine was a shot which hit the steamer, about 1.30 a. m. This shot was followed by six other shots in rapid succession, four more of them hitting the steamer. The steamer was badly damaged, her wireless apparatus being put out of commission by the first shot, her smokestack being knocked down by the second one. Five men, including the captain, mate, and chief engineer, were wounded by pieces of shell and by flying débris. The captain of the *Eric* judges that the shots were fired from a distance of about 2 miles. The *Eric* stopped immediately after the firing began. No torpedoes were used.

A few minutes after the firing had ceased the submarine was seen by the crew of the *Eric* right alongside the steamer by the stern. Some one aboard the submarine hailed the *Eric* and asked if anyone had been killed by the shells fired; on being told that no one was killed, the man aboard the submarine said that he was glad, as he was after ships and not lives. The submarine crew did not board the *Eric* when they came alongside but ordered the crew of the *Eric* to come on board the submarine. There was but one boat of the *Eric's* complement of lifeboats left, a small one capable of carrying only four persons. In this boat the *Eric's* crew rowed over to the submarine, four at a time.

When the captain of the *Eric* got on board the submarine, the submarine commander informed him that in view of the fact that there were not sufficient boats in which to put him and his crew, he would keep them aboard the submarine until he found a vessel with sufficient boats to accommodate them.

The captain of the *Eric* went below when he boarded the submarine; some of his crew, however, remained on deck. These men saw men from the submarine board the *Eric* and sink her by placing bombs aboard her.

On going below aboard the submarine the wounded men from the *Eric* had their wounds dressed by a doctor, a young man about 25 years old. The crew of the *Eric* were given coffee aboard the submarine and the officers were given coffee, brandy, and cigarettes. The commander of the submarine told the captain of the *Eric* that he would put him and his crew aboard the first vessel found having enough boats to accommodate them. He asked the captain of the *Eric* if he had passed a fishing schooner a few hours before and gave its position as best he could.

About 6 a. m. the submarine sighted the Newfoundland schooner *Willie G.* The submarine went alongside the *Willie G.* and the submarine commander inquired regarding the number of boats she carried. On being informed that she only carried six small dories, he said that these were not enough to accommodate the crew of the

Eric and the crew of the *Willie G.* and that therefore he would send the *Eric's* crew aboard the *Willie G.* and would not sink her, as he had intended doing. This was done, and the *Willie G.* brought the crew of the *Eric* to St. Pierre, arriving there about 10 a. m. on August 26. The *Willie G.* was only about 25 miles from St. Pierre when the submarine overtook her and put the *Eric's* crew aboard.

Three hours after the survivors of the steamer had been placed aboard the *Willie G.* the submarine was again in the midst of the little schooners and by noon had sent to the bottom the *E. B. Walters*, 126 tons, the *C. M. Walters*, 107 tons, the *Verna D. Adams*, 132 tons, and the *J. J. Flaherty*, 162 tons. The last mentioned vessel was an American, the other three of Canadian register.

The position of the vessels above mentioned at the time the submarine was first sighted was latitude 46° 33′ N., longitude 57° 33′ W. This was also their position when sunk, as they were all at anchor and did not move. The date of the sinking was August 25, 1918, the time about 10.30 or 11 o'clock a. m. At the time the submarine appeared the vessels were at anchor within about one-half to 1 mile apart. The crews of the first three were aboard the vessels, as the Canadian fishermen do not fish on Sunday.

The submarine was first sighted by the crew of the *E. B. Walters*. When first sighted, the submarine was about 2 miles NW. of the *E. B. Walters*. The crew of the *E. B. Walters* were not alarmed when they sighted the submarine, as they mistook it for a Canadian patrol boat. The submarine approached the *E. B. Walters*, traveling slowly on the surface. When the submarine was within about 50 yards of the *E. B. Walters*, the crew of the schooner saw the German flag on a small flagstaff just behind the small deck house or conning tower of the submarine. At this juncture a large man in uniform hailed the *E. B. Walters* from the deck of the submarine. He ordered the captain to come alongside the submarine in a dory, and ordered the crew of the schooner to leave the vessel as quickly as possible. Capt. Cyrus Walters rowed alongside the submarine in one of the schooner's dories. As he got alongside he said, "You are not going to sink my schooner, are you?" Some one from the submarine's deck answered, "That's just exactly what we are going to do." Four men from the submarine deck then jumped into the dory with Capt. Cyrus Walters and rowed to the *E. B. Walters*. These men boarded the schooner and Capt. Walters gave them the ship's papers. Capt. Walters reports that the men from the submarine ransacked the ship, even going through the chests of the crew in the forecastle. He saw them pile up a large quantity of canned goods from the vessel's stores near the dory in which they had come aboard. Capt. Walters and his crew hastily packed up a few personal belongings and got into the dories and pulled away from the vessel. About 10 minutes after they had left the vessel they heard an explosion aboard the schooner and in about five minutes they saw the schooner sink.

The four men from the submarine who had boarded the *E. B. Walters* and sunk her, rowed back to the submarine in the dory which they had taken from the vessel just sunk. The submarine towed the dory alongside the *C. M. Walters* which was lying about one-half mile distant. When the submarine was within about 25 yards of the *C. M. Walters* the four men rowed to the schooner in the dory and demanded the ship's papers from Capt. Wilson Walters, the master. They ordered him and the crew to leave the schooner as quickly as possible, which they did in about 15 minutes. Before they left the vessel they saw the four men from the submarine arranging the bomb with which to sink the schooner. The bomb was pulled under the keel of the vessel amidships. About 10 minutes after the master and crew of the *C. M. Walters* had left the vessel they heard an explosion and in about three minutes the schooner sank, stern first.

The submarine, with the dory of the *E. B. Walters* in tow, then approached the *Verna D. Adams*. The master and crew of this schooner had left the vessel before the submarine approached them. The four men who had sunk the two other schooners rowed over to the *Verna D. Adams* and boarded her. The men from the submarine stayed aboard the *Adams* longer than aboard any of the other vessels. Capt. Mosher of the *Adams* says that he had a large supply of stores aboard, especially of canned foods, and believes many articles were removed from the schooner and taken aboard the submarine. The *Verna D. Adams* was sunk by a bomb placed aboard in the same manner as was done with the other two vessels.

After disposing of the three Canadian vessels the submarine turned its attention to the *J. J. Flaherty*, which was boarded and destroyed in the same way as the others.

On the morning of August 26 the raider captured and sank by bombs the Canadian fishing schooner *Gloaming*, 130 gross tons, in latitude 46° 02′ N., longitude 57° 35′ W.

After the attack on the *Gloaming* the *U-156* began her homeward voyage. On August 31 the U. S. S. *West Haven*, 5,699 gross tons, a Naval Overseas Transportation ship, was attacked and shelled in latitude 44° 20′ N., longitude 51° 09′ W.; but succeeded in escaping. The *West Haven* sent a radio message from the above location: "8.25 a. m. Attacked by an enemy submarine which opened fire upon us. Immediately brought guns into action. At 8.46 a. m. enemy submarine ceased firing and turned broadside to."

The *U-156* was the only one of the enemy submarines dispatched to the American coast that failed to return to her base in safety. After remaining in the North Sea during the concentration there, this vessel which had worked such havoc with the fishing industry of the Atlantic coast attempted to run the northern mine barrage. She struck a mine and was so damaged that she sank in a short time. Twenty-one survivors were landed on the Norwegian coast shortly after the signing of the armistice; the fate of the rest of the crew is unknown.

THE CRUISE OF U-140.

Within a week (June 22, 1918) after the *U-156* had commenced her voyage to the American Atlantic coast the *U-140*, a cruiser submarine mounting two guns and commanded by Korvettenkapitan Kophamel, left Kiel for the same destination. She proceeded north of the Shetland Islands and had her first encounter of the voyage on July 14, when an allo was received from the U. S. S. *Harrisburg*,[32] giving her position as latitude 45° 33′ N., longitude 41° W.

On the 18th the American tanker, *Joseph Cudahy*, 3,302 tons gross, which had been obliged to fall behind her convoy because of her slow speed, reported that she was being gunned in latitude 41° 15′ N., longitude 52° 18′ W. Two days later the cruiser *Galveston* announced that she had received a radio purporting to come from the *Cudahy*

---

[32] The *Harrisburg* sighted the *U-156* three days later.

reporting her position from a confidential reference point. In view of the vessel's speed, which was known to be 9 knots, and of the fact that her armament consisted of 3-inch guns, it was believed that this message was a decoy; that the *Cudahy* had been captured and that her confidential publications were in the hands of the Germans. The message, however, proved to be genuine, the merchant ship having escaped without damage.

On the 26th the British steamer *Melitia*, 13,967 gross tons, was gunned in latitude 38° 42' N., longitude 60° 58' W., and later the same day the *British Major*, 4,147 tons gross, was attacked by the submarine in the same locality; both vessels escaped.[33]

The following day the *U-140* registered her first sinking when in latitude 38° 25' 36" N., longitude 61° 46' 30" W., she captured the Portuguese bark *Porto*, 1,079 gross tons, bound from Savannah to Oporto. Capt. Jose Tude d'Oliveisa da Velha made the following statement to the American naval authorities:

> The *Porto* sailed under the Portuguese flag. Including myself there were 18 in the crew. Every member of the crew was Portuguese. On the 11th of July we sailed from Savannah, Ga., bound for Oporto with a cargo of 600 bales of cotton and barrel staves. We had on board provisions for six months. The ship's stores were of a general nature. The *Porto* was not armed. The submarine was first seen July 27, about 11 a. m. It was then about 2 miles off the starboard bow. She was on the surface and gradually approached us. When the submarine was about 2 miles off she fired three shots, after which we hove to. The submarine then came alongside the bark, while we were still aboard, and tied up. The commander of the submarine and one officer and a seaman who spoke Spanish asked for the ship's papers. I gave the commander of the submarine all the ship's papers, including the manifest, bill of lading, and everything. None of the nautical instruments were taken by the Germans because we managed to conceal them. One of the first things they inquired about was whether or not we had on board any pork or chickens. When I replied yes, they proceeded to remove all the pork and chickens we had on board. While we were tied alongside, the Germans for five hours took the supplies from our ship and put them on the submarine by the use of planks. In addition to the pork and chickens the crew took practically all of the ship's stores. None of the crew of the *Porto* helped in removing the supplies from our ship to the submarine, it was done by the crew of the submarine. No member of the crew of the *Porto* at any time boarded the submarine. The crew of the *Porto* did not wait until all the supplies were removed to the submarine, but shoved off in the two large lifeboats from the *Porto* after about half an hour. After shoving off in the lifeboats we remained in sight of the bark and the submarine until the bark was sunk. The *Porto* was sunk at about 5.30 p. m. with bombs and shell fire. No ships were seen at any time while the submarine was in our sight.
>
> The commander was tall and slim, with a short mustache, dressed in brown. I did not notice whether or not he had on any stripes. The commander was about 35 years old. There must have been about 90 men composing the crew of the submarine, as they were all on the deck at one time or another. The *Porto* was 216 feet long, and as the submarine lay alongside she was just a little bit smaller.
>
> The submarine was painted gray. The gun on the stern was larger than the gun on the bow. I do not know the caliber of the gun. The stern gun was about 15 feet long.

---

[33] The *Melitia* exchanged shots with the submarine, but the range was too great for effective fire from either.

and the bow gun about 12 feet long. She had one conning tower located in the center. The number "U-19" was painted in white on the bow. The submarine had no flag or ensign. The German commander did not give me a receipt for my ship. Some of the crew of the *Porto* engaged in conversation with the submarine crew in Spanish, but it only concerned the provisions. Neither I nor any member of the crew ascertained how long the submarine had been out or what their plans were. The commander conversed with me through an interpreter who was a member of the crew of the submarine and who carried binoculars and did not wear a hat. The interpreter through whom the submarine commander spoke, spoke a very pure Spanish, and I believe he was not a German.

On July 30 the American S. S. *Kermanshah*, 4,947 gross tons, was attacked by the submarine in latitude 38° 24′ N., longitude 68° 41′ W. In an interview with Robert H. Smith, master of the ship, with the United States naval authorities, he says:

The *Kermanshah*, owned by the Kerr Steamship Corporation, arrived at New York July 30, 1918, from Havre via Plymouth, in water ballast. She carried three naval radio operators and an American-armed guard crew of 21 men under the command of M. Coffey, C. G. M., U. S. N. Her armament consisted of one 4-inch gun astern and a 2-pounder forward.

On July 30, at 11.45 a. m. (ship's time), while in latitude 38° 24′ N., longitude 68° 41′ W., the captain was standing in the chart-room doorway and sighted the wake of a torpedo headed toward the after part of the port side of the *Kermanshah*. He ran on deck, let the ship run off about four points to starboard, and the torpedo missed the stern by 10 or 15 feet. The helm was eased a trifle so that the ship would not be swinging too quickly to starboard in the event another torpedo was sighted. The ship had no sooner steadied a little when the wake of another torpedo was seen approaching amidships on the starboard side. The captain immediately put the helm hard to starboard with the idea of throwing the ship in a course parallel to that of the torpedo. In this he was successful, the torpedo passing the starboard bow about 5 feet away.

As soon as the second wake was sighted the commander of the armed guard fired one round from the 4-inch gun astern, the shot being directed at the spot the wake started from. The explosion that followed sounded like the bursting of the shell against a hard object, which gave the captain the impression that a hit had been made. After following a northerly course at full speed of 9.5 knots for about 15 or 20 minutes, the submarine was sighted on the horizon about 4 miles distant. the gun crew immediately opening fire. After a few rounds it was seen that the submarine was out of range and fire was stopped. As the submarine made no attempt to chase or fire on the ship, the captain believes there is some basis for assuming that the first shot had some effect.

Allo and S O S messages were sent out immediately after the first torpedo missed, giving position and stating that the *Kermanshah* was being attacked and pursued.

At the time of the attack there was fine, clear weather, the sea fairly smooth, with moderate south winds. The regular watch was on the aft gun platform; there were lookouts in the crow's nests on the fore and main masts, but no periscope was sighted.

There was no telescope aboard the ship, and Capt. Smith having viewed the submarine through ordinary binoculars, could furnish no identifying description. He did not know whether any guns were mounted on her deck.

At 7 p. m. (ship's time), when about 60 miles north (true) of his noon position, Capt. Smith was about to alter his course to the westward when the gun crew fired at a periscope sighted off the starboard beam. After dark several decided changes were made in the course and the submarine was not sighted again.

Earlier in the day one of the gun crew reported to the watch officer the sighting of a small two-masted vessel. Capt. Smith is of the opinion that it was a disguised submarine, but could furnish no further details or reason for his belief.

The next victim of the *U-140* was the Japanese steamship *Tokuyama Maru*, 7,029 gross tons, which was torpedoed 200 miles southeast of New York, in approximately latitude 39° 12′ N., longitude 70° 23′ W., on August 1 at about 8 o'clock in the evening. The ship struck "was hit on the starboard side under the bridge with a torpedo," remained afloat long enough to send an allo, but the submarine which launched the torpedo was never sighted.

Another large ship was successfully attacked by the raider three days later, when the tanker *O. B. Jennings*, a vessel of 10,289 gross tons, after successfully avoiding a torpedo attack, was sunk by gunfire after a battle lasting over two hours, in latitude 36° 40′ N., longitude 73° 58′ W. In his preliminary report to the naval authorities, Capt. George W. Nordstrom said:

While on a voyage from Plymouth, England, to Newport News, Va., in ballast, on August 4, 1918, in position 36° 30′ N., 73° 20′ W., a torpedo was sighted about 1,000 yards, four points on port bow; by maneuvering ship, torpedo missed and passed 3 to 4 feet astern. At 9.30 a. m. the submarine opened fire from a distance of about 8 miles, and we immediately hoisted our flag and opened fire, after we broke out smoke boxes out and made a smoke screen, changing course often to hide ship behind smoke screen. At this time the submarine was observed five points abaft port beam. The submarine followed us and kept shelling until 11.40 a. m., having our range finely all the time, several shells bursting so close to ship that ship's side was punctured in several places. At 11.40 a. m. a direct shot hit the engine room through the counter, smashing port engine and wrecking main steam line. Several men were wounded. At the same time another shell hit magazine and exploded, destroying all ammunition. Previous to this one man was killed by gunfire and some minor wounded on deck. I pulled my colors down and sent out wireless calls. I surrendered at 11.45 a. m., ordered all hands in the boats, and abandoned ship. Pulling away from the ship, the submarine came up and interrogated boat crews, took second officer prisoner, asking the boat crew where the captain was, and the crew answered, that the captain was killed. Then the submarine returned to ship and commenced to shell her. We pulled away to northward until out of sight, and then hauled around to westward. At 3 p. m. all boats together, sails set, course given by captain, compass regulated, and commenced to sail for land. During the night the first officer's boat and chief engineer's boat dropped out of sight. At 8.30 a. m. we were picked up by Italian steamship *Umbria* and given food and relief. This ship took us down off Currituck beach, put the boat into water, and we sailed for shore. We landed 3.30 p. m. August 5, 1918.

At 9.30 a. m. sent out allo call and at 9.50 approximately sent out S O S at irregular intervals thereafter. The surrender call was sent out on emergency set, as dynamo was smashed.

Breech locks for our guns were thrown overboard upon the approach of the submarine to the life boats. The telescope sights were left with the chief engineer's boat. Moving pictures were made of the *O. B. Jennings* and her lifeboats from the deck of the submarine.

A more complete description of the attack, together with the conversation of the survivors with the crew of the submarine, a description of the raider, and the account of the rescue of survivors by the U. S. S. *Hull,* is given in the report of the aid for information, first naval district, to the Bureau of Operations.

At 9 a. m. (ATS), August 4, 1918, while proceeding at a speed of 10 knots, a torpedo wake was sighted four points off port bow. Helm was put hard astarboard and quarters was sounded and full speed ahead ordered. *Jennings* had been zigzagging and continued to do so, holding the same course. About 9.30 a. m. several shots were fired by the submarine, which was then sighted. The *Jennings* opened fire on the submarine, which was then apparently 7 miles away. Shots from *Jennings* fell short. *Jennings* continued at full speed, zigzagging and using smoke boxes. Submarine continued firing, discharging about 40 or 50 shots at two-minute intervals. At 11.40 a. m. shot from submarine exploded in the engine room of the ship, disabling the engine and wrecking the main steamline. A few minutes later another shell hit the magazine, exploding and destroying all the ammunition remaining. Prior to this time the *Jennings* had fired about 60 rounds at irregular intervals, causing submarine to submerge twice. During the engagement submarine fired 150 rounds at approximately two-minute intervals. At 11.45 ship's flag was struck and wireless call sent out that the *Jennings* had been captured. In this connection it had been the intention to use the word surrendered instead of captured.

Preparations were immediately made for abandoning the ship, and at 12.20 p. m. all survivors had left the ship in three small boats. Position of *Jennings* at this time was latitude 36° 40′ N., 74° W. Submarine then approached the *Jennings* and continued shelling her. The boats drew away from the vicinity and at 2.20 p. m. the *Jennings* turned on port side and sank slowly, disappearing from view 15 minutes later. At this time the lifeboat in charge of the first officer, W. J. Manning, was about half a mile away from the *Jennings*. The lifeboat in charge of the chief engineer, Albert Lacy, was 2 miles ahead of the first officer's boat and the boat in charge of the captain was ahead of the chief engineer's boat, thus the actual sinking of the *Jennings* was observed only by the first officer's boat. After the crew abandoned the ship and before they were permitted to leave the vicinity the three boats were called to the side of the submarine, and a conversation between the second officer of the submarine and the men in charge of the three lifeboats took place as follows: The officer of the submarine said: "We got you at last; I knew we would. What damage did the shell in the engine room do?" Reply: "Put the engine out of commission." Question: "Where is the captain?" Answer: "He is dead." Question: "Where is the chief wireless operator?" Answer: "I don't know; he must be dead, too." The above conversation was carried on by one of the men in the captain's boat, during which time the captain and the chief wireless operator were both present, but the captain's clothes had been placed on the body of the second steward, who had been killed and left on the deck of the *Jennings*.

The chief engineer was in charge of one of the lifeboats, and in this lifeboat was also one Rene Bastin, second officer on the *O. B. Jennings*, who had joined the ship at Southampton, England. Bastin insisted that he be permitted to speak with the officer on the submarine and, despite the fact that he was slightly wounded, jumped from the lifeboat to the deck of the submarine and began speaking rapidly in German to the officer and men on the deck, finally shaking hands with them and without further conversation with his companions in the lifeboat went below decks of the submarine and never returned. The men and officers on the *O. B. Jennings* had been suspicious of this man during the entire voyage. At the time he joined the ship in Southampton he claimed to be a Belgian and produced proper credentials to substantiate his claim. He spoke French and German fluently. The captain of the *O. B. Jennings* feels confident that this man could have been carrying no confidential documents to the officers aboard the submarine.

The submarine was about 300 to 325 feet in length, and the top of the conning tower was about 20 feet from the surface of the water, very rusty looking, with a guard around the propeller. It was armed with two guns, 6-inch caliber, barrel 20 feet long. They were placed fore and aft and about 6 feet from the conning tower. There were two periscopes about 5 inches in diameter on the conning tower. No masts or wireless visible. Three officers and 30 men were observed on the deck of the submarine, all dressed in regulation blue uniforms. The hat of the men had the inscription: "Undersee Boat Deutchland Undersee Hamburg."

At 2.20 a. m., August 5, two boats in charge of the first officer and chief engineer were picked up by the U. S. S. *Hull*. About 30 minutes before this occurred a submarine was sighted moving slowly along the surface. Submarine passed about 50 yards from first officer's boat and about 300 yards from the captain's boat. Submarine was about 300 feet long, conning tower about 20 feet from the surface of the water.

The U. S. S. *Hull* searched the vicinity for 30 minutes, endeavoring to locate the captain's boat, but without success, as the captain refused to show any lights or answer any signals, believing, as he stated later, that the U. S. S. *Hull* was the supposed submarine sighted about 30 minutes earlier. The only fatality was that of the second steward. Several of the crew sustained minor injuries from shrapnel.

The reference to Rene Bastin made in the account of the rescue of the survivors of the *O. B. Jennings* is explained and amplified by the following letter from the American Consulate at Havre, France:

I have the honor to report that, on January 4, 1919, Mr. Rene Henry Bastin, formerly second officer of the American S. S. *O. B. Jennings*, of New York, came to this consulate and asked for relief and transportation to the United States, giving the following explanation of his situation:

The American S. S. *O. B. Jennings* (gross tonnage 10,289 and net tonnage 7,890), owned by the Standard Oil Co., Capt. Nordstrom, sailed from Plymouth, England, for Newport News, Va., on July 20, 1918. On August 4, 1918, when about 60 miles east of Newport News, it was attacked by a German submarine and sunk by gunfire. Mr. Bastin was taken aboard the submarine as a prisoner of war, remaining on the submarine for nearly three months, until its arrival at Kiel on October 25, 1918, when he was transferred to a prisoners' camp.

The enemy submarine was *U. K. 140*, being an armored cruiser submarine, 375 feet long, drawing 23 feet, with freeboard 3 feet above the water line, armed with four 6-inch guns, carrying 35 torpedoes and having eight torpedo tubes and seven sets of engines. Mr. Bastin says that the submarine carried a crew of no less than 102 men, including the captain, seven officers, and a special prize crew.

During Mr. Bastin's enforced stay aboard the submarine he had many exciting experiences. On August 5, 1918, the submarine sank the American S. S. *Stanley Seaman* (?), of Boston. On August 17 it sank the Diamond Shoal Lightship and four steamers, whose names are unknown to Mr. Bastin. On August 22, 1918, the submarine torpedoed and sank a large British passenger steamer called the *Diomed*, of Liverpool (gross tonnage 4,072). On September 20, 1918, the submarine attacked a British tanker, the S. S. *Lackawanna*, of Liverpool (4,125 tons), which, being armed, succeeded in shooting away the conning tower of the submarine. (Note: It might be stated here that on August 16 the *Lackawanna* had an engagement with the German submarine *U–156*, which is described in detail in this publication, under activities of the *U–156*.) On October 1, 1918, the submarine attacked a convoy but was driven away by destroyers. It succeeded, however, in torpedoing an unknown ship.

While confined in close quarters aboard the German submarine Mr. Bastin naturally suffered great hardship and mental torture. On several occasions the submarine was closely attacked by destroyers, which dropped depth charges in dangerous proximity. On these occasions Mr. Bastin said that the faces of the entire German crew blanched with terror and he himself and the four or five other prisoners from different ships sunk by the submarine awaited momentarily their end. The effect of this long continued mental strain may well be imagined. Only those of robust physique and well-balanced mentality could stand the strain.

Mr. Bastin said that the prisoners received the same food as the crew, this being, in rotation, boiled barley one day, boiled rice the next day, and boiled macaroni the third day, with roasted barley as a substitute for coffee. The prisoners were permitted on deck only one and one-half hours each day, of which one hour was in the morning and one-half hour in the afternoon. The remainder of the time was passed in the close and noisome atmosphere of the engine rooms in the depths of the submarine. While the ventilation was as good as can be attained on a submarine, the air was so heavy with odors that the men were in a drowsy condition and slept most of the time. On the whole, Mr. Bastin said that the treatment of the prisoners aboard was bad and the supply of food inadequate. He felt sure that the German crew had been forced aboard in Germany and everything was done according to the strictest military discipline. As above stated, the submarine arrived in Kiel on October 25, 1918. For some days previously there had been great discontent among the crew and plans were made to attack their officers and join with other submarine crews as soon as they landed.

On October 29 the crew received an order to put to sea to fight the British fleet. They refused to obey the order and, joining with other submarine crews under the leadership of a sailor from the *Seidlitz*, who had been for two years in a submarine, they began the revolt, the signal for which was a bombardment of the main street of Kiel by a German cruiser in port. The prisoners of war were released for the day only with orders to return aboard at night.

On November 5, Bastin, with his comrades, was transferred to Wilhelmshaven and was then interned on the German cruiser *Hamburg*.

On November 9 the prisoners were told that the armistice had been signed and that a revolution had broken out in the British, as well as the German navy; that Marshal Foch had been shot and that the peace conditions would be favorable for Germany. In confirmation of these statements the Germans showed the prisoners an article in a local newspaper.

On November 10 there was a great illumination of the German fleet and a celebration in the city of Wilhelmshaven. On November 11 the real terms of the armistice being known, everybody was depressed and everything was quiet.

On November 21 the prisoners were escorted from Wilhelmshaven to the American officers' camp at Karlsruhe, where, according to Mr. Bastin, there were about 20 American officer prisoners from the Flying Corps.

Mr. Bastin was released and left the camp at Karlsruhe on November 29 and proceeded to Villingen, about 20 miles from the Swiss frontier, where he was cared for by the American Red Cross. On December 1 he arrived at American Base Hospital No. 26, A.P.O. 785, and it was from that point that he came by rail to Havre and presented himself as a destitute American seaman, entitled, under our laws, to relief and transportation.

Naturally, Mr. Bastin had none of his original papers, all having been lost or taken from him by the Germans. He showed me, however, Special Order No. 445, of the adjutant of the American base hospital above mentioned, relating to him, and also a permit issued to him at the German camp. Mr. Bastin stated that he was born in Ostend, Belgium, on June 21, 1889, and that he went to New York in June, 1918, and took out his first papers for American citizenship. Not being yet an American citizen I could not issue to him an American seaman's identification certificate. As a destitute American seaman, however, I relieved his immediate needs, provided for subsistence and lodging and, after conferring with the American naval port office, I arranged with the master of the U.S.S. *Newton* to accept him as a consular passenger aboard that vessel to the United States. The U. S. S. *Newton* sailed from Havre for Newport News, Va., via Plymouth, England, on January 11, 1919.

On August 5 the *Stanley M. Seaman,* a four-masted schooner of 1,060 gross tons, bound from Newport News to Porto Plata, San Domingo, with a cargo of coal, was halted in latitude 34° 59′ N., longitude 73° 18′ W. by a shot from the *U–140.* The crew of the schooner took the boats at once and rowed to the submarine, where they delivered their papers. They informed the German officers that they "had left the schooner in a hurry and were without sufficient food and water," whereupon the submarine took their boats in tow and returned them to the schooner, where they were permitted to provision. They were ordered to run a line from the stern of the schooner to the bow of the submarine and after so doing were permitted to leave the vicinity.

The day following the sinking of the *Stanley M. Seaman* the *U–140* sank the American steamship *Merak* (formerly Dutch), 3,024 tons gross, 4 miles west of Diamond Shoals Lightship. The *Merak* was proceeding at about 8 knots an hour, when at 1.40 p. m. a shot from the submarine crossed her bows. The weather was so hazy that the submarine, which was 4 miles off the port bow, was invisible, but the flashes of her guns could be seen. The *Merak* put about at once and made for shore, steering a zigzag course. The submarine pursued, firing at intervals of about a minute. The *Merak,* which was not armed, ran aground after the submarine had fired her thirtieth shot and the crew took to the boats. The Germans drew up to the steamer, boarded her from the deck of the submarine, placed their bombs, and as soon as these had exploded, called the lifeboats alongside and questioned the captain of the *Merak.* After checking up the captain's answers in Lloyds, the submarine officer gave him the distance to shore and turned his attention to other vessels which were in sight at the time: The Diamond Shoals Lightship, 590 gross tons, the British steamer, *Bencleuch,* and the American S. S. *Mariners Harbor.* Of these vessels the first was sunk by gunfire, the second escaped after being chased and gunned for some time, and the third escaped attack of any kind. The *Mariners Harbor* was, however, close enough to the lightship to observe the attack upon her, and a summary of her captain's story as submitted to the naval authorities tells of the afternoon's work of the *U–140*:

The *Mariners Harbor,* of 2,431 tons gross, operated by the New York and Porto Rico Steamship Co., and commanded by Capt. Hansen, left Porto Rico for New York July 31, 1918, with a cargo of sugar.

At 1.45 p. m. (Saturday), August 6, 1918, in latitude 35° 01′ N., longitude 75° 24′ W., proceeding to Diamond Shoals Lightship at 9 knots, the report of gunfire was heard offshore and south of the lightship. At this time the sea was choppy, weather fine, visibility excellent.

The firing was off the starboard bow of the *Mariners Harbor*. The course was altered to NW. for about 15 minutes. Through the glasses the captain could see the lightship and one ship on either side of her. One of the ships appeared to be of about five or six thousand tons, and the other one was much smaller. The larger ship seemed to be inside the lightship and the smaller one appeared to be outside of the lightship.

Shells were observed to be dropping about the ships into the water, causing a considerable spray to arise. The firing was not regular. Usually two shots were reported with an interval of a few seconds between them. Then an interval of from three to five minutes and sometimes longer would follow. The captain estimated that about eight shells were fired during the first 10 minutes of the attack.

At 2.12 p. m. (Saturday) the *Mariners Harbor* intercepted the following radio message: "KMSL S. O. S. Unknown vessel being shelled off Diamond Shoal Light Vessel No. 71. Latitude 35° 05′, longitude 75° 10′."

The course of the *Mariners Harbor* was then changed to N. and it was observed that the report of the firing became more distinct. Subsequently the course was changed to NW. and then to due W. for a short time, and the report of the firing became quite faint. Finally the course of the *Mariners Harbor* was steered N. and the engines were stopped when the ship reached a point about 10 miles WSW. of Cape Hatteras, in 8 fathoms of water. It was then about 5 o'clock.

The firing seemed to cease for about a half hour, when it commenced again, SSW. of the ship's position, and continued until shortly after 6 o'clock.

At 5.50 (Saturday) the *Mariners Harbor* received the following radio message: "Gunned, steering S. 55 E. *Bencleuch*."

At 6 p. m. a ship was sighted astern of the *Mariners Harbor* proceeding at a low rate of speed on about an ENE. course. She came alongside the *Mariners Harbor* and Capt. Hansen hailed her captain through a megaphone. The name of the ship was the American S. S. *Cretan*, of about 1,000 tons, engaged in passenger service.

The captain of the *Cretan* inquired about the firing and asked Capt. Hansen if he was going out. Capt. Hansen informed him of what he saw, and stated that he intended to proceed after dark.

At 6.25 (Saturday) the *Mariners Harbor* received the following message: "Ceased firing after 37 shots, 23.25, steering toward Lookout."

The *Cretan* and the *Mariners Harbor* stood together until 6.30 p. m., when the *Mariners Harbor* proceeded along the beach, followed by the *Cretan*. After about a half hour the *Cretan* stopped, but the *Mariners Harbor* continued on her E. by N. course until Cape Hatteras was reached.

At dusk (7.15 p. m.) the *Cretan* came up to the *Mariners Harbor* and the course was resumed. When offshore about 7 miles the captain observed that the Diamond Shoal Lightship was not in sight, although the ship was in range of its visibility.

At 8.30 p. m., what appeared to be a small steamer was observed off the starboard bow coming from the southwest and steering northeast for the position of Diamond Shoal Lightship. She was showing a masthead light, and a red side light could be seen through the glasses. The lights were very low in the water and proceeding at a high rate of speed. The *Mariners Harbor* and the *Cretan* were running completely darkened. The night was dark, with no moon to be observed.

The captain believes this vessel to be a submarine, and the *Mariners Harbor's* helm was ported, followed by the *Cretan*, and a due west course steered for about 2 miles. The lights on the unknown vessel remained in view for about 15 minutes.

The *Mariners Harbor* and the *Cretan* then followed the course which the unknown vessel was steering.

Capt. Hansen is of the opinion that this unknown vessel was a submarine, and that it was steering this course expecting to meet his ship. The submarine undoubtedly observed the ship during the attack and saw her head for the shore. At that time the sun was between the submarine and the *Mariners Harbor*, and the captain believes this accounts for the fact that the submarine did not shell him, although his position was about the same distance away from the submarine as the lightship—the three positions forming a triangle.

During the entire attack the captain estimated that between 50 and 60 shells were fired.

At 10 p. m. a message was received that the Diamond Shoal Lightship had been sunk.[34]

On the morning of August 10, the following radio message was intercepted by several ships and stations: "S O S 36 N. 73 W. Help. We are running extreme danger. We are being attacked. Lat. 36 N., long. 73 W. S. D. Z." The U. S. S. *Stringham* hurried to the assistance of the endangered vessel, which proved to be the Brazilian steamer *Uberaba*. The result of her mission is evidenced by the following message received by the Bureau of Operations: "Enemy submarine sighted lat. 35° 51' N., long. 73° 21' W. Dropped 15 depth charges. Searching vicinity Brazilian steamer. Call letters S. D. Z. Escaped undamaged."[35]

Three days later the U. S. S. *Pastores* engaged the *U-140*. The story of this action is taken from the war diary of the *Pastores* dated August 13:

At 5.32 p. m., G. M. T., this date, in latitude 35° 30' N., longitude 69° 43' W., this vessel changed course from 269° true to 330° true in order to cross a restricted area in approach route before moonset. Zigzag combined plans Nos. 1 and 2 had been carried on all day. At 5.43 p. m., G. M. T., the officer of the deck noted a splash about 2,500 yards distant, a little on the starboard quarter, and heard the report of a gun. With his glasses he discovered a large enemy submarine lying athwart our course 6 or 7 miles distant, a little on the starboard quarter, and firing at this ship, apparently with two guns. From size of splash it appeared that these guns were of about 6 inches in caliber. Went to battle stations and commenced firing at submarine at extreme range with armor-piercing shell at 5.46 p. m., G. M. T. The enemy fired about 15 shots, none of which came closer than 1,500 yards, after which she headed around toward us or away from us and ceased firing. This ship fired nine rounds at extreme range from after 5-inch 40-caliber guns, all of which fell more than 3,000 yards short. Ceased firing at 5.50 p. m., G. M. T., after enemy had ceased, and proceeded on course at full speed. Submarine disappeared about 5 minutes later.

For a week following the engagement with the *Pastores* nothing was heard of the *U-140*, and when, on August 21, she resumed her activities she was far to the northward of the scene of her former operations. At that time she attacked and, after a brief fight, sank the British steamer *Diomed*, 7,523 gross tons, bound from Liverpool to New York.

---

[34] Statements of Louis Hansen, master of the *Mariners Harbor*, to United States naval authorities.

[35] On a subsequent visit of the S. S. *Uberaba* to the United States, in February, 1919, a request was made by the officers and men of that ship through the Brazilian naval attaché at Washington, for permission, which was granted by the Navy Department, to present to the officers and men of the U. S. destroyer *Stringham* an American flag in silk and a silver loving cup brought from Brazil to express their heartfelt esteem for the timely succor given, and to further strengthen the bonds of confidence and affectionate gratitude between the United States and Brazil.

We left Liverpool in convoy with the *Harrisburg, Plattsburg, Baltic* (White Star steamer), *Belgic* (White Star), *Katoomba, Dunvegan Castle,* and the guide ship *Lancashire*. We were joined afterwards by the *Ortega*. There were eight destroyers in the convoy. They left at approximately 15 W. As soon as the convoy was broken up, the various vessels dispersed and followed the routes and courses prescribed in the sailing instructions. All the vessels were transports so far as the chief officer is advised, and with the exception of the *Harrisburg* and *Plattsburg* were commanded by a captain of the Royal British Naval Reserve. The average speed of the *Diomed* was 15¼ knots. The day before the *Diomed* was sunk she ran 400 miles.

I came on watch at 4 a. m., relieving the second mate. At 4.30 a. m. I took stellar observations. I just finished the work on these observations at about 4.50 when an object was sighted on the starboard beam, distant about 4 miles. By this time it was about half daylight, perfectly clear sky, smooth water, and light air. I ordered the helm hard a starboard for the purpose of bringing the object astern. I sent the midshipman to tell the gunners to stand by, but not to open fire until they got further orders, as I could not tell from the first examination whether the object was a submarine or whether she was a torpedo boat.

In the meantime the ship was swinging and when the object was about a point off the starboard quarter she opened fire. I am under the impression that she was not moving in any direction. As soon as she fired her first shot we opened fire at about 5,000 yards distance, but I could not observe the fall of the shot. The captain was in the chart room when the submarine was sighted and came on the bridge whilst the ship was swinging under a starboard helm. As soon as our first shot was fired I left the bridge and ran to work the after gun, the captain taking charge of the ship. The gun was a 4.7-inch British Admiralty gun. The fourth shot that the submarine fired struck the *Diomed's* starboard quarters, and from then on the submarine registered several hits. By the time we fired 12 rounds the steampipe to the steering gear, which was on the poop, had been carried away and we could not get to our ammunition locker, which was located just on the foreside and underneath the steering engine house, on account of the dense volumes of steam; the shot which carried away the line completely disabled the steering gear.

We had a hand-steering gear, but it was impossible to hook it up and use it because it would have taken half an hour to rig it under the most favorable circumstances. No orders were passed to connect the hand-steering gear because the dense volume of steam which prevented our getting at the ammunition locker also stopped any possibility of so doing.

In the meantime the submarine was dropping shells all around and upon our poop. The splash of the German shells made our spotting observations almost impossible. We were spotting from the roof of a locker immediately forward of the gun, because under the circumstances it was impossible for the spotting officer to make himself heard by the gunner from the top, since there were no voice tubes from the after gun to the maintop.

As soon as I found that passing the ammunition was impossible on account of the dense volume of steam, and also from the fact that the officer in charge and his petty officer in the ammunition party were severely wounded, I gave the command to cease firing. We then made an attempt to ignite the smoke boxes, but as these did not ignite readily I ordered the poop to be left in order to try and prevent casualties.

As far as maneuvering of the ship is concerned, the chief officer is not in a position to give any information, except that from the time the steam line was carried away up to the time the vessel surrendered she was going ahead at full speed. She swung somewhat to port after the main steering line was carried away. When the chief officer left the quarter-deck the submarine was shelling the port side of the ship. After leaving the quarter-deck I reported to the captain that the gun was out of

AMERICAN S. S. O. B. JENNINGS AFTER HER FIRE.

(Page 73.)

GERMAN U-117 ANCHORED AT WASHINGTON, D. C., AFTER THE WAR.
Used in the Victory loan campaign.

GERMAN U-BOAT SHOWING SAW-TEETH ON THE BOW USED FOR CUTTING NETS.

SINKING OF AMERICAN S. S. FREDERICK R. KELLOGG.

(Page 92.)

action and offered the suggestion, in order to prevent unnecessary waste of life, that the ship be abandoned. The captain agreed to this suggestion and the ship was abandoned in good shape.

The captain's boat, in which I left the ship, was held alongside the ship as long as we thought it proper to hold her there. By the time we joined the other boats, which were lying about a quarter of a mile off the ship waiting for us, the submarine had steamed to a position quite close to the other boats. I was never less than 250 yards from the submarine, but I tried to observe all I could of her construction and general appearance. The submarine passed our boats as she went to take up her position to sink the ship, which she did by firing three salvos of two rounds each from a distance of about 300 yards, and the ship immediately commenced to list to port and finally sank on her port side about 15 minutes after the first salvo had been fired. When the ship sank we were about 600 yards from her. The position at the time of sinking was latitude 40° 43′ N., longitude 65° 15′ W.[36]

The day after the sinking of the *Diomed* the *U–140* attacked the American cargo vesse *Pleiades*, 3,753 gross tons, bound from Havre to New York. The submarine, which was lying awash and not underway, was sighted at 7.10 p. m. from the crow's nest of the ship by a member of the armed guard crew.

The *Pleiades*, of 3,700 gross tons, owned by the Luckenbach Co., left Havre August 4, 1918, for New York. On August 22, at about 7 p. m. (ship's time), in latitude 39° 43′ N., longitude 63° 11′ W., a member of the armed guard in the crow's nest reported a suspicious object two points off the starboard bow, distant 5 or 6 miles. The weather was clear, but the first officer on the bridge could not make out the object and ascended to the crow's nest. By this time the object was dead ahead. The first officer recognized that what the lookout had taken to be a funnel was the conning tower of the submarine.

The submarine was awash, not under way, and in the slight swell of the sea the first officer could make out the bow and stern alternately exposed below the water line. He noticed a gun forward and aft, but could not distinguish other details at that distance beyond the fact that she was a big submarine, at least 300 feet long, and that her conning tower was amidships.

At 7.10 p. m. the course of the *Pleiades* was changed from S. (true) to SW. by W. ¾ W., at her regular speed of 9½ knots. A few minutes later the lookout reported that the submarine had submerged.

At 8 p. m. the flash of a gun was seen off the port beam and a shell fell 1,000 yards short of the *Pleiades*. A submarine was sighted, lying awash, distant between 3 and 4 miles. The position of the ship was 39° 34′ N., 63° 25′ W. There was a full moon, in the rays of which the submarine lay, making an excellent target. The *Pleiades* swung her stern to the submarine and worked up a speed of 12 knots.

All told the submarine fired four shots, the interval between the first and second being three of four minutes and between the other two about two minutes. The second shot fell off the ship's port quarter from 500 to 1,000 yards short; the third and fourth shots struck astern from 700 to 1,000 yards short.

The *Pleiades* fired 13 shots from her after gun, a 4-inch 40. Beginning with the fourth shot the range was got and thereafter the shells fell close, although none of them hit the submarine. The submarine was heading S. and quickly moved out of the moon's rays after the first half dozen shots and no longer presented such a good target. Within 15 minutes after the first shot the submarine submerged. It was then

---

[36] From the examination of Chief Officer Alfred E. Batt by the aid for information at New York.

two or three points off the port quarter. The first officer believes the submarine fired only four shells, because the armed guard's shots were so well aimed as to lead the submarine to decide to submerge quickly.

The first officer explains the failure of the submarine either to pursue the *Pleiades* or to maneuver around her to get her in the path of the moon's rays on the grounds that she was not of a speedy type.

Two radio messages were sent out by the *Pleiades*. The first was an ALLO, sent at 7.15 p. m. The other was an S O S S S S S message, sent at 8.15, approximately. It was acknowledged by a shore station, but the first officer was unable to state which one.

The *Pleiades* arrived at New York August 25.[37]

After the attack on the *Pleiades* the *U-140* began her homeward voyage and on September 5 made an unsuccessful attack on the British tanker *War Ranee*, 5,559 gross tons, en route from Grangemouth, England, to Halifax, Nova Scotia, in ballast. At 11.30 a. m. in latitude 51° 27' N., longitude 33° 24' W., the *War Ranee* sighted a periscope and then the track of a torpedo close alongside, which passed immediately under the engine room, but did not hit the ship. The ship had been stopped for minor engine repairs and when the submarine was sighted orders were given for "full speed ahead." After a delay of five minutes she steamed ahead, zigzagging, until the submarine was well astern. The submarine came to the surface and gave chase. Later the submarine opened fire. Two rounds were fired at three-minute intervals between shots. The last seen of the submarine, she was heading south and the *War Ranee* escaped.

The *U-140* having sustained some damage resulting in a slight leakage, delayed her passage and she was joined on September 9 by the *U-117* which came to her assistance. The two then proceeded in company for a time toward Germany by way of the Skaw and Albach Bay. The *U-140* arrived at Kiel on the 25th of October, 1918.

THE CRUISE OF U-117.

The *U-117*,[38] commanded by Kapitanleutnant Droscher, left her base early in July, 1918. This vessel was one of the cruiser, mine-laying type of German submarines, and combined the errand of sowing mines on the American coast with that of destroying tonnage by direct attack. Her approach to the American coast was heralded by an attack on the British steamer *Baron Napier*, July 26, when in latitude 45° 26' N., longitude 32° 50' W.

On August 10 she attacked the fishing fleet in the vicinity of Georges Bank. Before the day had ended the submarine had sent to the bottom nine small motor schooners—the *Katie L. Palmer*, 31 tons; the *Aleda May*, 31 tons; the *Mary E. Sennett*, 27 tons; the *William H. Starbuck*, 53 tons; the *Old Time*, 18 tons; the *Progress*,

---

[37] Statement of John McNamara, chief officer of the *Pleiades*, to the American naval authorities.

[38] After the surrender at Harwich the *U-117* was one of the submarines sent to America for use in the Liberty loan campaign.

34 tons; the *Reliance*, 19 tons; the *Earl and Nettie*, 24 tons; and the *Cruiser*, 28 tons. The *Albert W. Black*, 54 tons, was fired on but succeeded in escaping, and the *Gleaner*, 45 tons, after seeing one of the victims disappear under the waves, fled without molestation.

All of the fishermen witnessed the sinking of at least one schooner besides their own; some had conversation with the officers and crew of the submarine, while others, who were taken aboard the submersible were able to furnish fairly good nontechnical descriptions of the raider.

I am a French Canadian,

said Fred Doucette, engineer of the *Aleda May*,

and 32 years old. Have been in the fishing business 15 years. We sighted the submarine when we were SE. of Georges Banks. I think that the water there is about 70 fathoms. We sighted the submarine between 9 a. m. and 10 a. m. I was engineer, and the first I knew about it was when I was told to start the motors. Just at that time I heard the first shot, which jarred the boat. I opened the engine wide open, then we heard another shot. The submarine was then about one-fourth mile from us, coming toward us. A shell struck and cut our mainsail off. The smoke from the shell was black. Then we got into our dories. They took the skipper, a young fellow, and myself and told us to go aboard the submarine. They took our dory and then three Germans, two of whom were sailors, got on board with *Aleda May*. The officer had a jersey sweater on, with blue serge pants. Had devices on hat. He spoke English. They took our picture from the bridge, as we came alongside, with a small camera.

They were aboard the *Aleda May* and took all our food. They took onions, candles, watermelon, bananas, and meat, and cleaned out all our provisions. They took a hose which I had there, also a can of gasoline and a can of cylinder oil. Took rubber boots and shoes. Also took the bow line and dumped it in the dory.

The bomb was painted red, about the size of a big tomato can. They screwed a fuse into the metal on the top of the bomb. They then lowered it down the side of the vessel. They tied the fuse with piece of rope when they lowered it down the side. They then took a screw driver and shoved it into the end of the fuse and it snapped. Then they said, "Row off quickly. We have seven minutes." About every minute there seemed to be a snap. It seemed more than seven minutes to me. I should say it was nearer 10 minutes. The officer began to look anxious, and then it exploded, without much noise. The boat settled slowly, and the officer said "There she is; that is war." There was a handle on the side of the bomb to carry it with. There was a second bomb in the dory and this gave me a good chance to get a description of it. It was 7 or 8 inches high; 6 inches around; nose was 3 inches long and about 1½ inches in diameter. The handle was just large enough to take hold of. We were on the deck of the submarine for a whole hour. The bow slanted; top was round; stern went right down to the water. There were two tight wires stretched from forward aft, over conning tower.

There was a steel plate (washboard) on each side of submarine to keep the spray off their feet. This board was about 2 feet high. There was a saw tooth for cutting the wires which ran about 14 or 15 feet from the bow, and seemed to be quite heavy. There were turnbuckles at after end of wire for torting up wire.

The submarine was about 300 feet long. Her hold was about 6 or 7 feet above water. There were two guns, one forward and one aft. The forward gun was about 50 feet from conning tower. The after gun was closer to conning tower, probably 30 feet.

The forward gun looked to be larger than the aft gun. The forward gun was about 12 feet long. The after gun was about 10 feet. The recoil cylinder was conspicuous on after gun.

There was a wire handrail the entire length of the submarine held up by iron.

When the crew got on deck they were covered by four men. They took an empty shell from the gun, which shell was about 5 inches, with a brass nose fuse, about 2½ inches. They loaded the empty gun again. They took up a wooden grating from floor where shells were kept. There was an iron bar holding wooden grating down. There seemed to be about 200 shells. They picked up the shell, turned it up, nose down, and unlocked case which held shell (brass case). They put the shell into gun and took the empty shell and put it with the other shells and covered it over again with iron bar.

No wireless or periscope was noticed. There was a pipe on each side of conning tower, about 6 feet above conning tower.

The smallest gun was aft. There was no flare on the submarine. She ran straight. There was a small German flag on after end of conning tower, red, white-black.

The deck of the submarine was perfectly smooth except for the grating. The conning tower was about 12 feet. She was battleship-gray color. She set up in water pretty well forward, and went down low aft.

The men stayed on deck about one hour. She was steaming up to sink the *Progress*, and made a sign to the captain to push away. They got into the dory, and they told us to come down the conning tower. We went down the hatchway through the conning tower, and when we got down we walked a few steps to another manhole about the same size, and then to another manhole, which made the third, and we had to stoop down to get through it. It was a little aft.

On the first level nothing was noticed. Nothing was noticed on the second level. On the third level, we went through manhole, and there were two big motors there, one on either side, probably dieselators. They were about 2 feet apart. They were very noiseless in running, and kept going all the time. The engine was started from up above by a turning wheel, and went very smooth. There was no vibration whatever. It was a reversible engine. When she ran on reversible she was just as noiseless. The engine room was short distance from conning tower.

The men sat on tool chest and there was a small dynamo running all the time. A bell would ring, and the switch was thrown, which would result in a loud noise. This would happen quite often. There were a number of men handling the motors. When bell would ring there would be indications above (lettered) and a certain man would throw lever on. There were five or six men handling the switches. They were kept busy all the time.

There were no crosspieces or wire running from bow. The men stood back of conning tower for about one hour. The beam was about 30 feet wide amidships. Conning tower was about 12–15 feet wide. Did not have double flare.

When they were sitting on the tool chest there was a manhole opposite, and it seemed as if the crew of the submarine did not want them to see into it. They were very careful about closing the door every time they went in, and when the door was left open, they hollered to close it. You would have to stoop to get into manhole.

The door on manhole opened inside port side. The crew of the submarine, went into manhole and brought out a large pot of pea soup. They gave Doucette a dish and offered the other men some, but they would not take it. Doucette took it. They gave him a large dish and spoon, but no marks on it. The soup was quite thick, with peas and beans. One of the crew of the submarine took enough to last Doucette a couple of days, and ate it standing at his post. The men had on leather suits and wooden soled shoes.

The captain of the *Lena May* asked one of the crew of the submarine if they had sunk many vessels, to which he replied that he had sunk quite a few. It was 1 o'clock when the men went down in submarine, and 3.15 when they came out. Quite a few men shook hands with them and wished them luck.

All the supplies of the crew of the *Lena May* were taken away. Also all their clothes.

This man on board the submarine, who appeared to be an officer, stated that he had been in New York and Providence. He stated that he was married. He said, "Do you think the people of America think they are going to win the war?" He said, "I suppose you people think the same." He said that nobody would win. He said that Germany had a good chance to win, as they had plenty of men. He asked about the draft. He asked Doucette how old he was, to which Doucette replied 33. He said that the draft age in America was between 20–30. He also asked if there was many training. He asked Doucette how many men there were in France, to which Doucette replied that there was three million in France, and one-half million in Italy. He wanted to know if we had any charts. They seemed to be very much afraid of mines, and wanted to know if there were any that we knew of.

They got some ketchup from the *Lena May* and were quite pleased with it. They said, "Oh look, Sniders." They threw open the hatch on the *Lena May* and found fresh goods.

They looked like a crowd of pirates, and were very yellow.

It was very hot in the submarine, the air was very foul from crude oil.

At about 9.50 a. m. on Saturday, August 10, according to R. A. Sanchez, owner of the *William H. Starbuck*,

the man on the lookout on the *Starbuck* first sighted the submarine. At that time the *Starbuck* was about 220 miles SE. by S. from Graves Light. It is believed that the *Starbuck* was the first one of the fishing fleet to sight the submarine, which was coming from E. by SE. and about 5 miles off; it was recognized at once as a submarine. She showed a great deal of foam and appeared to be coming fast. When at a distance of about 3 miles from the *Starbuck*, she started to shell that vessel, which was attempting to escape. The *Progress, Reliance, Aleda May*, and one other vessel were in the fleet. After several shells fell very close to the *Starbuck*, she hove to. This was after fragments of shell had fallen on the deck of the *Starbuck*. This was probably about 10 o'clock a. m. Three dories were prepared to abandoned the ship, and at about 10.30 the *Starbuck* was abandoned. The dories were close by and afterwards approached the submarine, and during this time witnessed the sinking of the *Aleda May*, the *Progress*, and possibly the *Reliance*, sunk in probably the above order. At about 2 p. m. the submarine sank the *Starbuck* with a bomb. No sound of the explosion was heard, but the concussion was distinctly felt in the dories.

Mr. Sanchez states that he thinks the submarine was somewhere between 200 and 300 feet long, and he thinks that she was certainly not over 250 feet. Her after gun was considerably smaller than her forward gun. The after gun appeared to be very large at the bridge, and what appeared to be the barrel itself was no longer than 5 or 6 feet, and the larger part toward the bridge appeared to be even longer than this. The caliber of the gun appeared to be about 3 inches. It was a peculiar looking gun and entirely different from anything the captain had ever seen in the American Navy. The forward gun apparently was about 25 feet long.

There was apparently a solid wire stay which stretched from bow to stern, running over the conning tower itself. The whole length of this stay, from the bow to the conning tower, had what appeared to be teeth like a knife fastened to it. This stay appeared to be about 3 inches in diameter, made of wire. Her bow was sharp, sloping forward from the water line like the bow of a schooner, and her deck ran down from amidships aft.

As many as 20 of the crew were standing in the conning tower laughing as the *Starbuck* was being rifled of all her provisions by some of their mates.

About 20 feet from the bow of the submarine appeared a contrivance, which looked like the davit on board a vessel for hoisting purposes. No boats were visible on deck. The submarine was painted lead color, as were also her guns. Attached to the stay running fore and aft was what appeared to be a wireless apparatus leading to the conning tower. Mr. Sanchez is absolutely positive that the after gun was much smaller than the forward gun and appeared to be about half the caliber. About 10 feet from the bow there appeared to be a spar, which lay on deck, and which apparently could be forced forward to an upright position. This spar appeared to be about 20 or 25 feet long and appeared to be fitted to a hinge on deck.

At about 2 p. m., shortly after leaving the submarine and when about 4 miles distant, the submarine opened fire on the dories of the *Starbuck*. There is no question in Capt. Sanchez's mind but what they fired on the dories, the shells landing in their vicinity, and the submarine afterwards coming toward them and looking them over.

About 6.30 p. m., Sunday, August 11, after sailing since Saturday afternoon about 2 p. m., the trawler *Acushla* was met and the crew of the *Starbuck* went on board of her and were brought to Boston, arriving at 9 a. m., Tuesday, August 13, 1918.

James Nickerson, the master of the fishing schooner *Reliance*, gives the following account of the attack:

> It was about 10 o'clock Saturday morning and I was lying down, and one of the crew came down and said there was a shot fired alongside of us. There were four boats close together, all fishing boats. So I came on deck, and just as I came up a shell struck alongside and I saw them lower sails off of her. Then he shelled one outside of us a little, and we started our power and swung away from her, and then he threw two shells at us; one struck about 50 feet from us and the other about 150 feet.
>
> She was not a mile away from us when we sighted her, and, of course, then we stopped our machine and let her lay. There was no use in trying to get away, and we put our dories over and took some provisions and water and got all ready to leave, and then we went back on board.
>
> I don't know the first one sunk; she was about 2 miles away from us. The second, the *Progress* of Edgartown. We went aboard, then got some canvas to make sails and stayed there until the second one went down, and when he came toward us we pushed off and lay perhaps 200 or 300 yards from her. He had a yellow dory at the stern of the submarine. He came within about 200 feet between us and the boat. Of course some of our dories were farther off; we had three dories. One man I saw

getting over the side of the submarine with a bag. I think he was an officer. He had a white cap and oilskins; all of them had. It was an officer's cap. They were perhaps 20 minutes aboard her before they left her, and they just got aboard the submarine and did not move very far before she went up. There wasn't much of an explosion; she went down stern first. We saw three more schooners just about the time we left; the *Starbuck* was about north by west from us. After he sunk the *Starbuck* he steamed in that way. There were about 10 or 11 shots fired there at those other three.

The wind was about ENE. She wasn't going very fast. She had the dory astern. There was very little noise; just smoke. She fired perhaps 10 or 11 shots. Just about noon the *Starbuck* went down and we got aboard the *Katie Palmer* about 5.30. Ten minutes before we boarded her we heard four more shots. We got aboard and started power and started about west by south. We didn't go 40 minutes when we saw her coming behind us, and, of course, when she was about 2 miles from us we sighted her. Her bow was about 12 or 14 feet out of water and her stern was awash. The center was about 6 or 7 feet out of water. So, of course, he says there is no use of us trying to get away. He stopped his engine and we got into our dories again and started out. The *Katie Palmer* is owned, I think, in Boston. The master is Edward Russell. He had no dory out that time and had no boat of any kind because the first of his dories came along with us, and the submarine was perhaps 300 yards from us and there was a fellow signaling to one of the last dories that left her and that dory went alongside. It was getting dark then. We heard this slight explosion. Of course we started then for land. We never saw anything after we left her until Sunday night about 8 o'clock we heard—I suppose there was a fishing vessel coming up. About noon Monday we were picked up by the schooner *Corinthian* about 14 miles around South Channel. The owner of my boat is John Nelson, of Gloucester. The crew of the *Katie Palmer* all left her. The *Palmer* looked like a dory alongside the submarine. He was about 17 miles about west from where we were. Her bow was round, just like a schooner bow. I was within 200 feet of her when she came down alongside of our boat. They all had some kind of coats on. She had two guns aft. One heavy gun on the bow. It was covered. It was as long as one of those 6-inch guns. Must have been 50 men on her forward deck. There wasn't over 12 men in sight when she was alongside us. She was twice as long as the *Starbuck*, and the *Starbuck* I should judge to be about 90 feet. She was 250 feet at least. She was close to the *Starbuck*. She was newly painted. The *Starbuck* looked like a jolly boat alongside her. There were no rough spots on her. She looked new.

The following is the statement of Manael Dias, captain of the schooner *Mary E. Sennett*:

The crew consisted of seven, all being saved.

Saturday, August 10, 1918, between 3 and 4 p. m., SE. part of Georges Bank, known as latitude 41°, 160 miles SE. Island Light; weather very good. Friday night, August 9, 1918, weather was stormy, raining, and rough.

The *Cruiser* from Boston, a fishing boat, told me that they heard some shots east of them and that they thought we had better go to port, but owing to the fact that the captain had heard these reports from other fisherman from time to time, did not pay any attention to this report. *Cruiser*, *Old Time*, and this boat, the *Mary E. Sennett*, were all fishing together around 1 o'clock, and captain was on mast looking for sword fish when two submarines were sighted ESE. of where this boat was. One submerged and was never seen again, and the other was making circles trying to fool the fishing boats—that is, the submarine zigzagged around so that the fishing boats would come near to it. Whereas, the captain thought these were other fishing boats at first, and sailed toward them. *Cruiser* and *Old Time* sighted and recognized what they really were.

All boats tried to run away toward the NW. Then speed was put on; when about a mile off three shots were fired at same time, one at each one of the fishing boats. Then we faced vessel SE. and then two more shots were fired, one at stern and one at bow. Then we took to dories and went WNW. and the vessel SE. jogging along by itself. Only saw one shot hit water and went under keel. *Cruiser* was sunk and *Old Time* was also sunk; none of men believed saved.

Germans were not seen going on board any of these vessels. After *Cruiser* and *Old Time* were sunk, it went toward the *Mary E. Sennett.* Lost sight of vessel and did not pay much attention as we were using our best efforts to get away.

Around 5.30 or 6 p. m. nine shots were heard in direction where submarine was seen. Sailed NW. for home. Sailed until Sunday 2 p. m. *Goodspeed*, a knockabout trawler on Clarkes Bank, brought us to fishing grounds. We then got on board a United States chaser and were brought to the S. S. *Rijndijk*, which was at Island Light, and it brought us to harbor, where we were taken to the immigration office.

The submarine was about 200 feet long, nothing less, and looked gray. We saw two brass guns, one on stern and one on bow. The gun on the stern was of solid shell. Fire came from forward gun and smoke from the stern gun when fired. Believe there were more guns on it.

There was no wireless seen. No flag. Conning tower quite high, about 8 or 9 feet. Lost sight of vessel and therefore do not know whether or not they boarded my vessel.

Statement of Edward Russell, captain of the *Katie L. Palmer:*

The *Kate L. Palmer* was a fishing schooner formerly owned by William and W. S. Jerden and taken over by Mr. Jack O'Hara, Boston, Mass. She plied between Boston and the fishing banks.

It left Boston, August 6, with a crew of seven men, including the captain, bound for Georges Banks, about 200 miles off the coast of Massachusetts.

On Saturday three gun shots were heard about 10 a. m. The weather was clear and the wind was NE. During the day several shots were heard, but nothing was seen till about 3.30 p. m., when a submarine was seen about 8 miles away. It continued coming nearer until it arrived alongside the ship. The submarine was about 300 feet long and was a war-gray color. It had two guns, fore and aft. The fore gun was 6 to 8 inch and about 15 feet long and looked to be about 3 feet in diameter. No overhead wires were seen. The conning tower was about 25 feet high. On the outside of the submarine were about 20 or 25 men. Later I boarded her and saw several men on board. I was questioned as to whether or not I was armed. Four of my men boarded the submarine, but the other three did not. I was told to go below. The crew were sociable and said, "Don't hurry," and asked if we had water and provisions. I replied that we had. The submarine crew then took our stuff out of the dory. I had a drink with some of the members of the crew and was given a bottle of cheap rum, unsealed. An officer of the crew asked about the mines and tried to get us to talk. We said we were not permitted to know anything about these matters. He then asked if we would like to have peace. I answered, "Yes." He next asked if our people wanted peace, and I said that I thought they did. He asked when I thought the war would be over and I answered that I did not know. He then said, "What do your people think about it." I said that they had different opinions. He said, "I suppose President Wilson knows." I did not answer. He said, "I saw President Wilson's picture with a great big nose," and he laughed.

The submarine crew were all Germans. They spoke broken English. I asked the length of the submarine and was told that it was about 300 feet and they had 500 different types of submarines in Germany, some 500 feet in length. He said, "I suppose you have submarines over in this country?" I answered, "Yes." The officer to whom I was talking seemed to feel that Germany knew all about submarines and that America knew nothing. He said, "You have about 100 men in Europe, haven't you?" I said that we have more than 1,000,000. He evidently did not believe it, and shrugged his shoulders. He told me not to go ashore and tell any lies. I answered that I would not.

Before leaving, the crew of the submarine returned all of my goods to my dory. We left the German sub about 8. We exchanged greetings and headed west. The submarine headed south. I was asked by the crew of the submarine about how many fishermen were about and I answered 25 or 30 eastward. I said that for the purpose of going west ourselves, in the hopes of finding a boat to help us. The officer said that they were going to give us a boat but later said they had changed their minds. We were aboard the dory until about 11 p. m.

When we were sunk, we were about 200 miles SE. of Highland Light in 50 fathoms of water. We went west toward the South Shore Lightship for the purpose of meeting some vessel to take us up. We were picked up about 10 o'clock by the *Helen E. Murley* and landed at New Bedford, Mass., about 3 a. m. The officer I talked to looked like the second mate. I don't think he was the captain. The men were dressed in leather jackets and wore regular German hats.

The officers wore slate-colored clothes and caps. The machinery looked as if it were operated by electricity. All the bells and lights were electric. They had two engines running lengthwise in the vessel. There were three passageways. I headed through the conning tower, then through another deck and then another and then another deck into the submarine. It was divided into compartments, with round doors that closed so that the compartments could be shut off. The engines were aft of the submarine. The galley was aft of the sub. I saw no anchors, ammunition, torpedo tubes, or numbers. There was a life rail about 3 or 4 feet in height.

Evidence that the German plan of breaking the morale of the American people and leading to a demand for the recall of the destroyer division was not badly calculated is shown by the fact that James J. Phelan, assistant States administrator of Massachusetts, at the instance of the mayor of Gloucester, reported to Washington that the fishermen and their families were greatly alarmed by the U-boat activities and desired additional naval protection on the fishing grounds.

The statement of Louis Amirault, a member of the crew of the schooner *Katie L. Palmer*:

On August 10 at about 10 a. m. gunfire was heard to the eastward which was repeated several times during the day up until about 2 o'clock, when it was distinctively recognized as being gunfire.

About 3 p. m. the man at the masthead reported three dories which came from the eastward. These dories proved later to belong to the American fishing schooner *Reliance*, a swordfish vessel from Gloucester. There were two men in each dory.

The crew of the *Reliance* stated that the *Starbuck*, *Progress*, and *Lida May* were sunk about 7 or 8 miles to the eastward of the position of *Katie L. Palmer*. The *Reliance* was sunk some time between 12 m. and 2 p. m. All of these vessels were sunk by bombs after shots had been fired across their bows to bring them to.

About 4 o'clock the submarine was sighted, coming from the northeast. She was coming very fast, and it was said by the crew of the submarine that she was making about 21 knots an hour. When first seen she was about 5 or 6 miles away. During this time the *Katie L. Palmer* was trying to get away from the submarine but was overtaken in 45 minutes. As the *Palmer* was going about 6 knots an hour, it is estimated that the submarine was making about 12 knots.

When the submarine came to about 100 yards of the *Palmer*, the *Palmer* was abandoned by its crew and that of the *Reliance*. After they had got into the dories, the submarine crew beckoned to one of the dories of the *Palmer* to come alongside. In this dory were Capt. Edward Russell of the *Palmer*, Fred Quinlan, Forman Belliveau, and the subject, Louis Amirault.

The submarine appeared to be about 300 feet long. Her deck appeared to be about 9 feet above the sea level. Conning tower was about 13 feet long, 6 feet wide. She had two guns, the one forward appearing to be 12 feet long and the caliber is estimated as being about 6 inch. The after gun was very much smaller, and appeared to be not more than 4 or 5 feet long. The forward gun appeared to be mounted about 30 feet forward of the conning tower. The other gun appeared to be about 20 feet aft of the conning tower.

She had a hand rail which began about the forward gun and ran aft slightly behind the conning tower. She appeared to have two hulls, and had square holes out of which the water was running.

The four men of the crew of the *Palmer* remained on the deck of the submarine about one-half hour, standing between the conning tower and the forward gun, chatting with the crew of the submarine of which there were about 30 or 40, and three of whom spoke English. The majority of the crew were dressed in khaki trousers and undershirt, some barefooted, and only one appeared in white uniform.

One of the three men who could speak English asked the subject, Amirault, from what port he hailed, to which he replied, "Boston." He told them that they were 150 miles from the nearest land, and that they would be picked up Saturday.

One of the officers of the submarine later asked the captain of the *Palmer* if he had any information in regard to mine field off the United States coast, to which he was given the answer that such information was secret, and that they knew nothing about it.

After standing for about one-half hour on deck, the four men were ordered below, where they went, going down a manhole in the conning tower, by climbing a ladder on the starboard side. The manhole appeared to be about 3½ feet in diameter.

They went through three manholes to get to deck below. At the foot of the manhole he found himself in an alleyway about 3½ feet wide, with a steel floor.

The men then went aft down the passageway through three or four bulkheads, which had round manholes about 2 feet from the floor. These manholes had steel doors. When they reached this compartment they were told to sit down on some small boxes. On either side of this passageway was machinery which they were told was electric on one side and motor power on the other side.

A member of the crew of the submarine, who stated that he was mate on the submarine, conversed with the crew of the *Palmer*, and asked them how long the war was going to last. They stated that they did not know, and the mate answered that Wilson knew anyway. At this time a member of the crew in white uniform brought in a bottle of liquor and were told to drink it as it was not poison.

This man asked if the United States had 100,000 soldiers over there, and we told them that they had 1,000,000. He said, "I saw an American paper, and the Americans captured 24 Germans, and the next day the Germans captured twice as many." He said, "You have got a lot to eat in this country anyway." He also said, "I hear you have got a lot of aeroplanes in this country. I would like to get a couple of them."

He asked the skipper whether he was a pilot and asked him if he knew the location of any mine fields on the United States coast. He asked the same question of the members of the crew. It appeared to Amirault that mine fields were the only thing that they were afraid of. The mate of the submarine stated that he had been in New York and in the Southern States. It is understood that he said that he was on a steamer. He stated that there were 500 U-boats in Germany, and said that he was going back to Germany in six months.

The crew of the *Palmer* remained in the compartment about one hour. All the time that they were below the engines were running and after about one hour they stopped and the men went on deck. Amirault does not know whether they submerged or not during this hour.

The crew of the *Palmer* were then put into their dory and were told by the man on the submarine to tell the truth about the way they had been treated on the submarine, and he wished them good luck.

While on board the submarine the cook of the *Palmer* was questioned as to whether there were any potatoes on board the vessel. At the time they came on deck of the submarine there was no vessel visible, and it was thought that the *Palmer* was sunk. When the crew of the *Palmer* went below deck of the submarine, some of the crew of the submarine went over to the *Palmer* carrying with them what appeared to be a bomb. This was red in color, flat on both ends, somewhat like a tomato can and about the same size. It appeared to have a fuse 1 inch long coming out of one of the ends.

No boats were seen on the deck of the submarine, but the crew of the *Reliance* stated that there was a dory on the submarine.

The submarine was painted a light gray and appeared to have been freshly painted. What could be seen of the bottom appeared clean.

She had two heavy wires about 1 inch thick strung from the bow over the conning tower to the stern. No anchor or other devices were noticed.

The guns appeared to be darker in color then the hull of the submarine, and the forward gun had a tampion on the muzzle. No plug was visible, and the cook of the *Palmer* told subject that he noticed a periscope about 25 feet long. It was very hot in the hold of the submarine.

At 11.20 p. m. on August 10 the dory of the *Katie L. Palmer* was picked up by the *Helen E. Murley*, of New Bedford, and immediately set sail for shore water on Georges bank and from there headed for New Bedford, arriving there about 12 p. m. August 11.

The man who said he was mate on the submarine stated that he was 38 years and that he was the oldest man aboard. The mate of the submarine was questioned as to how many vessels he had sunk, and he replied that the *Palmer* was the ninth vessel sunk on August 10.

They had about three or four weeks' growth of beard. About 75 men in the crew. Stated that they had been here for six months. The crew of the submarine seemed to be tired of the war, and one said that he wished it would end shortly. He said that the submarine business was a hard job and that he did not like it.

Mate on submarine stated to Amirault, "Don't put any guns aboard any fishing vessel because if you do we will consider you pirates and cut your throat." He stated that the French had placed guns aboard their fishing vessels.

After sinking the fishing fleet off Georges Banks the next activity of the *U-117* was two days later, when on August 12 she torpedoed and sunk (about 25 miles SE. of Fire Island) the Norwegian S. S. *Sommerstadt*, 3,875 gross tons, in latitude 40° 10′ N., longitude 72° 45′ W. The officers and crew of the ship declared that the torpedo fired by the submarine made a circle and returned, exploding against the side of their vessel.

A summary of the report of Capt. George Hansen tells the story:

The *Sommerstadt* left Halifax August 9 in water ballast. A little after 8 o'clock on the morning of August 12, 1918, I came out on the bridge, where my chief officer and second officer were at that time. I went over to the port side of the bridge and looked out, and I thought I saw something on the water. I went and took the glasses, but I could not make out what it was. I stood for a few minutes looking through the glasses and then saw a torpedo coming along a little aft from abeam of the ship about 150 fathoms away.

As soon as I saw the torpedo I stopped the vessel and ordered the engines reversed and full speed astern. The torpedo went under the vessel, barely missing it, a little on the fore part of the bridge, and came up on the other side.

I walked across to the other side and I then gave the orders for full speed ahead.

The torpedo went about 1,300 fathoms on the starboard side; then it started to turn to the left. When I saw the torpedo start to swerve around I gave orders for full speed ahead. After it passed the bow it made two turns, making a complete circle, and then struck our vessel aft on the port side exactly between the third and fourth hold, right at the bulkhead.

The submarine didn't come to the surface, but after we got into the boats I saw a stick, and somebody said, "There's the periscope." I was expecting the submarine to come to the surface.

My ship was drawing about 7 feet, and when the torpedo passed under the ship she only missed it by about a foot. At first she was traveling at a depth of about 8 feet, but gradually started to come to the surface, and when she finally struck us she was about 5 feet under.

At 6.25 the next morning the British steamer *Pyrrhus*, when 1 mile north of Fire Island Lightship, sighted a periscope abeam. A little over an hour later the periscope was again sighted, this time astern. The *Pyrrhus* opened fire at a range of 2,600 yards, and the enemy submerged. Late in the afternoon of the same day the *Frederick R. Kellogg* was torpedoed and sunk 30 miles south of Ambrose Channel Lightship. The statement of Capt. C. H. White is as follows:

My ship, the *Frederick R. Kellogg*, was torpedoed at 5.10 p. m. August 13, 1918, 12 miles north of Barnegat and 5 miles off shore. Latitude and longitude is not given for the reason that the ship was sunk in 15 seconds.

I was steering at the time of the attack north by east magnetic. The ship is owned by the Pan-American Petroleum & Transportation Co., and was carrying a cargo of oil for the United States Government. It was coming from Tampico, Mexico, bound for Boston. The *Kellogg* had a gross tonnage of 7,127 tons, net tonnage of 4,418 tons. The port of registry is Los Angeles, Calif., where the ship was registered when built. Immediately she was taken around to the east coast.

At the time of the accident there were moderate southerly winds, water smooth. No sign of a submarine, no periscope, nothing suspicious before the attack was seen. Nothing was seen until after the torpedo exploded, and then for about 150 yards the wake of the torpedo was seen by me. No warning was given, and for about an hour after the attack I looked for some trace of the submarine, expecting that the bow would be shelled, and absolutely nothing was seen. The ship went down in less than 15 seconds in shallow water, stern first, and it looked as though the stern were resting on the bottom. It is my opinion that this ship might possibly be salvaged if immediate action were taken.[39]

The torpedo struck the ship in the engine room in the after part of the ship on the port side, and I attempted to give the signal to clear the engine room, but communication had already been cut off, and stepping out on the fly bridge I pulled the whistle until the steam was out, and turning my head once more toward aft I saw the ship completely under water and sinking rapidly by the stern. The engine room and fireroom were together.

---

[39] The *Frederick R. Kellogg* was salvaged before the end of the month of August.

The torpedo must have been close to the water for the reason that it blew up two steel decks and a wooden deck and a lifeboat on the port quarter clean into the air. There was one engineer, the third assistant, one fireman, and one oiler on watch, and all three were killed. Four others were killed or drowned. These men were in the vicinity of the engine room. They were the second engineer, one mess boy, and two cadets.

The ship was unarmed. However, she was measured last trip for gun platforms. It was impossible to do anything for the defense of the ship, for she was torpedoed without warning and the sinking was instantaneous. Even if the ship had been armed nothing could have been done.

On the 14th the *U–117* halted the American schooner *Dorothy B. Barrett*, 2,088 gross tons, about 6 miles from Five Fathom Bank Lightship. The crew of the *Barrett* took to their boats and the submarine after following them for a time returned to the prize and destroyed her. William Merritt, master of the schooner, tells the following story of his escape from his ship, his rescue by the U. S. S. *Kingfisher*, and the action of the latter vessel in warning an unknown tanker of the presence of the raider:

The schooner *Dorothy Barrett* was at 9 o'clock about 6 miles NE. of Five Fathom Bank Lightship, heading NNE., when from the WNW. a submarine on the surface about 4 miles away ESE. fired one shot. The *Dorothy Barrett* hove to and lowered her jib sail and abandoned ship. The submarine came within 2 miles and submerged. I started my boat NW. to try and get some assistance. After getting within 1½ miles of the submarine I stopped the boat for awhile and then thought I had better try to secure some help.

I was to the north and west of the submarine. Then he made a short circle and then I had to go on the outside. I then had him on a line between me and the ship. Now I was between him and the shore. He waited a while to see what I would do. I thought if he wanted that vessel he would take it, and in the meantime I would try to get some help. I then gave our boat a NW. course, then headed WNW. and ran in on that until I found the *Kingfisher*. The submarine followed me for a while and then stopped and showed his conning tower. I kept going and bye and bye I got away. He was going to the ship again, and worked on to a line between me and the ship with his conning tower still up. Then for about 10 minutes after that I saw the *Kingfisher* coming from the northward. I laid my course to the *Kingfisher* to see if he could not give us some assistance. He swung around as soon as I signaled him and I went aboard.

I asked the captain what he had to fight with. He said he had three-inch guns, and I told him that the submarine was too big for him to tackle with that kind of gun. I then went up on the bridge and asked him what he was going to do. He said he was going to run for shoal water. We had been running about west only a short time when we sighted the oil tanker. I said to the captain, "He is going to get that fellow, also, and to shift our course to warn the tanker." The submarine was on our starboard quarter and we commenced firing. We were then heading about west and that submarine was about 2½ miles on our stern, just so we could fire by the pilot house. I did not see the conning tower then, but the gunner said he saw it, and he fired a couple of shots.

When I saw the tanker she was headed SE. By this time she had also seen the submarine, I guess. We did not have but little time to go down toward him, and started to fire on this submarine, and then we had to watch the fellows. We kept right on down that way toward him and started to fire and put on all the steam we could; but, as I said before, we wanted to get in shoal water.

Then the submarine came up and went right ahead of us and we fired about three shots. From the time we abandoned our ship to the time these shots were fired, I judge it was about three-quarters of an hour.

Some of them came pretty near. Just before we shot the last few times a big black smoke cloud came up out of the water. It was coming up just like steam. Then, about five minutes later, another big black steam cloud seemed to rise from the water from near the vicinity of the submarine and kept coming up for about 10 minutes. I called the captain's attention to it, but he said he could not tell what it was. I do not believe it was over 5 fathoms deep where that submarine was. The last thing I did before I left my vessel was to heave the lead and it showed 15 fathoms. If we had only had one of your fast submarine-chasing boats there we could have gotten that fellow because he was in shallow water and could not turn very fast.

Capt. Frederick Rouse, master of the Brazilian motor schooner *Madrugada*, which was the next victim of the *U-117*, made the following report of the loss of his vessel:

The *Madrugada* had a gross tonnage of 1,613, and a net tonnage of 1,288. Her home port was New York, and she left on August 13 at about 11 a. m., bound for Santos, Brazil, with a general cargo.

On August 15 at 7.15 a. m., in latitude 37° 50′ N., longitude 74° 55′ W., the first mate sighted a vessel about 2 miles off. This vessel was entirely out of the water, and did not look like a submarine when we first saw her. The first mate called me and said, "I don't know what to make of her; she looks like a destroyer to me." She then opened fire on us, her first shot falling about 100 feet over the starboard bow, and the next shot falling about 20 feet ahead. She then fired a third shot, which fell slightly over her port bow. By that time we had stopped our engines, putting the wheel hard down. A fourth shot was then fired, which struck the engine room. They then fired a fifth shot right on the water line, and seeing there was no chance to save the vessel, I ordered the crew to take to the boats, which we all did without mishap. While we were pulling away they fired two more shots, staying at the same distance from the ship all the time. They did not fire at the lifeboats. After we got well away from the ship the submarine steamed right up under her stern and put two shots in her stern, at a distance of about 20 feet, and then put another shot through the cabin, setting fire to the oil tank. She was burning as she went down, and the last we saw of her the whole bowsprit was sticking out of the water. She had 1,000 tons of cement on board at the time, and I think when this cement settles to the bottom it will cause the bowsprit to remain above the water, making it a menace to navigation. The submarine did not signal us at any time, nor did she offer to render us any assistance. The sea was calm during the attack.

After they had fired the first shot at us, my wireless operator, F. L. Cook, who is stationed at the City Port Barracks, Armed Guard, Brooklyn, N. Y., sent out an S O S call, but we had not time to wait for any response. My vessel was not armed. At the time my ship was sunk the weather was a little hazy, and as the submarine was about 2 miles off, I could not get a good look at her; I could barely make out the forms of two or three men at the guns.

The submarine was the ordinary type, about 400 feet in length. This I judge from the fact that my ship was about 250 feet long, and when the submarine was standing by before sinking her, she overlapped my vessel on both ends. The submarine had a wireless rigged up. She had two guns, one fore and one aft of the conning tower, which I judge to be 6-inch guns. She was painted dark and had no distinguishing marks at all on her. Owing to the fact that she did not come near us at any time, and the weather being hazy, I did not get a very good look at her. After sinking my ship she kept right on to the westward, without submerging, and disappeared. We were picked up by the *Taunton* at about 11.30 a. m. 10 miles southwest of Winter Quarters Shoals. Nobody from the submarine boarded the *Madrugada*.

The day after the sinking of the *Madrugada* the Norwegian bark *Nordhav*, 2,846 gross tons, bound from Buenos Aires to New York with a cargo of linseed, was halted by shell fire in latitude 35° 42′ N., longitude 74° 05′ W. The statement of Capt. Sven Marcussen of the *Nordhav* may be summarized as follows:

On August 17 at 6.30 a. m., when his vessel was 120 miles east southeast of Cape Henry, heading north northwest, a submarine was sighted 1½ miles astern coming slowly. The submarine proceeded until it was abreast of the ship on the port side still 1½ miles distant.

At 7 a. m. the submarine fired a shot over the ship followed quickly by two more shots. The *Norhdav* was hove to and the lifeboats made ready. The submarine signaled for papers to be brought aboard. The captain took 12 men in the ship's boat and was rowed to the submarine. He delivered the papers to the submarine and was asked where ship came from and where bound and what cargo she had. These questions were answered.

Capt. Marcussen with his men together with four Germans, one of whom was an officer returned to the ship. The German officer spoke excellent English. He said that he had been first officer on vessels trading between Hamburg and South America. He asked the captain if he had any potatoes on board.

When the ship was reached the crew were allowed 20 minutes in which to get together their effects. During this time the Germans placed hang bombs over the port side of the vessel, one forward and one aft and one amidships.

The captain and his crew then returned to the submarine and were all ordered below except four sailors, who were left in the boats. The men were kept aboard the submarine four hours; when they came on deck, their ship was laid over at an angle about 45°. She sank in half an hour. The men remained in open boats for 29 hours and were picked up on August 18 about 6 p. m. by the U. S. S. *Kearsarge*. They arrived at Boston on August 20 about 3.30 p. m.

The following is a description of the submarine which attacked the *Nordhav*: 250 to 300 feet long, 25 feet beam. She was painted dark gray. In places the paint appeared to have been chipped which made some spots on her hull darker than others, which the captain said somewhat resembled camouflage. The hull of the submarine was fairly clean and in good condition except in places where chipped as previously described. The captain did not see any name or number on the submarine, but states that his steward claims to have seen *U-117* on the hull. The bow was nearly straight being but slightly curved and a little slanting from the peak to the water line. The captain did not get a good view of the stern and declined to describe it.

The main deck was about 4 feet above the water. The conning tower was located amidships, and was 8 or 9 feet high from the deck forward, and about a foot lower aft. The metal plate around the forward part of the conning tower was carried about three feet above the deck of the tower, serving as a protection to the men stationed there. The remainder of the tower about 1 foot lower than the forward part was surrounded by a railing a little lower than the plate.

She had three guns, one large, probably a 6-inch, forward, half way between the bow and the conning tower and two others which he thought were smaller than the 6-inch gun, located aft, about half way between the conning tower and the stern. His recollections of the appearance of the after guns was a little hazy, and he declined to commit himself on these points. The captain did not see any periscope.

Capt. Marcussen stated that he had not seen any torpedo tubes or cables on board the submarine. She had no boat so far as he knew.

At the bow she had a sawtooth arrangement running fore and aft for a distance of about 4 to 6 feet. It started low over the bow and was higher at the other end being about 4 feet above the deck at the point where the wireless was attached. There was a railing running around the whole main deck.

The captain entered the submarine through a hatchway, just aft of the forward gun. He passed through the chart room. (He declined to give any description of the chart room, stating that he only passed through it and did not notice anything about the furnishings or navigating instruments, etc.) He next passed into a room about 6 feet by 9 feet, having two bunks on one side and a sofa on the other. He thought that this made sleeping accommodations for four men. This room had no other furnishings so far as he could tell. None of the remainder of the interior of the submarine was visited by the captain. He saw 20 to 25 men on deck. The commander of the submarine informed him that he had a crew of 40. The men looked well fed, but had a pale yellow color and appeared dirty. He thought the officers were from 25 to 40 years of age, and the men were mostly younger. All the officers had uniforms of material similar to khaki, with some sort of a mark on the shoulder. They wore caps with visors, having an insignia over the visor. The crew were mostly dressed in dungaree and khaki. Some of the men said that they sunk a ship nearly every day. When asked how long they had been away from Hamburg, one of the men said four weeks, and others laughed at this remark and said it was nearer six months.

On August 20 the Italian S. S. *Ansaldo the Third* encountered the *U-117* in latitude 38° 57' N., longitude 70° 48' W. The submarine was first sighted at 7 o'clock in the morning. She attempted to cross the bow of the steamer and was prevented from so doing by gunfire. Thwarted in this she drew up abeam the *Ansaldo* at a distance of 2½ miles and began a gun duel which lasted for almost three hours during which 200 shots were exchanged. The steamer having exhausted her supply of ammunition, put on all possible speed and succeeded in making her escape. Several shells from the submarine took effect; the afterpart of the *Ansaldo* was damaged, one gun put out of commission, and three members of the crew wounded.

At 9 a. m. the following morning the British S. S. *Thespis* sighted the periscope of the *U-117* in latitude 39° 54' N., longitude 69° 25 W. The *Thespis* turned stern to and made off at full speed. The submarine then dove and it was believed she had been shaken off. At 10.40, however, the wake of a torpedo was observed. The steamer having succeeded in avoiding injury by the narrow margin of 20 feet, the submarine rose to the surface and opened fire. The *Thespis* replied and after a running fight lasting half an hour outdistanced her enemy.

At 6 p. m. the same day, when in latitude 40° 30' N., longitude 58° 35' W., Capt. Eric Risberg, of the Swedish steamer *Algeria*, 2,190 gross tons, sighted the raider about a mile off, on the port beam of his ship.

The captain states that the next thing he knew the submarine fired a shot which fell about 600 feet off the port beam; he then stopped the engines and gave two long

GERMAN U-155 (EX-DEUTSCHLAND) AS A WAR SHIP.

(Page 100.)

LARGE GUN MOUNTED ON U-155 (EX-DEUTSCHLAND).
(Page 100.)

GERMAN U-155 (EX-DEUTSCHLAND), AFTER SURRENDER, ANCHORED WITHIN THE SHADOW OF THE FAMOUS TOWER BRIDGE, LONDON.

U-155 (EX-DEUTSCHLAND) AFTER THE WAR, IN THE THAMES NEAR LONDON.

blasts of the whistle to indicate that there was no headway of his ship. The submarine then hoisted the international code letters "T. A. R.," and the captain of the *Algeria* replied, "I can see your letters but can not make out the meaning."

The submarine then fired the second shot, which fell on the port side very close to the ship. After the second shot the captain ordered the boat lowered and proceeded to board the submarine. The submarine in the meantime swung under a starboard helm and came astern of the *Algeria*, laying starboard side to the stern of the *Algeria's*, distant about one-quarter of a mile. While in this position the captain pulled alongside and boarded the submarine from the starboard side.

When he approached the submarine, he was told to go up on the conning tower, and when he got on the conning tower the commander first said to him, "Why did you not lower a boat at once when you saw the submarine; your actions were not those of a neutral." The captain answered, "You were showing no flag, and it not being the first submarine I have seen and being so close to American waters, I assumed it to be an American submarine." He then asked where the captain was bound. He replied Gothenburg to Sandy Hook for orders.

He then took the *Algeria's* log and examined it, and when he found that she had been operating on the United States coast he said that was the "end." The captain replied, "You should not be guided by what I have been doing in the past but by what I am doing in the present." The chief officer of the submarine said to the captain of the submarine that the captain of the *Algeria* was correct; that they had nothing to do with what he had been doing before. At this point several of the officers of the submarine joined in the conversation, all of which was in German, and took the side of the chief officer, stating among other things that if they sank the *Algeria* the German Government would have to pay for it.

The discussion lasted about 45 minutes to an hour. The commander of the submarine then turned to the captain of the *Algeria* and stated he was sorry, but he would have to let him go; but the next time he caught him, he would sink him without warning. He asked the captain if he would give him his word of honor that the *Algeria* was not under charter of the United States Shipping Board, and the captain said "Yes," but added that all he knew was that he was under sailing directions to report to New York for orders. The other officers on the submarine addressed the commander, who was the man the captain of the *Algeria* spoke to, as (Herr Kapitän-Leutnant.) The captain of the submarine was not over 5 feet 4 inches tall, thick set, round face, black hair, dark eyes, clean shaven, and about 35 years old. The first officer of the submarine was about 5 feet 8 inches, and had light hair. The submarine was about 300 feet long, high bow, but stern was not awash. The conning tower was about 10 to 12 feet, on top of which was a wireless leading from the bow to the conning tower and to the stern, insulated at places with glass. The captain saw no periscope, and no identification marks; she had two guns, the forward one appeared to be 6-inch and the after gun was 75-mm.; there were no torpedo tubes. There was a hatch midway between the conning tower and the after gun, which appeared to be an ammunition hatch. The submarine was of the double hull type, with numerous portholes on her outer shell. According to the marks, she was at the time drawing about 4.2 meters of water. Capt. Risberg saw no net-cutting device. There was a life rail around the midship portion of the submarine, but whether it extended clear forward and aft, the captain is unable to tell.[40]

On the 24th, the Canadian three-masted schooner *Bianca*, 408 gross tons, bound from Brazil to Canada with a cargo of tobacco, was attacked by shell fire in latitude 43° 13′ N., longitude 61° 05′

---

* Report of the Aid for Information, New York, N. Y.

W. The crew abandoned the vessel and the Germans boarded and bombed her. They apparently did not remain to see the vessel sink, for three days later she was picked up at sea by a Boston fishing schooner and towed to Halifax, her cargo of tobacco having swelled and stopped the leaks.

The next victim of the *U-117* was the American steam trawler *Rush*, 162 gross tons, which was overhauled and sunk in latitude 44° 30′ N., longitude 58° 02′ W., on August 26.[41]

Statement of Joseph Golart, seaman from the American schooner *Rush*:

The *Rush*, owned by the Commonwealth Fishing Co., of Boston, Mass., under the command of Alvro P. Quadros, left Boston on August 20, 1918, on a fishing voyage to Quero Banks. At 5.45 a. m., August 26, 1918, in latitude 44° 30′ N., longitude 58° 02′ W., or about 135 miles southeast of Canso, we sighted a submarine and it came within 50 feet of us across our stern. They told us to lower our forward sails, which we did, and the captain and three members of the crew, Joseph Golart, Joseph Telles, and Joseph Tasida, got into one of the boats and we went alongside of the submarine. When we got alongside, they took our boat and ordered us to go below, and we stayed below on the submarine for three hours, and when we came on deck again we saw the wreckage of our vessel, but we did not hear any explosion.

The submarine was about 250 feet long, painted a light gray, with a dark-brown daub above the water line; no distinguishing mark; large conning tower; no masts seen; two guns, one forward about 12 feet long, one aft about 6 feet long, both looked to be of 5-inch bore, wireless running from the conning tower forward and aft; side lights on the conning tower; had German Diesel engines, depth about 50 feet.

There were about 60 men in the crew and we only saw 2 officers. They were not dressed in uniform, but wore brown leather trousers and some wore leather coats. The captain of the submarine was short, thick set, blond hair and beard, wore an officer's cap, but no coat. When we were taken below, they put us in the motor or battery room, and from there we could see the engine room and its force. Several of the crew in the engine room spoke to us in English and told us that they had sunk nine vessels off Georges Banks. The captain of the submarine showed our captain a list of the vessels he had sunk. I do not recall all of the names, but some of them are: *Progress*, *Old Time*, *Katie Palmer*, and *Mary Sennett*.

The second officer was short, thick set, blond, clean shaven; spoke Spanish, Portuguese, and very good English. Said that he had been at St. Michaels in the Azores, but did not state whether he was in a submarine or not. Also, stated that he was outside of Boston Light 14 days ago. One of the engineers told us that they could not keep us on board because they did not have enough room, but that they had larger submarines. I think they were short of fuel, for when we came aboard they measured their oil tanks and found only 4 inches in the tanks. They took 1,200 gallons of fuel oil from our vessel. They said that they had been getting newspapers and magazines, and the captain of the submarine told our captain that others had been reporting they only had four guns on board the submarine, and that he was to report they had eight. They treated us courteously.

We came on deck about 8.35 a. m. and they ordered us to shove off. Our captain told the captain of the submarine that we had no food, and they supplied us with two buckets of fresh water and some of our own crackers, which they had taken from our vessel. They took everything from our vessel, including stores, fuel oil and tools.

---

[41] The *Pluos* was reported sunk on the same day, but the United States Commerce Department report that there was no such American ship as the *Pluos* and that the report undoubtedly referred to the *Rush*.

We pulled away from the submarine about 9 and at 11 a. m. we sighted the *John J. Fallon*, who picked us up and landed us at Canso.

The sea was calm and there was a thick fog. The vessel was unarmed and nobody was injured.

The day following the sinking of the fishing vessel, the Norwegian steamer *Bergsdalen*, 2,550 gross tons, was sunk by a torpedo in latitude 45° 10′ N., longitude 55° 10′ W., about 110 miles SW. true from Cape Race. The attack was made without warning and the submarine was not sighted by the crew of the steamer. The *Bergsdalen* sank so rapidly that there was not sufficient time to launch all the boats. Many of the men had to leap overboard and one was lost in so doing.

The last operation of the *U–117* on this side of the Atlantic was the sinking of two Canadian fishing schooners on August 30, in latitude 50° 30′ N., longitude 47° W. The two vessels, the *Elsie Porter* and the *Potentate*, were overhauled while in company and were both sunk by bombs. Some of the details of the encounter as given by W. M. Rheinhard, master of the *Elsie Porter*, are as follows:

Submarine first sighted approaching the schooner from the eastward and fired rifle shots to stop the schooner. The submarine showed no colors at any time. All the provisions were taken off the schooner and the captain of the submarine asked the master of the *Porter* the course that steamers usually took from Newfoundland to Canada. Master replied that he did not know. Submarine commander then threatened to take the master to Germany or make him do pilot work. He took the ship's papers.

Submarine had no number, appeared to be from 300 to 400 feet long. Had the whaleback deck forward and steel slats in front of conning tower. Conning tower was 15 to 18 feet high. Had large gun forward, but could not see whether there was a gun on the bow to conning tower and from conning tower to stern. No wireless gear seen. Submarine was painted a dark steel color and paint looked to be about two months old. No marks of damage were seen on the submarine. Officers and crew wore leather uniforms and naval caps. Commanding officer was about 35 years old, medium height, thin face, sharp nose, dark complexion, black hair, and appearance dirty. The master and crew were treated humanely and were offered tobacco, matches, and compass on leaving submarine.

Submarine crew stated that they were tired of war and were only being made to fight by their officers. The submarine claimed to have sunk the schooner *Bianca*, and from charts seen submarine had come from Cape Race.

The steamship *Solberg* picked up part of crew of the *Elsie Porter* in latitude 47° 40′ N., longitude 51° 08′ W. at 1.15 p. m. on September 1. The same ship picked up crew of *Potentate* which was sunk by submarine at 8 p. m. on August 30.

The sinking of the two schooners evidently took place while the raider was on her homeward way.

On September 9 she went to the assistance of the *U–140* which had been forced to call for aid because of a leak, also on her return voyage, and the two spent the day in company in latitude 54° 10′ N., longitude 22° 30′ W.; and then proceeded into the North Sea.[42] The

---

[42] See page 82 (U–140).

U-117 passed the Skaw and Albach Bay safely, but apparently ran short of fuel oil later, for in October as she approached the German coast, torpedo-boat destroyers were sent out to tow her into Kiel.

THE CRUISE OF U-155.

The *U-155* was the original German submarine of the converted mercantile type having been, before her conversion into a commerce destroyer, the famous submersible cargo carrier, the *Deutschland*. After the entry of the United States into the war this vessel together with others built for merchant service were refitted and soon after made their appearance as raiders. It seemed fitting to the Germans that this vessel, which had in her peaceful character made two trips to American ports, now to be dispatched to western Atlantic waters to attack the commerce of the United States.

It was early in August of 1918 that the ex-*Deutschland* under the command of Kapitanleutnant Erick Eckelmann left Kiel on her errand of destruction. She was sighted off Udsire (lat. 59° 19′ N., long. 4° 50′ E.) on August 16, going north.

The first attack made by the *U-155* was directed against the American steamship *Montoso*, of 3,129 gross tons, on August 27, 1918, in latitude 40° 19′ N., longitude 32° 18′ W. The following is the statement of A. O. Forsyth, master of the steamer *Montoso*:

On the evening of August 27, 6 p. m. (A. T. S.), in latitude 40° 24′ N., longitude 31° 41′ W., it was reported to me that a suspicious looking wake had been seen on our port beam, resembling that thrown up by a small steamboat. I was at dinner at the time, and it had disappeared by the time I had reached the bridge.

I gave orders for an especially good lookout to be kept, and remained on the bridge myself. Signaled to U. S. S. *Rondo* and the U. S. S. *Ticonderoga*, which were in company with us, and asked the *Rondo* (who was acting as commander by mutual consent) if he did not think it advisable to make a radical change in our course after dark, in order to prevent our being followed successfully. He changed the course 20° and to starboard.

At 9 p. m. (A. T. S.), latitude 40° 19′ N., longitude 32° 18′ W., I distinctly saw the outline of a long, low dark object on our port beam about 2,000 yards away, showing about 4 feet. I called the attention of the chief boatswain mate, commanding the Armed Guard, to it. He immediately went to the after gun and opened fire, in the meantime I ordered course to starboard to bring the object on our port quarter, leaving it a little open so that forward gun would bear on it. We fired six shots from aft and four from forward, and the *Ticonderoga* fired two, the *Rondo* was unarmed. Submarine making about 10 knots, we about the same.

Just after we opened fire, two shots fell a few hundred yards astern of us, evidently the submarine had lost sight of us and was firing at the flashes of our after gun; if so, his range was good, but direction poor.

I did not see him after the first shot was fired from our forward gun, as the flash of the gun blinded me, but when I first observed him he was directly under the star "Antares" and I could see that our shots were good as far as direction was concerned. If we did not hit him, we prevented his surprise attack, and scared him badly.

Lost sight of *Ticonderoga* and the *Rondo* for the balance of the night, but picked them up the next morning. Signaled the *Ticonderoga* and compared notes. He said be was of the opinion that there were two submarines. I saw only one, however. He also said submarine had fired three or four shots. I only observed two under our stern and they were so close I had to see them. I can not give too much credit to the crew of this ship for the manner in which they conducted themselves, both the Armed Guards and the civilians, every man being in his place in the shortest possible time, and absolute discipline prevailed.

Four days after this encounter the submarine scored her first success, capturing and sinking with bombs the Portuguese schooner *Gamo*, 315 gross tons, in latitude 46° N., longitude 32° W.

The day following, the U. S. S. *Frank H. Buck*, 6,077 tons gross, was attacked in latitude 45° 38' N., longitude 37° 17' W. The gun crew of the tanker bested the submarine in an engagement which lasted half an hour, some of their shots thought to be direct hits. The commander of the American vessel reported his belief that the enemy had been sunk, but the submarine continued to operate.

U. S. S. *Frank H. Buck*, Capt. George E. McDonald, lieutenant commander, U. S. N. R. F., from Fairhaven Island, left August 27, and reports that on September 1 at 8.25 a. m.—weather clear, fresh breezes from northwest, sea choppy, in latitude 45° 38', longitude 37° 17'—sighted an enemy submarine on the starboard beam at 14,000 yards. Submarine opened fire with two 6-inch guns. We answered fire with forward 3-inch gun. We saw the shot fall about 400 yards short and immediately swung stern forward to submarine, using after gun of 6-inch caliber. Our shots were very close to submarine and the submarine's shrapnel was bursting very near to us, some of the pieces falling upon our deck amidships. We changed the course frequently in short swings, which seemed to upset the submarine's aim and range. As soon as submarine saw our range was equal to hers she hauled away from us. Up to that time she had been closing in on us so that the range was down to 10,000 yards. Before submarine could get out of range our twenty-eighth shot from the 6-inch gun apparently hit her stern. The twenty-ninth shot hit her just forward of the conning tower, near and under the water line. The bow immediately shot up into the air very suddenly, then settled and then went down out of sight, the stern making a half turn toward us and then it disappeared.

Upon shot striking submarine we very clearly saw a terriffic explosion and black smoke. The charge of the shot was T. N. T. The whole submarine was enveloped in a cloud of smoke. I am positive that we destroyed her, as she disappeared almost instantly after the shot struck her.

On September 2 the Norwegian steamer *Shortind*, 2,560 tons gross, was sunk by torpedo in latitude 45° 15' N., longitude 30° W., about 400 miles north of Fayal.

On September 7 the British S. S. *Monmouth*, 4,078 tons gross, was chased and shelled in latitude 43° N., longitude 45° 50' W., without warning.

The excellence of the Allied intelligence service is shown by a message received in Washington on September 9:

S. S. *Monmouth* reports that on September 7th, she was chased about latitude 43° N., longitude 45° 40' W. Should this report prove reliable submarine would be one of the two converted mercantile type which were expected to sail from Germany about the middle of August, and she would reach the American coast about September 15. It is known that the other had not left Kiel on September 2.

The other submarine spoken of was the *U-139*, which left Kiel about the end of the first week in September, 1918.

At 6.10 a. m. on the morning of September 12 the *U-155* torpedoed and sank the Portuguese steamer *Leixoes*, 3,345 tons gross, in ballast, from Hull to Boston, in latitude 42° 45′ N., longitude 51° 37′ W. The captain of the *Leixoes*, Joaquim F. Sucena, gave the following account of the loss of his ship:

The torpedo struck on the starboard side of No. 4 hatch; submarine was not visible. As soon as the ship was hit I saw she was going to sink, and I ordered all hands to take to the lifeboats, and all of my confidential books were sunk. The ship was heading east by south true. Fifteen minutes after the ship was struck the submarine appeared on the starboard beam about one-quarter mile distant. Our vessel sank in about 15 minutes and before we got alongside of the submarine.

The submarine was about 500 feet long; four guns, two aft and two forward, about 6-inch; straight flat deck, sharp bow, no railing; wireless running from conning tower aft; one very small periscope; painted black and it looked like brand new paint; was not flying any colors, nor did she have any number. The captain of the submarine was of light complexion, dark mustache, wore no uniform, but had on a cap; was heavy set and he spoke splendid English, very much like an American. He asked what ship it was, and we said it was a Portuguese ship, and then he asked if there were any Englishmen on board, and I said no, and then he ordered all hands up on deck. There were about 50 men in the crew of the submarine. When he ordered us to shove off he did not give us any course, neither did he give us any provisions. The submarine went to the eastward, steaming on the surface.

One man lost his life on the ship. He was probably asleep when the ship was struck and did not wake up. Two other men lost their lives from exposure and cold.

On September 13 the *U-155* was worsted in another running battle with an armed British merchant ship, the *Newby Hall*, of 4,391 tons gross. The following is a statement of F. O. Seaborne, master of the *Newby Hall*, to the United States naval authorities:

The *Newby Hall* left Barry on August 30, 1918, and left Milford Haven on September 1, 1918, in convoy, bound for New York. On September 3 at 6 p. m. we were ordered to detach convoy and proceed to destination according to secret orders. All went well until Friday, September 13, at 9.52 a. m., in latitude 42° 18′ N., longitude 58° 22′ W. We sighted a torpedo coming toward us from three points on the port bow. We immediately put helm hard starboard. The torpedo missed by about 6 feet, passing our bows from an angle over to the starboard side. I then steered parallel to track of the torpedo, and at 9.56 a. m. (approximate) I altered to SSW., thereby bringing position of the submarine astern and instructing engineers to give all speed possible.

At 10 a. m. we sighted submarine coming to surface bearing north; I then kept him astern steering an irregular zigzag course (about 3,000 yards).

We saw their gun crews coming out of the conning tower and manning the two guns. They commenced firing immediately and we replied with our gun. He was then steering in a westerly direction and going at a moderate speed, and to keep him astern we had to gradually alter course to the eastward.

The enemy was firing rapidly with both guns. The forward one appeared to be of larger caliber than the other. After about 50 rounds with our gun a direct hit, smoke, flash, explosion put his forward and largest gun out of action. When the smoke cleared we found this gun had tilted over to an angle of about 30° and no gun crew was to be seen. Soon after we scored another hit on his forward end, the fore part of the forward gun causing an explosion and a volume of smoke. After that we scored another hit on his after end, about 20 feet aft the after gun. He then reduced his speed and seemed to be under difficulties, but continued firing with his after and smaller gun.

At about 13,000 yards we outranged him and he ceased firing. He headed toward us and appeared as if he was chasing us, but in a few minutes he was broadside on to us again and stopped and suddenly disappeared. Action lasted from 10 a. m. to 11.20 a. m., when firing ceased. Enemy commenced and ceased firing first.

During the action the enemy used shrapnel and high explosive shells, but none hit the ship except shrapnel. None of the crew was injured. Two boats on the port side were riddled and one plate amidship on the port side dented and badly cut in numerous places by shrapnel or burst shell. All the crew behaved splendidly throughout the action, and special praise is due to the gun layer for his coolness and the masterful way he handled the gun, and also the gun's crew who worked very hard; also the officers and engineers who assisted in passing up the ammunition.

Distress signals were sent out by wireless for assistance and answered immediately by United States patrol, who endeavored to come to our assistance but as the weather became thick and rainy we saw nothing of him. All secret books and codes were thrown overboard during the action.

The submarine was about 250 to 300 feet long; black in color; cutter bow; flush deck; gradually sloping into the water at the stern. There was a platform about 3 feet high amidships and 40 to 50 feet in length; in the center of the platform was the conning tower about 10 feet long at the base and 4 or 5 feet high. The after vertical portion of the conning tower was not parallel with the forward portion as the conning tower was smaller at the top than at the bottom. The forward gun was about 20 to 30 feet from the forward part of the platform. A mast or periscope extended from the forward portion of the platform and another was situated on the after portion. They were the same height as the conning tower.

During the ensuing seven days the inactivity of the *U–155* against ships may be attributed to the fact that it was reported in advance that one of her purposes was to lay mines off Halifax and the Nova Scotia coast. The sighting of an enemy submarine there and the discovery of mines off Halifax confirm the correctness of that report.

The American steam trawler *Kingfisher*, 353 gross tons, was the next victim of the ex-*Deutschland*. The fishing vessel was stopped on September 20 when in latitude 43° 31′ N., longtitude 61° 53′ W. After the trawler was abandoned, her crew were ordered alongside the submarine where they were questioned and then ordered to proceed. They heard what they took to be the explosion of bombs after they were out of sight of their vessel but could not be sure that their ship, the *Kingfisher*, had been destroyed. The officers and crew of the submarine were described as follows, by the crew of the *Kingfisher:*

The commanding officer was about 6 feet tall, thin, ruddy complexion, sandy hair, wearing short side whiskers, and appeared to be between 25 and 30 years of age. Another officer of the submarine was about 5 feet 8 inches tall, light complexion, clean shaven, and weighed about 180 pounds. About 53 men were counted on the deck of the submarine, wearing various kinds of uniforms. The crew were all young men and apparently healthy and contented.

It was more than a week before the submarine was again definitely located, although the allo of an unknown vessel was reported September 26 from latitude 43° 15′ N., longtitude 65° W., the approximate whereabouts of the submarine.

On the twenty-ninth, the British S. S. *Reginolite*, 2,246 tons gross, was attacked at 12.25 p. m. by gunfire, in latitude 40° 51′ N., longitude 66° 40′ W. The submarine opened fire at a distance of about 5,000 yards and continued firing for 45 minutes without result. The *Reginolite* returned the fire while steering a zigzag course at her best speed. The submarine being outdistanced gave up the chase and submerged.

On October 2 the British steamer *Nevasa*, 9,071 tons gross, sighted the submarine in latitude 38° 31′ N., longitude 68° 23′ W. The submarine which was about 8 miles away when first seen attempted to overtake the steamer without success; then swung broadside to, fired one shot which fell far short and abandoned the chase.

On October 3 and 4 the *U-155* scored two successess; the first the torpedoing of the Italian S. S. *Alberto Treves*, 3,838 gross tons, in latitude 38° 20′ N., longitude 67° 10′ W.; the second the destruction by bombs of the British schooner *Industrial*, 330 gross tons, in latitude 37° 57′ N., longitude 66° 41′ W., about 250 miles SE½ S. (true) from Nantucket Island.

On October 12, the American S. S. *Amphion*, 7,409 tons gross, formerly the German S. S. *Koln*, and belonging to the United States Shipping Board, in ballast from Bordeaux to New York, was attacked in latitude 36° 06′ N., longitude 62° 59′ W. The submarine appeared at 10 a. m. and at once opened fire on the steamer, the second shot carrying away the wireless. A battle lasting over an hour ensued during which time the *Amphion* gradually drew away from her pursuer. The submarine fired almost 200 shots, a number of which took effect. Two men were mortally wounded and a number of others were seriously injured by shrapnel; five of the steamer's lifeboats were riddled and her superstructure was badly damaged. The *Amphion* fired 72 shots in return, the last of which appeared to be a hit. Immediately after this the submarine, by this time well astern, abandoned the chase and submerged.

Five days after the attack on the *Amphion* the *U-155* scored the final success of her cruise, by sinking the U. S. A. C. T. *Lucia*, of 6,744 gross tons, owned by the United States Shipping Board, and bound from New York to Marseilles, France. In the report of C. F. Leary, master of the *Lucia*, to the United States Shipping Board, he says:

> At 5.30 p. m. on October 17, 1918, the U. S. A. C. T. *Lucia*, bound for an European port in convoy (without escort), was torpedoed in the engine-room on port side, killing four men. The position at the time was latitude 38° 05′ N., longitude 50° 50′ W.

There was no sign of any submarine to be seen. I had just finished my supper and was going on the bridge. The commander of the armed guard, who was on top of the chart house several minutes before I got on the bridge, said he saw the wake of the torpedo about 100 yards off, and had guns trained in that direction. There was an efficient lookout kept at all times. Our speed at that time was $10\frac{1}{2}$ knots. The S. S. *Hawaiian*, our guide ship, was about two or three points on our port bow, about 1,000 yards distant. We immediately sent out S O S calls and our position, and semaphored the guide ship *Hawaiian*, to broadcast same. We sent out S O S calls from time to time on auxiliary set, until five minutes before leaving ship.

As we fully expected the U-boat to return and send another torpedo into us or shell us, I decided after a consultation with the commander of the armed guard and officers, to lower three boats and put civilian crew afloat and hold on to bow and stern of the ship. As our No. 4 lifeboat was destroyed by the explosion, and her complement was 22 persons, four of whom were killed in the engine room, 18 persons were left to divide up in the remaining boats. There three boats hung by ropes from the stern of the ship all night until morning of the 18th of October. I had civilian crew come on board and get some food and return to their boats. Our after decks were awash at this time (1 a. m.). Our engine room and fireroom and No. 4 and No. 5 hold were full of water, No. 6 was one-half full and gradually filling and deck load breaking loose. The wind and sea was increasing, and seas breaking over our after decks. About 10 a. m. we put No. 2 boat afloat, bringing her on lee with three men and stood by, as ship was slowly settling down.

About this time I heard a noise below, which I believed was the carrying away of the bulkhead between the fireroom and No. 3 hold as the ship settled more by the head after this, which I believed was due to the flooding of No. 3 hold. At 1.30 p. m. we launched No. 5 boat, which was on starboard quarter, and hung her off to leeward, standing by. We also launched after life raft and forward life raft. The after gun crew had to abandon their gun as the sea was breaking over gun platform and they were ordered to their boats immediately. At 2.20 p. m. I left for ship in No. 2 boat with the commander of the armed guard and forward gun crew and three others of the civilian crew. No. 6 hatch was broken in by deck load and filled. Stern settled down, with after decks under water. All boats hung at leeward of ship until 3.15 p. m. when her stern sank until ship was perpendicular with her upper bridge just underneath and sank in that position. At 3.20 p. m. she disappeared beneath the waves. After the ship sank, all boats hauled away clear of floating wreckage and laid to sea anchors. A very heavy sea was running now and our boats were taking considerable water on board and we had to keep bailing continually. At 9.26 p. m. October 19, we sighted the U. S. S. *Fairfax* coming to our rescue. At 10 p. m. we in No. 2 boat were all landed safely on the destroyer, and at about 12.05 a. m. the last boat was landed on board the destroyer without any mishaps.

If the *Fairfax* had not arrived at the time it did, I do not think our boats would have weathered the heavy seas, as they were all overloaded. I and my officers and crew think that great credit is due to the commanding officer and crew of the *Fairfax* in the skillful way he handled his ship, in the heavy seas, and effecting the rescue of our crew without any mishaps.

All confidential books, codes, and papers were dropped overboard immediately after we were hit, in presence of armed guard commander and ship's officers. I also witnessed all armed guard books and papers, and radio confidential books and papers dropped overboard.

After this attack the *U-155* cruised toward the Azores and probably received the order to return to her base while operating in the waters about these islands. It is believed that she is the submarine that made the unsuccessful attack upon the British steamer *Clan Mac-*

Arthur of 7,382 gross tons on October 25 in latitude 41° 20′ N., longitude 32° 30′ W. This was her last recorded activity; she is next heard of as arriving in Kiel November 15, four days after the signing of the armistice.

THE CRUISE OF U-152.

The *U-152* was a submarine of the converted mercantile or *Deutschland* type. In the latter part of August, 1918, she left Kiel under command of Kapitanleutnant Franz and made her way north of the Shetland Islands on her cruise to American Atlantic waters.

The first attack of the voyage resulted in the sinking of the Danish sailing vessel *Constanza* on September 11 in latitude 62° 30′ N., longitude 35′ W. Her next attempt was directed against the British steamer *Alban*, 5,223 gross tons, which was fired upon September 24, when in latitude 44° 22′ N., longitude 29° 45′ W. Five days later another unsuccessful attack was made in latitude 43° 40′ N., longitude 37° 42′ W. upon the U. S. S. *George G. Henry*, 6,936 gross tons. The submarine was sighted at 8.50 a. m. and the *Henry* opened fire. The submarine fired in return. At 9.05 a shot struck the *Henry*, causing an explosion in the magazine in the ship, causing a fire. At 9.50 a. m. the fire was under control. After a hot running fight the submarine ceased firing and submerged at 10.40 a. m. The following day, September 30, the U. S. S. *Ticonderoga* (ex-German *Camilla Rickmers*) a vessel of 5,130 gross tons, which because of engine trouble had fallen behind her convoy during the night was attacked at 5.20 a. m. by the *U-152* in latitude 43° 05′ N., longitude 38° 43′ W. The *Ticonderoga* manned by a navy crew made a gallant defense and the account of their action and the sinking of their ship form a story of heart interest, not exceeded by any episode of the war. It was not until the end of a two-hour battle, when both the ship's guns had been disabled and many of the men aboard killed or wounded that the submarine dared to approach near enough to fire the torpedo that ended the engagement.

Of the 237 men aboard the *Ticonderoga* only 24, the majority of them wounded, were rescued, including the two officers, who were taken prisoners by the submarine and taken to Germany.

A part of the story of Ensign Gustav Ringelman, who was officer of the deck at the time the submarine appeared, is quoted here:

> The submarine was sighted at first about 200 yards off our port bow awash, the whole length showing. I reported to the commanding officer immediately and ordered the forward gun crew to open fire. The forward gun had its gun cover on because during the night it had rained, and there was a heavy spray, and we needed the gun cover on to protect the gun. Immediately the captain put his helm hard to starboard and came within 25 feet of ramming the submarine. Before we could get a shot off the submarine fired an incendiary shell which struck our bridge, killing the helmsman

and practically putting the navigation of the ship out of commission, crippling the steering gear and setting the amidships section ablaze.

Lieut. Commander J. J. Madison, U. S. N. R. F., captain of the *Ticonderoga*, was severely wounded by a piece of this shell.

This all took place in just as short a time as I am telling you this. I was going back—I had charge of the 6-inch gun aft.

The submarine fired with the aft gun at our 3-inch forward gun, killing the gun crew. They fired six shots putting the gun out of commission. She then steamed around our starboard side and opened up her distance a little bit, opening fire again. We replied with our 6-inch gun.

I am not exactly sure, but I should say the distance was now about 4,000 yards. That was my range, I believe, and the submarine gradually opened up the distance between us to about 4 miles. Meanwhile the submarine was shelling us and we were answering her shots. During this time most everybody on board our ship was either killed or wounded to such an extent that they were practically helpless from shrapnel. The lifeboats hanging on the davits were shelled and full of holes, others carried away. However, we kept the submarine off until our fire was put out and our boats swung out on the davits, ready to abandon the ship with the few men left on board. Possibly 50 were left by that time—the rest were dead. Well, at 7 o'clock up comes the submarine again, off the starboard quarter.

Meanwhile we had also several boats which were swamped immediately, due to the falls carrying away—the submarine had shot them away before—and holes in the boats, and there was not another boat got away that I could see. Every boat that attempted to get away was either swamped, or something happended to it. The submarine fired at us again for the second time at a range of 10,000 to 12,000 yards, and there were only three left on our 6-inch gun as a gun crew—a chief boatswain mate, a gunner's mate, and myself. We manned that gun until a shell struck us underneath the gun and put the gun out of commission, as well as ourselves, disabling us. The submarine still continued to shell us, and then came alongside off our starboard beam and fired a torpedo which struck amidships in the engine room. The ship thereafter slowly settled.

There was a life raft left on the top of the deck house. We got our wounded men together, lashed them to the life raft—that is, those who were able to do this—and shoved the life raft off from the ship. Possibly three or four minutes after that she took the final plunge. After the *Ticonderoga* had sunk the submarine came alongside and had already picked up the executive officer out of the water and made him a captive. They took the first assistant engineer off the life raft and made him a captive also.

They asked us several questions; wanted the captain and the gunner; where bound for, and where from; threatening us. After getting no information they shoved off. Now, before she came to us she had been to this only lifeboat that had stayed afloat, and the captain was in that, but they did not see him. The captain was severely wounded and was lying on the bottom of the boat. One of the German sailors went into the lifeboat and made a line fast by which she towed the lifeboat a few yards, but the line parted when they speeded up. After that the submarine made off but stayed in the vicinity. Several shells before this had fallen rather close to the life raft and it also looked as if they meant to shell the boat but gave it up. Now, I will tell you how we got into the boat. This lifeboat, the only one afloat, drifted down onto the life raft, and the captain of the ship, who was in the boat, called for myself and several others to get into the boat, as there was not a single sailor in that boat to handle her, there being nothing but soldiers in it, and a high sea running called for somebody to be in that boat to handle it. Well, a few of us got into the boat, which still left a few on the raft—a few unconscious men and some that were not very badly hurt. The sea separated the raft and the boat and we made sail and attempted to get back to the raft in order to tow it, as they had no food on it. The wind and sea grew in violence and after many futile attempts to come alongside of the raft we had to give up the idea of getting a line to it. We made sail in the small boat to get away from the submarine, and in case another ship or a rescue ship should come along we would be away from the submarine. We sailed day and night for four days and three nights, and on Thursday morning at 8 o'clock we sighted a steamer heading west at a distance of 5 miles. She, however, ignored us.

At 2 o'clock in the afternoon we sighted another steamer dead ahead. The steamer bore down on us. When she came alongside she picked us up. The name of the steamer was the *Moorish Prince*, British, bound for New York in command of Capt. Birch. We received all the comforts and attention they could give us. They had no medical officer aboard, but the steward, who knew his business very well, attended the men to the best of his ability. While on board the *Moorish Prince* on Sunday, October 6, this steamer, the *Grampian*, came alongside and seven of us were transferred to this ship. There were 22 in the lifeboat altogether. We were transferred to this ship because better medical attention and better facilities could be had aboard of her for the wounded. But two men, the commanding officer and a soldier, who were too severely wounded to be transferred and moved, were kept aboard the *Moorish Prince*, with three other men, soldiers, to attend them—and here we are now.

Ensign Clifford T. Sanghove, U. S. R. N. F., third engineer of the *Ticonderoga*, gave the following version of the attack, to the aid for information at New York, N. Y.:

On September 30 at 5.30 a. m., in latitude 43° 05′ N., longitude 38° 43′ W., the vessel sighted a submarine. At the time I was in my room; an 8-inch shell which crashed through the room woke me up. From that time on I was busy. This first shell struck the bridge, setting it afire and destroying the wireless and preventing the sending out of any wireless messages.

The *Ticonderoga* was armed with a 6-inch gun astern and a 3-inch gun forward. I do not know, however, how many shots were fired from the vessel. The after gun fired some shots; also the forward gun, but shortly afterwards both gun crews were shot away.

The sea was fairly rough at the time. The ship was darkened, but I do not know whether she was zigzagging or what her course was.

When I saw the submarine she was abeam of the *Ticonderoga* and a couple of hundred yards away. She was off the port bow and on the surface well out of the water. The submarine remained in the vicinity all day until after dark that night.

I went down to the engine room and organized gangs to fight the fire. Some of the men would be shot away and I would have to organize a new gang. I was the last man to leave the engine room, and I tried to get fresh water started to relieve the wounded men on deck.

While I was down in the engine room a torpedo struck the ship and I was pinned up against the bulkhead and the grating by the bulge of the bulkhead from the explosion of the torpedo. This torpedo was nearly the last thing fired by the submarine, and it struck right aft of the engine-room bulkhead on the starboard side. I was crushed about the chest and hips at this time.

During the attack I was at various places down in the engine room, on deck and near the steering gear. As the first assistant engineer was on watch, I assisted wherever I could.

No shells struck the engine room except around the upper hatches. From the time the torpedo was fired until the vessel sank approximately 15 minutes elapsed. From the time the first shot was fired until the vessel finally sank 2 hours and 15 minutes elapsed, and it was about 7.45 a. m. when the *Ticonderoga* sank. The ship commenced to turn before we left her at 7.45. Her amidships rail was right on the water level.

After the torpedo was fired we got some of the wounded together and got some water and blankets together, and then placed a few of the wounded on the raft, which I helped to launch from the deck house, which was 20 feet above the water at the time. The raft went into the water with two or three wounded men on it, who still clung to it. This raft was the last thing to leave the ship. There were 13 lifeboats altogether aboard.

The boat the captain was in was fired at by the submarine while it was in the water. The two shots which were fired at it missed; I was on the raft at the time of this firing and I know that a couple of shots were fired, and the men in the boat claim that these shots came past them. There were eight or nine men on the raft with me; this was the same raft on which the wounded men were launched. We had tied a line to it before launching and then drew it in toward the railing and jumped on it ourselves after launching it. I was the next to the last man off the ship. The captain had been placed in a lifeboat, which was the only one which was safely launched to my knowledge. He had been placed in this boat after he had been wounded in the leg.

There were a number of potatoes and boxes on the afterdeck, which floated off the vessel as the after part sank, and the submarine picked up a number of these boxes, cruising around meanwhile. When I first saw the submarine the *Ticonderoga* fired three or four shots from the after gun. This gun became totally disabled, having been struck by a shell from the submarine.

We remained on the raft until 2 o'clock in the afternoon, when we drifted toward the captain's lifeboat and five men left the raft and got into the lifeboat, as when the raft came close to the lifeboat they shouted that there was no one in the boat who was able to man same, all of them having been wounded. The five men transferred were Turner, the carpenter (Edward J. Willoughby), the quartermaster (George S. Tapley), Mr. Ringleman, and myself. This boat contained all the survivors.

I did not see many of the lifeboats launched, as I was below most of the time, rigging fire mains, getting water, etc. I did see two boats launched, on one of which the forward fall burned away and she capsized as she was being launched. She had at least eight men in her.

The submarine came alongside the raft and spoke to us. She asked who it was tried to ram them and where was the captain and where was the gunner; how many soldiers were aboard; where we left and where we were going. Mr. Ringleman answered a couple of them and the chief machinist's mate, who I believe was lost, also answered some questions. The chief machinist's mate was taken aboard the submarine for a time and then finally returned to the raft, and was probably lost, as the sea was high and we never saw the raft again.

The first assistant engineer was also taken aboard the submarine and kept a prisoner. His name is Fulcher. He was a lieutenant (j. g.). I believe the executive officer, Mr. Muller, had been picked up from the water and also taken aboard the submarine and kept a prisoner. I believe the executive officer, Mr. Muller, speaks a little German, but I know Mr. Fulcher could not speak a word of German, as he wanted to answer them but could not. They were the only men of the survivors who were in uniform. One or two of the men asked for first-aid packages, but received a very gruff answer. I held a German second assistant engineer's license in the Adriatic service of the Hamburg-American Line and the North German Lloyd Co.

The story of the Chief Quartermaster, George S. Tappley, adds many details to the reports above and shows the bravery of the American sailors in the face of hopeless odds:

I was in my bunk at the time the general alarm was sounded (5.20 a. m.) and immediately got out and dressed. I ran out of my room up to the bridge which was all afire. Just at that time the whistle blew for "abandon ship." I saw the captain coming along, trying to make his way aft. He was badly wounded, and I helped the paymaster bring him aft and sit him in a chair. The executive officer was lowering the forward boat on the port side of the bridge alone, so I went over and helped him lower it. I also helped lower the two boats on the port side. The steering gear was out of commission, and I went aft into the after steering quarters and disconnected the steam from the hand-steering gear, and tried to steer the ship by hand; but finding the steering gear jammed, it was necessary to connect back again, so I went down to the steering engine to see what could be done. Our wireless had been carried away the first thing, so we couldn't send out any messages. We were firing our guns all the time, but apparently didn't make a hit. When the submarine had first been sighted she was about 200 yards off our port bow. The first two shots hit our bridge, setting it afire, and the third shot carried away the 3-inch gun and killed all the gun crew. Our speed at the time was about 10 knots, and the captain bore directly down in the submarine's path and tried to ram it, but missed by about 25 feet. The submarine was firing all time, and our deck was covered with dead and wounded men. The submarine then submerged for about 20 minutes, but reappeared about 2 miles off our starboard quarter and then started shelling us with shrapnel. She next fired a torpedo which struck us directly amidships, breaking the steam pipes and causing considerable steam to come from the engine room. The ship then started to settle. The Germans' markmanship was excellent, and they seemed to hit all parts of the ship. Most of the lifeboats were full of holes from shrapnel. At about 7.15 the captain was put in the last boat on the vessel, together with 14 soldiers, and the boat was lowered away. That was the only boat that got away clear. At that time there were about 35 or 40 men still left on board the ship, alive. I reported to the executive officer that our 6-inch gun had been disabled by shell fire, and the vessel could not be steered from the steering engine room. By his orders I tied a white blanket on the aftermast, near the top mast, but the submarine paid no attention to it, and continued shelling us, killing four or five of the remaining men. I picked up a piece of plank near where the executive officer and five other men were standing, but for some reason I thought better of it, and looking around I saw a raft on top of the boat deck. I made my way up to that, and there found twelve men, three of whom were very badly wounded, lying on top of this small house alongside the raft. I asked them why they were lying there, and "damn" soon found out, for just then a shell struck about two feet under me, going directly through the small house. We then put the three badly wounded men on the raft, and pushed it into the water, about 20 feet below; but the raft capsized and the three men were thrown into the water. Then the rest of us got down on the raft, 15 in all. It was then 7.30 and by that time the submarine had stopped firing. She had fired in all about 200 shots. A few minutes after getting on the raft the vessel went down, stern first, sinking completely in about 10 seconds. We then drifted off on the raft. I saw the submarine fire two shots at the only open boat left.

The submarine then went alongside the lifeboat and inquired for the captain, chief engineer, and gunner. On being told that the captain was not aboard, they took aboard the submarine two seamen, tieing the boat to the stern of the submarine. The last I saw, the two seamen were on the submarine. The submarine then went over to the driftwood, and picked up considerable potato crates, etc., from the water, also picking up the executive officer and taking him prisoner. In about 15 minutes the submarine came over to the raft on which we were, tied up alongside, and took on board Chief Machinist Mate, Rudolph Alicke. They questioned him for some time, he being of German extraction, and then put him back on the raft.

They asked for the captain, chief engineer, and gunner, all the time keeping us covered with revolvers. We told them the chief engineer had been killed, but that the first assistant engineer was on the raft, so they took him aboard the submarine, putting the two seamen back on board our raft. That left the first assistant engineer and executive officer on board the submarine. We asked them to give us medical assistance, a number of the men having been seriously wounded, but they ignored our request. Then the submarine let go of our line, and we drifted away. The only boat that got away was about 1 mile to windward of us, but all the time drifting nearer. When it came alongside five of us from the raft got in the boat, intending to tie a line to the raft, but the wind was so strong that we couldn't do so. We tried for four hours to get back to the raft to give her a line, but the wind prevented us from doing so. We then hoisted a small sail on the bow of the boat, in order to keep her stern to the wind, and this way we spent the night. The next morning we took an inventory of the supplies, and found we had 8 gallons of water, 2 cans of hardtack, 1 case of apricots, and 1 case of pineapples. There were 22 men in all, including the captain, who was very badly wounded. We at first decided to try and make Newfoundland, but the captain said northwest winds started blowing about this time of the year, so we abandoned the idea and commenced to steer east-southeast for Spain. Bad weather had set in and we thought we saw two ships on the horizon, but were not sure. Each man's rations consisted of one apricot and two spoonsful of juice twice a day. We continued pulling on our course all that day. That night the sea started to run very high, and we had great difficulty in keeping the boat from swamping. On the third day the sea became more moderate, and we made perhaps 60 miles to the eastward. The captain was feverish and delirious at times, and it was necessary to give him water at frequent intervals to keep his fever down. The men in the boat were behaving as well as could be expected, except that they were constantly complaining about not having water. On the fourth day the weather calmed down, and the sea was moderate.

At about 7 a. m. we sighted a ship away off on the horizon heading west, but apparently she did not see us. At about 1 o'clock smoke was sighted dead ahead, and in the course of an hour's time the S. S. *Moorish Prince* came alongside and picked us up. Everybody was very weak, and the captain was in an extremely bad condition. They kept us on board for three days and then transferred us to the *Grampian*.

The executive officer F. L. Muller, lieut. (j. g.), U. S. N. R. F., and the first assistant engineer, J. H. Fulcher, lieut. (j. g.), U. S. N. R. F., of the *Ticonderoga*, were the two officers taken prisoners by the *U-152*. Lieut. Muller collected many of the wounded on a raft secured to the deck house and cut the lashings as the ship sank. Muller took to the wherry which was badly holed and soon filled. Both he and Fulcher were in the water about 40 minutes. Fulcher finally got to the last raft. The following is a report of Lieuts. Muller's and Fulcher's experience:

Muller and Fulcher were taken separately, sent below and isolated. Neither knew of the other's presence on board for four days. Muller, whom Capt. Franz of the submarine, supposed to be the captain of the *Ticonderoga*, was picked up at 9.20. Franz, standing amidships, demanded: "Where's the chief gunner? Where's the chief gunner's mate?"

"Dead," replied Muller.

Franz was under the impression that the *Ticonderoga's* after gun had continued firing after the sheet had been hoisted.

Alicke, a machinist's mate of German descent, already hauled aboard the submarine, interpreted for Fulcher. Franz was ordering him to the raft alongside when he pleaded to be kept on board. "Speak for me," he begged his officer; but the German captain replied: "Get back on the raft. What do you mean by fighting against us, against your country? Only God can save such as you now!"

Wounded men on the raft pleaded: "Won't you please take us? * * * * We have no food or water; no chance." But Franz answered, "We have room for no more," and cast them adrift.

Fulcher was taken to Chief Engineer Heine's room, where shrapnel was cut from his leg, and he was given brandy and overalls by the ship's surgeon, whose name, by coincidence was Fuylcher. He was kindly treated, and the pair conjectured upon their relationship. Meanwhile Heine kept saying, "Why do you call us Huns? We are no more cruel than you." This soreness, testifying to the effect of Allied propaganda, prevailed insistently among the submarine's officers. Their tune at first was "Why did the United States enter the war? See what you get now for coming in."

Fulcher was questioned about the speed, cargo, and number of ships in the *Ticonderoga's* convoy, but in return "gave the hand of Esau, speaking with the voice of Jacob."

The captain came in and said to Montau, a C. P. O., "Take the prisoner and show him where he will sleep." Fulcher went to the forecastle, where about 35 men were quartered in permanent bunks. He was given a lower one, which he occupied for the rest of the voyage. The surgeon came each day and dressed his wounds. He messed with the warrant officers, as did Lieut. Schwarz, radio officer. Muller ate in the ward room, but the food in both messes was the same, white bread twice a week, plenty of wurst and butter, canned brown bread, etc. Muller also was continually asked why we came into the war: "Why do you call us barbarians? We are only doing our duty," was repeated over and over. There was a copy of Hearst's magazine on board. An article in it on Harry Lauder's visit to France showed a Hun soldier standing with a bayonet over a wounded French soldier. "That is not true! That is not true!" exclaimed the officers.

U-152 had left Kiel September 5 on an outbound voyage to the American coast. It was only her second trip. All the time that they were aboard, the two Americans were allowed on deck, except during the various actions with merchant ships that ensued. They were then sent below, but managed to secure information of happenings there. They also learned, chiefly from the crew, many of the orders that came by radio. They were always well treated. The *U-152* remained on the surface except when forced by the presence of Allied craft to dive.

Between September 30 and October 11, the submarine's course was SW. (true), speed 4 knots; but as she was continually in the Gulf Stream, her position did not vary much. She was on the lookout for Allied shipping. Up to the latter date, when the first intimation of the armistice negotiations were received, no attacks were made. The submarine's engines were in bad condition, and it was stated that she could not make more than 10 knots on the surface. Her proper speed was 12 knots, but she never made more than 11 on her first voyage. The engines were overhauled every day, and appeared to lack copper and other metals.

On October 11 this message came in code—as did all others: "Engage men of war only. The merchant war has ended." The Americans were told that this was, "The first act of our new government." Course was now changed to SE.

On October 12, the Norwegian bark *Stifinder* was sighted about 4 p. m. and two shots sent across her bows. The crew took to the boats. Lieut. Wille went over to her with a boarding party, and returned with many provisions, onions, canned fishballs, etc., from the United States, besides three live pigs. The Norwegians were given compasses and food, then told to set sail for the nearest land, which was Newfoundland, some 1,000 miles away. It was impossible to protest against this barbarity. The *Stifinder* was sunk by the submarine the next afternoon. She contained contraband, light oils—none of which were of value to the *U-152*—en route from New York to Australia.

October 15, an unescorted steamer, unarmed, was sighted in the afternoon. Sixty shots were fired at her. She had apparently fallen behind her convoy; for she radioed: "Help! For God's sake, Help!" At length the submarine's alarm for diving rang, and she plunged at about an angle of 45° (she usually dived at 30°) to a depth of 55 meters. The limit of the depth dial was 50 meters, but Muller was told "We don't

SURVIVORS OF THE U. S. A. C. T. LUCIA LEAVING THE SHIP.

(Page 104.)

MOTOR BOAT ARRIVING ALONGISDE THE U. S. S. FAIRFAX WITH A LOAD OF SURVIVORS FROM THE U. S. A. C. T. LUCIA.
(Page 104.)

U. S. S. TICONDEROGA.
(Page 106.)

TYPE OF U-BOAT WHICH OPERATED IN AMERICAN WATERS.

worry about that." A cruiser and a destroyer were reported. Five minutes later, nine depth charges exploded. The boat shook, but no lights went out, and the Americans were told that no one "worried" unless that happened.

Various courses on the surface were now steered for a few days. A torpedo was fired at a British steamer on the 17th, but as it was not heard to explode, probably missed. The submarine dived, but ten minutes later came to the surface and engaged the steamer in a gun duel. The latter fired 40 shots, none of which hit *U-152*, and the submarine 83; range and effect not learned by the prisoners. This was in the late afternoon, and had continued for two hours. The steamer was making more speed than the submarine, and now escaped.

October 20 came the radio "All submarines return to Kiel." *U-152* set course NE., till she had rounded the Faroe Islands. She entered the northern mine barrage at 4 p. m., November 11. She proceeded at full speed on the surface, through its center, and the Americans were told that the mines had been passed at 4 a. m., on the 12th. They woke to learn that the officers had heard of the signing of the armistice. All hands seemed pleased that "the war was over." Lieut. Schwartz admitted that for months Germany had been waging a losing fight, because the United States had intervened.

The Skagerack was entered on the night of the 12th. *U-152* encountered *U-53* (Hans Rose's famous sub), and tied up to her from 9 to 11 p. m. Von Schrader had replaced Rose in command. He stated that about six weeks previously *U-53* had torpedoed a United States escort ship at the entrance to the Bristol Channel. *U-53* was not certain of her name, but it sounded like *Tampa*. (Note: Time and location of the unexplained loss of U. S. S. *Tampa* would confirm this. It is known, however, that about that date *U-53* fired a torpedo at U. S. S. *Chester*. The *Chester* was not hit, but as she dropped depth charges the submarine may have been deceived by their explosion.)

U-53 stated that after she had torpedoed U. S. S. *Jacob Jones* (Dec. 6, 1917), she had recognized in the latter's dory Lieut. Commander D. W. Bagley, "Who had been aboard an American destroyer off Newport when we torpedoed enemy merchant men in 1916." She also declared that she had sent out a radio message when the *Jacob Jones* was sinking, and that this was the only call for help that any submarine had ever given in the case of a torpedoed ship. (Note: A radio message whose origin has never been accounted for, signaling the sinking of the *Jacob Jones*, was intercepted at Queenstown on the afternoon of Dec. 6, 1917.)

U-53 also declared that she had left Kiel owing to the revolution; that her officers and men were loyal to the Kaiser, and that she was bound for Sweden. Apparently uncertain about this step, however, she proceeded back toward the Baltic on the morning of November 13, leading *U-152* through the mine fields. The latter continued into the Sound, after the *U-53* went ahead at 15 knots for Kiel, and she anchored near Copenhagen on the evening of the 14th. Here two radio messages were received: One from *U-53*, saying that all was calm at Kiel, but that she was leaving to intern in Sweden (which she has supposedly done). Another from the Commandant at Kiel ordering *U-152* to return to port.

Capt. Franz now held a meeting of the officers and crew, and took their vote as to whether the sub should go to Sweden or to Germany. Of the crew of 80, about 10 favored interning, and 70 Kiel. As the submarine got underway, Franz said to Muller and Fulcher: "You two gentlemen are now free. You are no longer prisoners of war. I don't know whether we shall finally reach Kiel or Sweden, or Denmark; but rest assured that in any case you will be safe. I shall protect you at all hazards. Whatever we do, you will be well off.

U-152 had received many radio messages concerning mutinies and the chaos ashore in Germany. The Americans were advised to proceed to their consulates if a neutral port was reached. "I, Mr. Muller," continued Capt. Franz, "was a gunnery officer at the Battle of Jutland. But during the years since, I have been in submarines. And the submarines have been doing all the Navy's work in the war. The battleships and cruisers of the High Seas Fleet have been doing next to nothing." This feeling of chagrin and anger was from now on constantly phrased both aboard *U-152* and the ships visited by the prisoners at Kiel.

Kiel was reached at 5 p. m., November 15. The Americans were quartered on the submarine mother ship *Kronprinz Heinrich*, where they got hot baths and rooms. But they continued to mess on *U-152*, which was the outboard submarine of the seven U-boats alongside. The executive officer of the *Heinrich* formally released them as prisoners. "Naval officers have no more power over you," he said. He blamed the collapse of Germany upon the United States entry into the War. "You have ruined our country," he added. "See what you have done." He told them that they were free to go ashore, but advised against it.

On the 16th, they were told that they would leave for Copenhagen at 10 a. m. the next day. Nothing was done to carry this out, and the executive of the mothership asked apologetically whether his guests minded waiting until the following day. That afternoon (Saturday) they went ashore with a chief boatswain's mate of the *U-152*. They were told there that the mutiny in the High Seas Fleet started on October 28, the day fixed for it to go to sea to meet the Grand Fleet. The black gang in a certain ship started the revolt. Between 250 and 300 of the crew were put in the lockup, but a crowd of 10,000 ratings surrounded the ship (apparently alongside dock), released them, and hoisted the red flag. Ashore in Kiel, the Americans visited five restaurants. There was little to buy except bad beer. Many British, Belgian, and Russian soldiers were encountered, but no Americans. Conditions did not appear abnormal.

The executive of the mothership on the 17th stated that he no longer had any authority to deal with his guests, in any way. He said that to arrange for reaching Copenhagen or elsewhere, they must treat with the soldiers' and workingmen's representatives aboard. He referred to them as "soldaten," although one was a chief boatswain's mate, and the others two able seamen. They also had charge of the submarines alongside.

"The submarines are going to England with transports," they said. "We will arrange accommodations for you on one of the transports." But when the crew of *U-152* heard this they protested. They held a vote, and elected to take Muller and Fulcher with them. "We wish to insure your safety," they said, among other evidences that the Americans were popular aboard. They had no relations with the officers of the ship, but the divided authorities were not antagonistic, and ship discipline was maintained by the latter. Muller and Fulcher stayed on the *Heinrich* until November 20, and were given clean underwear and shoes.

On the morning of that day, they went aboard *U-152* again, and at 2 p. m. left through the Kiel Canal, arriving at Brunsbuttel the following afternoon. They reached Heligoland 11 p. m. the same day, and left for Harwich at 7.30, November 22. The 24 submarines en route, preceded by a transport, were in two columns, one led by *U-152* and the other by *U-155* (*Deutschland*). Harwich was reached on Sunday, the 24th.

Preceding the departure from Germany, half of the *U-152*'s crew had gone ashore, some home, others to man merchant ships at Hamburg. There had been no objection by any of them to visiting England. Capt. Franz, several warrant officers, the chief engineer, first officer, and Lieut. Schwarz also stayed behind. A meeting was held to elect a captain. Lieut. Wille was chosen, and he kept good discipline on the trip to Harwich. The messes were maintained, the men and officers not eating together. Throughout, the officers and crew had been friendly to the Americans, doing everything possible for their comfort, giving them cigarettes, etc. When they left the ship in Harwich, the stock of provisions aboard was divided up equally among all the men and officers. They insisted that the Americans take their share of them, and out of politeness Muller and Fulcher felt that they had to do so. They stepped ashore with packages of cheese, and flour, and wurst. "We have more than we need to take back to Germany," said the crew.

Every German they had seen expressed himself as being glad that the war was over. It was declared that surrender had been necessary to save the lives of women and children; that except for this the fight would have continued. All officers stated that Germany months ago would have won if the United States had not come in. This was the opinion even of those still loyal to the Kaiser. All were enthusiastic over the new Government, which was to be a republic.

"Take all our submarines, and battleships, and battle cruisers," the soldation on the *Kronprinz Heinrich* had said. "Sink them in the mid-Atlantic. We don't want them any more. What we do want from now on are ploughs and picks and shovels, to get back to work again."

After the sinking of the *Ticonderoga* there was no definite report of the whereabouts of the *U–152* until October 13, when she sank the Norwegian three-masted bark *Stifinder*, 1,746 gross tons, bound from New York to Freemont, Australia, Tarwald Frehe, chief mate of the sailing vessel, made the following report of the loss of the ship to the American naval authorities:

Our position was 37° 22′ north latitude, and 53° 30′ west longitude. We first sighted the submarine at 1.45 p. m., when three shots were fired at us, none of which hit. I, personally, only heard the last shot, as I was below deck when the first two shots were fired and had gone up above when I heard shouting by the members of the crew. Well, after I heard the shot I went up on deck and saw the submarine, which was on the surface in a westerly position from us, off our stern about 3 miles away. We at once hoisted the Norwegian flag and drew in our sails. We then lowered our boat, and at the request of the captain I took eight men with me and sailed over to the submarine in the small boat with the ship's papers, it being the idea of our captain that they would want to see them as that had been our understanding of their practice in the past. On arriving alongside the submarine I asked if they wanted me to come on board, and on being told to do so by one of the officers on the submarine, I went aboard. I gave an officer the ship's papers. They immediately asked the name of the ship, where bound from, where to, and for information as to the nature of the cargo. I answered him that we were bound from New York to Australia, with a cargo of oil. He was looking over the papers, standing just outside the conning tower, and said, "You have turpentine also on board, have you not?" "Where is this stowed?" "Where are your plans?" I told him that we had turpentine on board, but that I did not have the ship's plans, as these were kept by the Standard Oil Co., of New York. I understand a little of German, and I heard him say to another German officer that this boat had turpentine and "we have none in Germany." His attention seemed to be centered on the turpentine, and was apparantly not interested in the kerosene and benzine.

The commander of the submarine would not talk to me in English, but he did talk to one of the officers in German, who, in turn, talked to me in English. After finishing looking at our papers he said, "I see you are going from one enemy country to another and that your cargo is contraband, so you know what that means." I told him ours was a neutral ship, but he replied that it did not make any difference, as he would have to sink us, talking to me in English. This last conversation was with one of the minor officers on the submarine. This officer asked me if I could talk German, and I said "No." The men were talking between themselves in German all the time. I did not hear all they said, but they seemed to want the turpentine. They also asked me if we had any potatoes on board, or any pigs. I told him "Yes," and the chief said then, "We will tow the boat up to the ship; go aboard, and see what we can use." They then made a rope fast to our lifeboat in tow, made about a half circle around the *Stifinder*, and came alongside. I understood the commander's orders to be full speed ahead, and I imagine he was making about 10 to 11 miles per hour. I was on board the submarine all this time. They tied up alongside the *Stifinder*, and I asked if they would return the ship's papers to me. The officer said "No," and at that moment a sailor on board the submarine pushed me from the back and into the lifeboat. That was the only rough attack made against me. They were very businesslike and had three or four cameras with which they were taking pictures, but I did not notice any moving-picture machine. A German officer then took charge of 10 or 12 of the crew from the submarine and ordered us all on board our boat. This officer then put one man in the crow's nest and placed guards at the different hatches. One of the men brought on a bag of bombs. I did not get a very good look at these, but one of them seemed to be about the size of a ball, painted black, and brass riveted. The German officer then went up to our captain and began talking to him but instructing me to throw some food and clothes into our lifeboat and beat it. I asked him if I could get the ship's instruments, and on being allowed went to my room, but before I got all I wanted they looked me up and told me to get out. I did get a few of my personal things and food and water enough for 11 men for about 20 days, the ship's sextant, and the lifeboat compass. After putting these in the lifeboat I again approached the German officer, who was still talking to the captain, and asked him for a chart, as we had two lifeboats and only one chart. He instructed what I took to be the navigating officer of the submarine to give me a chart. They let us take all the provisions we wanted and made no complaint about the quantity we took, and he gave orders to his men that nothing was to be touched until we left the ship and then they would take what they wanted after. No special remarks were made that I can think of which would be of interest to you, and I did not hear the conversation between the officer and our captain. We then lowered our captain's boat, which had been fully provisioned, and both our boats sailed away a few hundred yards and came together to talk over our position, where to land, and we decided to try and reach Nova Scotia. There were 11 men, including myself, in my lifeboat, and 8 men, including the captain, in the captain's lifeboat. My boat was sailing the fastest, so we gave the captain's boat a line and tried to tow it. It was about 4 p. m. when we left our ship, and at 5 p. m. we lost sight of our ship on account of darkness. We had made about 5 miles in a westerly direction. The last we saw of the *Stifinder* the submarine was still alongside, and we saw the German crew still on board and breaking open the hatches, with one man up in the rigging to keep a watch out. The captain had all of the confidential papers in the chart room, and I do not know what disposition he made of them. The stowage chart was one which was made by me for my information, and I had previously destroyed it.

I was on the submarine for about one hour's time, but only on deck, as I was not allowed inside. She was between 280 feet and 300 feet long; had one conning tower; two 5 or 6 inch guns, one fore and one aft; and each gun had two men in charge; the barrels of the guns appeared to be 25 or 30 feet long. I did not notice any machine guns on the deck. There was one 2-inch pipe immediately forward of the conning tower, which I took to be a periscope, but the eye had been removed; this pipe was about 12 feet high. There were two masts, one about 30 feet high and the other possibly 15 feet, the highest one being aft. There were wireless wires hanging down from them. The two large guns on the submarine were mounted on the raised portion of the deck, and my sketch will explain this better to you. I should judge there were 25 or 30 men on the deck, and there also were some below decks, as I heard them shout below to men in the engine room. They did not steer on the bridge, but the commander stood inside the conning tower. The commander was dressed, as I judged, like a chauffeur. He had on a short overcoat, of khaki color, with a large sheepskin collar, and a heavy white sweater inside. He looked to be between 32 and 35 years old and was about 5 feet 10 inches high, rather skinny; reddish face and a mustache between a blonde and red, with a rather big nose; I did not hear his name called. The general run of the men was as follows: Their clothes were very dirty, oily, and ragged; their clothes were a sort of khaki dungaree. They all appeared to be happy and well fed, and all were smoking cigars. Three or four of the men wore small arms, and all of the officers had revolvers in belts on their side. The officer who gave me the chart, and who I assume was the navigating officer, wore a dungaree suit and a sailor's cap. When he gave me the chart I asked him to mark our position on it and he did, but I think his latitude was wrong by possibly 10 degrees.

The lifeboat containing the captain and seven of the crew of the *Stifinder* landed at Turks Island November 5, having been at sea for over three weeks. The second boat, containing the mate and 10 men, was picked up by U. S. S. C. *No. 294* on October 28, after 15 days at sea.

On the 15th of October the *U–152* attacked the British S. S. *Messina*, 4,271 tons gross, in latitude 37° 20' N., longitude 53° 30' W. The *Messina* was armed with one 4.7-inch Japanese gun and was attacked by gunfire at 18.28 G. M. T., while en route from Plymouth to Baltimore in ballast. When the submarine was sighted the ship was steering S. 82 W. (true) at 7 knots. There was a strong WSW. wind, heavy sea, and fair visibility. Speed of submarine about 14 knots, steering W. by N. (true), and was sighted on the port quarter. On sighting, the ship brought the submarine astern, and put on full speed and zigzagged in accordance with the fall of the enemy shots. The submarine opened fire at 18.32 with range of approximately 8,000 yards and fired about 100 shots of two rounds per minute. The ship was hit once on the port side abaft the bridge and two plates were fractured in the side. The ship opened fire at 18.35 at about 7,000 yards range and fired 15 rounds, but the submarine was not hit. After two hours' running fight the chase was abandoned in approximately latitude 37° 37' N. and longitude 52° 48' W. The master of the *Messina* reported that the submarine was about 10 to 15 feet out of the water. Two 6-inch guns were seen, one forward and one aft of the conning tower. She was painted dark gray.

The last action of the *U–152* was her attack on the British steamer *Briarleaf*, October 17, in latitude 36° 05' N., longitude 49° 12' W.

The British S. S. *Briarleaf* arrived at Sabine, Tex., on October 29, and the following information was obtained from Capt. G. E. Patterson regarding the encounter with German submarine:

Capt. Patterson stated that on October 17, 1918, at 4.10 p. m., in latitude 36° 05' N., longitude 49° 12' W. (about 1,200 miles off American coast), a submarine came to the surface about 600 yards off the starboard beam, showing superstructure, conning tower and periscope. The submarine immediately opened fire with an explosive shell, which burst and fell short. The *Briarleaf* replied with one shot, which also missed. The submarine submerged, coming up astern and again opened fire on the vessel, which replied. The submarine fired in all about 150 shots, making no hits, although some fragments of shells dropped on deck. The *Briarleaf* fired 39 shots, and then ceased firing, as the submarine was out of range; however, the submarine contined firing for about 30 minutes, as it was equipped with heavier caliber guns. At 5.55 p. m. the submarine ceased firing and dropped astern. Capt. Patterson, while not positive, believes that he must have scored a hit which caused some slight damage, as otherwise the submarine would not have given up the engagement, as it seemed fairly able to maintain an even speed with the *Briarleaf*.

The submarine is described as follows: Length about 300 feet, with superstructure entire length, said superdeck being about 5 feet above conning tower; painted light gray, with periscope being either brass or painted yellow. Capt. Patterson was of the opinion this submarine is one of the latest type. No guns or gun crews were visible, the guns being situated under the superstructure, as all that could be seen were the flashes as the guns were fired. The submarine used two guns while in action, both of which were either 5-inch or larger, as they had much longer range than the guns on the *Briarleaf*, which is 4.7.

Capt Patterson advised also that while the submarine was shelling his vessel, a wireless message was received from the S. S. *Lucia* calling for help. The *Lucia* said in her message that she had been torpedoed and was sinking, and gave her position as about 100 miles north of the position of the S. S. *Briarleaf*.

It was formerly believed that the *U-152* was responsible for the sinking of the *Lucia* on the same day that the attack on the *Briarleaf* took place. Both the *U-152* and the *U-155* were in the vicinity at the time, and it is the testimony of Capt. Patterson and the War Diary of the U. S. S. *Princess Matoika* that leads to the decision that each was engaged in a separate attack:

At about 4 p. m., August 17, the signal from the *Briarleaf* came in. Plotted on the chart the *Briarleaf* bore from the *Princess Matoika* and the *Pastores 219* true distance about 15 miles. By inspection of the chart would pass within 6 miles of the allo. About 4.40 p. m. gunfire was heard ahead—sometimes to port and sometimes to starboard. At 4.52 sighted object ahead on horizon resembling heavy smoke. Firing could be heard and gun flashes visible. Transports changed course to bring objects abeam where they were last seen. Firing no longer heard. *Briarleaf* escaped and headed for Bermuda. Shortly after the change of course was made at 5 p. m. the allo from the *Lucia* was received. The allos were 150 miles apart.

The *U-152* may have been responsible for the allo sent by the Japanese *Kirin Maru* on October 20, but this can not be stated as a conclusion.

On October 20 the *U-152* received the German order for all submarines to return to their bases and in obedience turned homeward, entering the northern mine barrage area on the day of the armistice. She passed through the field running at full speed on the surface, completing the passage in safety on the morning of the 12th and arriving at Kiel three days later, November 15, 1918.

CABLE CUTTING BY THE U-151.

The possibility and probability of the interruption of transatlantic cable service by the enemy was a subject of serious consideration even before the United States entered the war. The conclusion of those most familiar with transatlantic cable traffic was that the reason the Germans did not interrupt these cables was not that it was impracticable for them to do so but because it was probable that they were using them for German messages and did not desire to do so. There seemed to be good reasons to suspect that either through friendly diplomatic channels or through apparently harmless messages, by which the British censorship was evaded, the Germans were making use of the cables for the transmission of their own messages.

All of these matters were discussed and carefully considered by the United States authorities and seemed to offer the most reasonable interpretation of the situation.

When the United States entered the war it was thought that the attitude of the enemy might be entirely changed toward the cutting of the cables and that the time might come when the advantages to the Germans of cutting the cables might outweigh the disadvantages. The advantages which the Germans might gain by cutting the cables were increasing rapidly as the United States forces in Europe were increasing. At the same time, the chances of the use of the cables by the Germans to carry their messages, were being eliminated because of the vigorous methods that were adopted by the Office of Naval Intelligence through naval censorship. These factors all tended to introduce a new enemy motive into the situation and gave the United States authorities both at home and in France much concern because they considered that our transatlantic electrical communications presented a vulnerable point of attack which he might be tempted to exploit whenever the advantages of doing so looked sufficiently promising; or when, in the final struggle, in his various measures of desperation, he might include cable cutting and interference in every possible way with the radio system.

On April 29, 1918, the Office of Naval Operations sent a memorandum to the Director of Naval Communications, saying: "A new phase of the employment of submersibles has developed in the cutting of cables. Evidently one of these vessels is specially fitted for the purpose, as there have been four cables cut within the last six weeks, presumably by the same vessel." The receipt of this warning produced additional activity and alertness so as to be sure to be ready in case the cables should be cut, which was then regarded as being something that might occur at any time.

The service on the Commercial Cable Co.'s No. 4 Canso-New York cable was interrupted at 12.35 p. m., May 28, 1918. On the same day the Central and South American Cable Co.'s New York-Colon cable began to fail at 3.30 p. m. and went out of service entirely at 9.30 p. m. The cable ship *Relay* made the repairs to the latter on June 25. At the break there was little sign of chafing or dragging on the surface of the cable. The armored strands were, however, somewhat distorted and showed indications of having withstood considerable pressure and wrenching. The strands of the armor appeared to have been cut approximately half through, either with a saw or possibly some rough-cutting tool, and the other half of each strand wrenched or broken off.

The Commercial Cable Co.'s No. 4 was repaired at 4 p. m. on July 4. This cut was an exceptionally clean shear, the cable sheath within half inch of each side of the break being in almost normal condition, very little distorted and showing no signs of chafing or anchor rubbing on the surface. In this case also the armored strands were cut approximately half through and broken off the rest of the way. The Commercial cable was cut at 12.35, three hours prior to the first indication of trouble on the Central and South American cable, at a distance of approximately 28 miles north of the Central and South American cable failure. The water at both points was approximately 25 fathoms.

A study of the causes of the failure of these two cables was made by various cable experts including Mr. Loriot, cable engineer of the Central and South American Cable Co., Mr. Pierce, cable engineer of the Commercial Cable Co., and Capt. Oldham, the commander of the cable ship. It is their opinion that the cables were cut on the bottom or near the bottom and were not raised to the surface to be cut. They believe the cables were cut maliciously by someone who came to the spot with the intention of cutting the cables. They do not think they were cut by a ship in clearing its anchor. The day was calm with a slight westerly wind. Normally there would be no occasion to anchor in this locality except during a storm with extremely adverse wind conditions. Neither of the breaks occurred in a normal route of ship travel. Both breaks were within sight of ship channels frequently used. The captain of the repair ship stated that it was his opinion that a submarine could hardly work there many hours in the daytime without being seen by passing ships.

These opinions were concurred in by Col. John J. Carty, vice-president of the American Telephone & Telegraph Co., who personally examined the cut in each cable.

While these facts are not conclusive, the evidence indicates that the two cables were cut by parties with malicious intent, possibly by an enemy submarine. The latter supposition seems quite probable.

On May 25, 1918, the *U-151* attacked and sunk the American schooner *Hattie Dunn*, *The Hauppauge* and *Edna* off the Virginia coast. Nothing more is positively known of the activity of *U-151* until June 2, 1918, when she sank the *Isabel B. Wiley*, *Winneconne* and *Jacob M. Haskell* off Barnegat Light, N. J. During these seven or eight days it is supposed that she was laying mines, and it is not improbable that during that time she may have cut the cables on May 28, and as will be plainly seen by reference to the chart, she was in a location on May 25 from which she could easily have reached the position of the cable cutting on the 28th, and afterwards reached the position of her sinkings on June 2.

UNITED STATES AND ALLIED RADIO SERVICE ADEQUATE FOR THE TRANSACTION OF IMPORTANT OFFICIAL BUSINESS IN CASE OF THE DESTRUCTION OF TRANSATLANTIC CABLES.

When the United States entered the war it was considered very necessary to provide a system of transoceanic radio communication, which would be capable of handling all official messages between the United States and Europe, in case the enemy should cut any or all of our cables; or in case the enemy made it difficult for us to repair such cables as were put out of commission either by the enemy or from natural causes.

In October, 1917, an Inter-Allied Radio Conference, consisting of representatives from the United States, Great Britain, France and Italy, met at New London, Conn. At this conference it was decided that the United States would make provisions for the use of its stations at Marion, Mass. (then under construction); Sayville, L. I. (taken over from its German owners); New Brunswick, N. J. (under construction by the Marconi Co.); Tuckerton, N. J. (taken over from the German constructor); and Annapolis, Md. (a naval high-power station just completed). The Allies were to organize their stations at Carnarvon, England; Lyons, France; Nantes, France and Rome, Italy.

In the spring of 1918 the Navy Department, having been given control of all high-powered transatlantic radio stations, was operating stations at Sayville, Tuckerton, Annapolis and New Brunswick, which were then capable of transmitting to Europe approximately 30,000 words per day. The European stations were capable of transmitting approximately 25,000 words per day. Inasmuch as both the United States stations and those in Europe were capable of transmitting and receiving simultaneously, this indicates a capacity of 55,000 words per day in transatlantic communication. This capacity was adequate to handle the important messages between the War and Navy Departments and the forces in Europe.

Inasmuch as the cables were not all cut, or put out of commission, the transatlantic radio system handled only a small amount of the total traffic between the United States and Europe. It is estimated that the greatest amount of traffic handled by radio was 50,000 words per day. However, this comparatively small amount relieved the cables to a certain extent and was not only a means of facilitating communication but served as an insurance for effective communication; and gave assurance that the enemy could not completely interrupt transatlantic communication. Had the enemy cut all the transatlantic cables it would have been impossible for him to have stopped effective communication between the War and Navy Departments and our forces in Europe.

MINE-LAYING OPERATIONS.

As all destruction of vessels by mines on the Atlantic coast was by mines planted by the Germans, it is of interest to know what submarines carried on these operations and how.

As we have no reports from them the procedure is largely a matter of conjecture. Any conclusion as to the respective dates and places of planting mines by the submarines can be, at this time, only a logical deduction, taking into consideration the general German policy regarding mine laying, the character of the cruises of those submarines, the speed, longest period of apparent inactivity, the lapse of time between sightings of or attacks by the submarines, and the dates and locations of reported sightings or destruction of enemy mines.

This procedure has been followed: A careful analysis of the track of the submarine with dates of her presence in certain localities and the corresponding date and locality of the damage to a ship by a mine.

According to Lieut. Commander Lafrenz, of the German submarine *U-65*, which was sunk by the French submarine *U-15*, on November 3, 1917, the German policy as to mine laying is to sow mines in the vicinity of harbors and in harbor approaches. The object of all mine laying, as Lafrenz pointed out, is not merely to sink ships, but it is considered just as important to keep enemy mine-sweeping craft so that those vessels are not available for offensive operation. Mines are nearly always laid in slack water and in theory, according to the German officer, it is best to lay four mines off one harbor and then four off another, and so on, as the same sweeping operations are necessary to sweep up four mines as eighteen. In practice, he said that the submarine commanders are usually too anxious to get rid of their mines and so lay them in groups close to one another. It is left to the commanding officer as to where his mines are to be laid. Lafrenz stated, also, that there was little danger in laying mines in the same place in which mines had been previously laid, but that if he went to the same place a second time he would always make it a point to come in at the high-water mark.

THE U-151.

From the character of the operations of the *U-151* just after she arrived off the American Atlantic coast, it is apparent that her commanding officer was extremely anxious to plant his mines as soon as possible before engaging in his other activity. After the submarine had engaged the steamship *Crenella* in latitude 37° 50' N., longitude 75° 50' W., on May 21, 1918, she seems to have taken a course southward and to have proceeded to the vicinity of Currituck Sound where she possibly laid mines near False Cape. Then moving northward she came to the entrance to Chesapeake Bay where she laid mines near Capes Henry and Charles.

Having completed her mine laying in these waters, the submarine continued her course northward. On May 25 she made the attacks on the American schooners *Hattie Dunn, Hauppauge,* and *Edna,* within about 30 miles of the coast. The commanding officer did not see fit to begin his active raid upon coastwise shipping at this time, however, but continued his northward route, planting mines as he went. On or about the morning of the 26th, the submarine possibly visited waters along that portion of the coast south and north of Winter Quarter Shoals.

In moving northward the submarine soon reached the vicinity of the entrances to Delaware Bay. Here she planted mines near Cape May and Cape Henlopen. On June 3, at 3.35 p. m., the *Herbert L. Pratt,* an unarmed American steamship of 7,145 tons gross, owned by the Standard Refinery Co., of Philadelphia, Pa., was damaged by a mine at his point. This fact furnished the only convincing evidence of the mine-planting operations of the *U-151* up to this time, for as no mines had been placed by the United States Government, and as it was known that the *U-151* was in this vicinity two or three days previous, it is evident that she laid the mine that damaged the *Herbert L. Pratt.*

On May 28, 1918, the *U-151* probably found and cut two cables leading from New York, one to Europe and one to Central America, 60 miles southeast of Sandy Hook.

On June 23, the steamship *Gloucester* reported sighting a mine off Shrewsbury Light, Ambrose Channel. This report indicates that the *U-151* may have visited the neighborhood of the entrance to Ambrose Channel. Even though the *U-151* may have laid a few mines along the coast of Long Island, it is thought that the mine that sank the cruiser U. S. S. *San Diego*, July 19, near Fire Inlet, was one of those deposited there by the *U-156* which later appeared off the American coast and was engaged in mining activities from July 8 to July 18.

The majority of the mines swept up in waters that the *U-151* possibly visited, conform to the description of the mines that the *U-151* was known to carry. The dimensions in the main were: Diameter, 19½ inches; length, exclusive of horns, 4 feet 9½ inches. They held in their center a charge of approximately 200 pounds of trinitrate of toluol. They were usually of the four-horned variety with a single mooring.

Having unburdened herself of her mines, during the interval May 25 to June 2, the *U-151* recommenced her activities against coastwise vessels, beginning her harvest with the attacks on the vessels *Isabel B. Wiley* and the *Winneconne*.

THE U-156.

As no activities of *U-156* were reported between July 8, 1918, when she sank the Norwegian schooner *Manx King* in latitude 40° N. and longitude 53° W., and July 17, when she was sighted by the U. S. S. *Harrisburg* in latitude 40° 10' N., longitude 68° 55' W., it is probable that the interval of eight days was utilized in laying mines in the approaches to New York. The chart evidence shows that *U-156* was in a position from which she could easily have performed this task which was, of course, a part of her mission. It is, therefore, altogether probable that the mine which sank the U. S. S. *San Diego* on July 19, 10 miles from Fire Island Lightship, was laid by this submarine.

THE U-117.

On August 29, 1918, the U. S. S. *Minnesota* struck a mine 20 miles from Fenwick Island Shoal Lightship in latitude 38° 11' 05" N., longitude 74° 41' 05" W., sustaining considerable damage but was able to make port. The chart evidence indicates that this mine was in all probability laid by the *U-117* while she continued her course southward off the coast of Maryland. The steamship *San Saba* also struck a mine on October 4, 15 miles southeast of Barnegat, in latitude 39° 40' N., longitude 73° 55' W., which was probably in one of these same mine fields.

U-155.

Between the attack by *U-155* on the *Newby Hall* on September 13, 1918, in latitude 42° 18′ N., longitude 58° 22′ W., and her next reported attack on October 20, when she captured and sunk the American fishing vessel *Kingfisher* in latitude 43° 31′ N., longitude 61° 53′ W., it is probable that the intervening seven days of her inactivity may be attributed to the fact that it was reported in advance that one of her purposes was to lay mines off Halifax and Nova Scotia coasts. The sighting of an enemy submarine there and the chart evidence showing that *U-155* was in that vicinity and that mines were discovered off Halifax confirm that report.

SUBMARINE MINES ON THE ATLANTIC COAST OF THE UNITED STATES.

The story of the submarine mines on the Atlantic coast can be briefly told.

There were no mines laid on the Atlantic coast either by the United States Government or any of the Allies. All destruction was, therefore, by mines placed by the enemy.

The sailor does not fear any of the terrors of the sea or of the enemy, so long as those terrors are in sight. Whether the vessel be under sail or steam, he enthusiastically prepares to meet the storms or the enemy. It is the hidden, invisible enemy that gives him greatest concern. These enemies were the fog and the submarine mine, to which in this war has been added the submarine vessel.

Seven vessels, three of which were of great value, were damaged on the Atlantic coast by the enemy's mines. These were the steamship *Herbert L. Pratt*, U. S. S. *San Diego*, steamship *Mirlo*, U. S. S. *Minnesota*, steamship *San Saba*, steamship *Chaparra*, and the U. S. S. *Saetia*. Some details are herewith given concerning these vessels.

Steamship "Herbert L. Pratt," June 3, 1918.—On June 3, at 3.35 p. m., the *Herbert L. Pratt*, an unarmed American steamship of 7,145 tons gross, owned by the Standard Refinery Co., Philadelphia, Pa., came in contact with one of these mines and sent out a S. O. S.:

> Overfalls Lightship Delaware Breakwater: Have either struck mine or am torpedoed.

Upon striking the mine the *Herbert L. Pratt* headed for the shore and was beached before she sank. Capt. H. H. Bennet, master of the *Herbert L. Pratt*, stated the following in regard to his vessel having been mined 2½ miles S. 45° E. of Overfalls Lightship:

> We sailed from Mexico May 26 bound for Philadelphia with full cargo of crude oil in bulk. We experienced very good weather on the voyage from Tuxpam, and nothing unusual occurred until we got warnings of submarines operating along the Atlantic coast, by a wireless which was warning ships to make the nearest port. To the best

of my recollection this message was received by us at 8 in the morning on June 3. I ordered the chief engineer to connect up a boiler that was out of operation, for the purpose of getting all the speed possible in case of attack. We were at this time approximately off the Winter Quarter Lightship. I was keeping the regular course and followed up the usual track.

Nothing further occurred until about 3.35 p. m., when I heard a slight explosion and felt the vibration of the ship which lurched forward apparently striking a submerged object and with indications of bouncing over; only one explosion occurred. I stopped the engines and started them immediately heading ship for the beach, ordered men to lifeboat stations, went below for my signal code books, and ordered wireless to send the position of the ship, her name, and that she had been either mined or torpedoed. I then went back on bridge of ship, gave chief officer orders not to allow the men to take the boats until I had given orders; I ran the ship for approximately 15 minutes until she refused to stir, then I ordered the men out of the engine room, and all hands into boats. We then left the ship.

Just previous to this, I hailed a guard boat (I don't know her name or number) and ordered her to stand by that I was sinking. This guard was approximately 2,000 feet on my port side. He signaled me "All right," and stood by until we left in boats. The pilot boat came up in the meantime.

We rowed over to the pilot boat where the crew was taken aboard, and I was put on board the guard boat. The guard boat started for Cape May and met another guard boat and hailed him. We then turned around and started for Cape Henlopen. We hailed the same guard boat again. While speaking to this guard boat I saw the wake of what appeared to be a submarine approximately 1,000 feet from starboard. This wake, I should say, was about 2 miles from where my vessel, the *Herbert L. Pratt*, was struck. I do not suppose the time or duration of this wake lasted more than a minute. I desire to state again in connection with the explosion that prior to the explosion I observed nothing that led me to believe that a submarine was operating in this vicinity. Both guard boats started immediately, the one I was on running toward Cape Henlopen and the other toward Cape May.

Shortly after, we heard guns fired from the guard boat that had gone in the direction of Cape May. I could distinctly see from my position a hitting of the shells in the water. I do not recall how many he shot, but I heard the explosion at least three or four times. We continued on to the naval base at Lewes, landing there and waiting for the crew which was being brought in by the pilot boat. All the crew was landed and taken to the naval base where they were fed.

Immediately upon the receipt of the S O S message from the *Herbert L. Pratt*, a number of S. P. boats were dispatched to the rescue. On June 3, at 9 p. m., the *Herbert L. Pratt* was visited by Naval Constructor Davis and at 4 p. m., June 4, preparations to raise her were begun; on the same date she was floated and brought to anchor in the breakwater. The *Herbert L. Pratt* left the Breakwater at 11 p. m., on Wednesday, June 5, 1918, and arrived in Philadelphia on the same day.

Armored cruiser San Diego, July 19, 1918—The court of inquiry which investigated the sinking of the U. S. S. *San Diego* reported the following conclusions:

The court is of the opinion that the loss of the U. S. S. *San Diego* was due to an external explosion of a mine.

That the loss of the ship, loss of life, and injury to personnel incurred was in no way due to any negligence, failure to take proper precautions, or inefficiency of the captain or any of the personnel of the ship.

That the loss of life and injury to personnel was incurred in the line of duty and in no way due to their own misconduct.

That at the time of the disaster and thereafter the conduct of the captain, officers, and crew was in the highest degree commendable, and that the remarkably small loss of life was due to the high state of discipline maintained on board.

That no officer should be held responsible for the loss of funds or property for which he was accountable, and that no further proceedings should be held in this case.

The court in its report reviews the main points in the testimony as follows:

The U. S. S. *San Diego*, under the command of Capt. H. H. Christy, United States Navy, was making passage from Portsmouth, N. H., to New York, N. Y., and at or about 11.05 a. m. July 19, 1918, she was in approximate latitude 40° 30′ N., longitude 73° W., on base course 304 true, and zigzagging by an approved plan; speed, 15 knots.

The captain was steering a safe and proper course at the time to minimize the submarine and mine dangers in those waters. A careful inspection watch had been maintained while last coaling ship to prevent the introduction of any foreign matter in the coal bunkers. All lookouts, gun watches, fire-control parties, etc., as prescribed by the "Orders for Ships in Convoy" of the commander cruiser and transport force were at their stations and on the alert. All reasonable and necessary orders to safeguard the water-tight integrity of the ship in dangerous waters had been given and were being carried out.

The following is a report by the Secretary of the Navy regarding the sinking of the U. S. S. *San Diego:*

At about 11.05 a. m., July 19, 1918, an explosion took place in proximity of the skin of the ship, at about frame No. 78, on the port side and well below the water line. As a result of this explosion the ship began to list to port and she finally rolled over and sank bottom up at about 11.25 a. m., July 19, 1918. The explosion was an exterior one and as a result of this explosion the skin of the ship was ruptured in the vicinity of bulkhead No. 78, at the level of the port engine room; and bulkhead No. 78 was so deformed that water-tight door No. 142, between the port-engine room and No. 8 fireroom, was opened to the ingress of water to No. 8 fireroom. The effect of this rupture was to immediately fill the port-engine room and adjacent compartments, and No. 8 fireroom was soon filled also. The effect of this water would give the ship a list of $17\frac{1}{2}°$ to port. With the increased displacement water entered through 6-inch gun port No. 10, which was justifiably open to permit using that gun, when the ship had listed $9\frac{1}{2}°$. This resulted in flooding the gun deck and accelerated the heeling of the ship and her final capsizing. Relatively small quantities of water entered the upper dynamo room through nonwater-tight voice tubes, but this had no appreciable effect on the sinking of the ship.

The captain properly withheld the order to abandon ship until he was certain that the ship would capsize and sink. The ship was abandoned in good order, and excellent discipline prevailed. Gun crews remained at their guns and continued firing at all suspicious objects until they were forced to jump into the water. The captain was the last to leave the ship.

The radio apparatus was put out of commission by the explosion. As no radio reports of this disaster had been sent, Lieut. C. J. Bright, United States Navy, was ordered to proceed with a dinghy crew to Long Island to report the disaster and request rescue vessels. The boat reached shore safely and carried out its orders.

The steamships *Malden*, Capt. Brown; *Bussum*, Capt. Brewer; and *F. P. Jones*, Capt. Dodge, hove in sight later and rescued the men in the water and transported them to New York. The court states the captains of these steamers showed courage and a splendid spirit in taking their ships into these waters, where a submarine had apparently been operating, and deserve commendation for their actions and it is recommended that suitable acknowledgment be made by the Navy Department of their gallantry.

On the day subsequent to this disaster six contact mines were located by the naval forces in the vicinity of the position where the disaster of the U. S. S. *San Diego* occurred.

As a result of this disaster six enlisted men were injured and six lives lost.

The six men lost in the sinking of the *San Diego* were Clyde Chester Blaine, engineman, second class; Thomas Everett Davis, fireman, first class; Paul John Harris, seaman, second class; Andrew Munson, machinist's mate, second class; James Francis Rochet, engineman, second class; Frazier O. Thomas, machinist's mate, second class.

THE SINKING OF THE S. S. MIRLO.

The British steamship *Mirlo*, 6,978 gross tons, was sunk at 3.30 p. m. on August 16, 1918, about one-half of a mile off Wimble Shoal Buoy; caused by an explosion. The ship took fire, being loaded with gasoline, and was abandoned after an attempt to beach her. Due to later explosions, she broke in two, in approximately latitude 35° 30′ N. and longitude 75° 18′ W.

The credit for the destruction of the *Mirlo* has formerly been given to the activity of the German submarine *U-117*, which was operating off the Atlantic coast at that time. The commanding officer claimed that the ship was torpedoed. However, no one saw a submarine or the wake of a torpedo. There was nothing to confirm the first report that a submarine was sighted.

There were nine other vessels in the vicinity, one within sight of the *Mirlo*, and no reports of sighting a submarine were made by any of them. The *Mirlo* was located at the time of her destruction over a now well-known mine field. (See Chart No. 2.) The U. S. S. *Taylor* sighted a floating mine the next day 1 mile east of the wreck. It, therefore, seems highly probable that the *Mirlo* was sunk by a submerged anchored mine, notwithstanding the captain's very positive statement that the ship was torpedoed.

STATEMENT OF CAPT. W. R. WILLIAMS, MASTER BRITISH S. S. "MIRLO."

On August 16, 1918, at 3.30 p. m. A. T. S., when the steamer was steering a north course off Wimble Shoal Buoy, bearing north by west half a mile distance, she was struck on the starboard side aft by a torpedo, bursting No. 2 tank and blowing up the decks, which was immediately followed by another torpedo, which struck farther aft and set fire to ship in stokehold and after end. The explosion causing the dynamos to be put out of commission, also breaking engine room, and destroying telegraph and putting wireless gear out of commission.

The orders were then given to make boats ready for lowering and efforts were made to put the ship toward the shore with some success. The starboard lifeboat was then lowered first, which got away from the ship. The port lifeboat was then lowered

EXPLOSION OF 450 POUNDS OF T. N. T.

GERMAN AND AMERICAN SUBMARINES AT HARWICH, ENGLAND.

AMERICAN TANKER HERBERT L. PRATT AFTER BEING MINED.
(Page 125.)

DAMAGE TO THE AMERICAN TANKER HERBERT L. PRATT BY MINE EXPLOSION.

(Page 125.)

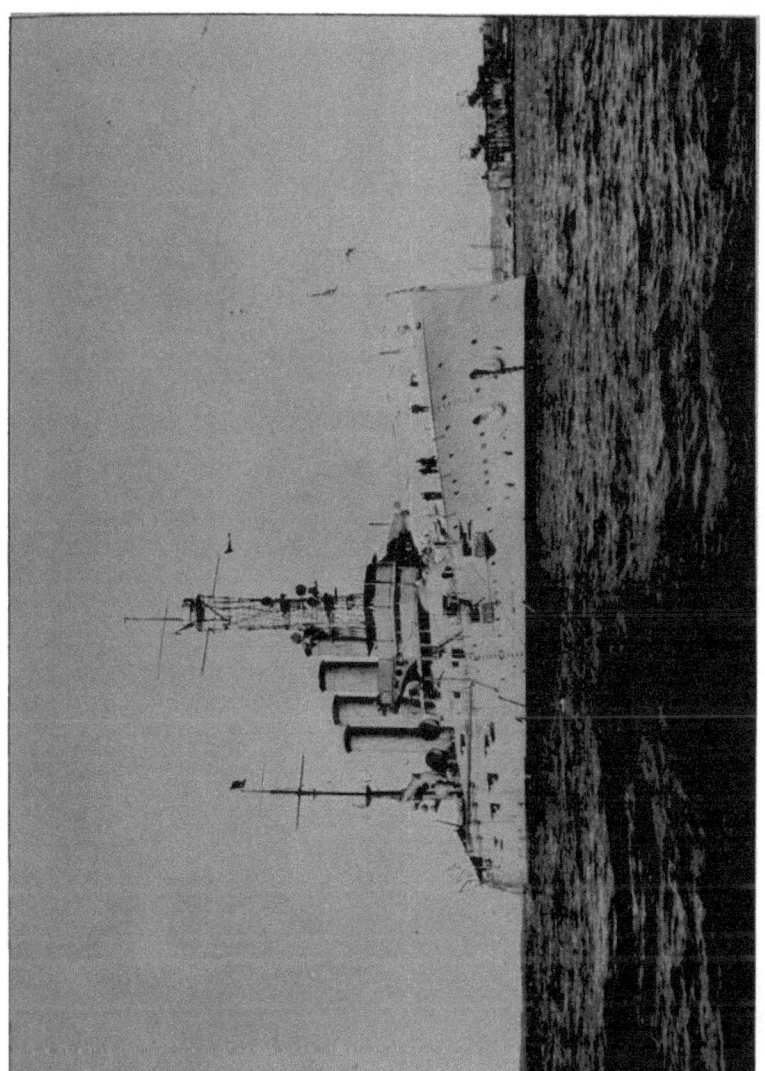

U. S. S. SAN DIEGO.
(Page 126.)

U. S. S. MINNESOTA.
(Page 130.)

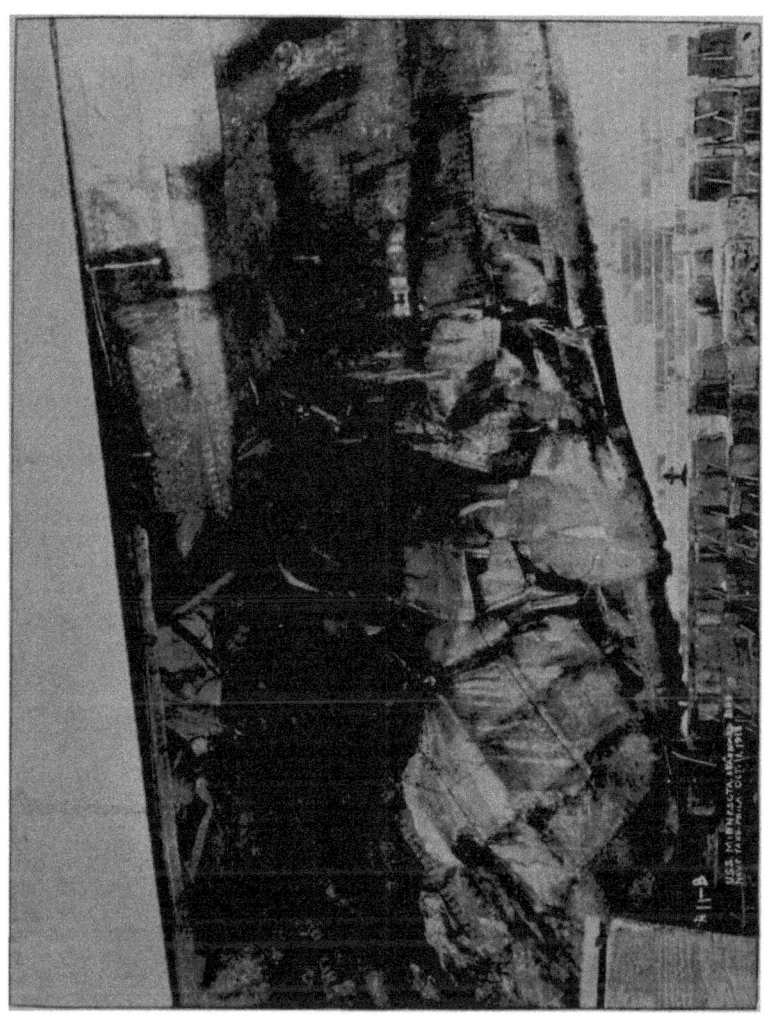

DAMAGE TO THE U. S. S. MINNESOTA BY MINE EXPLOSION.

(Page 130.)

PIECE OF THE MINE REMOVED FROM THE U. S. S. MINNESOTA AFTER MINE EXPLOSION.

(Page 130.)

and entered the water all right, when it was noticed that the tiller fouled the after falls, causing the boat to shear off from the ship and capsize. All the men that were in her were thrown into the water. At the same time the boat capsized she cleared herself from the ship. The starboard boat tried to go to the rescue. The orders were given to clear the after boats and lower same.

After ascertaining that all hands were off the ship we lowered away. During these operations the boat's falls caught fire, and it was with great difficulty that we succeeded in pulling away from the vessel. In a few minutes after leaving it the ship exploded with terrific force fore and aft, at the same time catching fire fore and aft. It was with difficulty that we managed to clear the fire and smoke that was floating on the water, caused by the ship bursting and all the cargo coming out.

The ship had been towing her otter gears from Florida Straits, and was towing them at the time of accident. The ship was steering a straight course north, magnetic, and in my opinion it would have been impossible for these explosions to have been caused by mines—the explosions being 12 to 14 feet below the water line. The two explosions were almost simultaneous.

A careful lookout had been maintained throughout the passage, and neither submarines nor mines had been sighted. There was no wake of either torpedo observed nor warning given.

The ship was armed with one 4-inch breech-loading gun aft and manned by a gun crew of three men, British Navy ratings. As soon as the torpedoes struck, the ship took fire aft. The gun crew was on the lookout, but nothing was seen to fire at.

After clearing the ship I lost sight of the other two boats, owing to the fire and smoke which I thought had enveloped them. After pulling away and sailing clear of the fire and smoke we looked for the other two boats, but nothing was seen of them. It was then decided to take the boat inshore. After proceeding inshore for sometime a motor boat was sighted, which came to us and spoke to us, and turned out to be from Coast Guard Station No. 179. He asked if there were any other boats about, and I requested him to go to the fire, as there were two other boats with 34 men in. He then directed me how to make for the landing and he went away toward the fire, as nothing was then seen of the ship.

The captain of the Coast Guard station succeeded in locating the upturned boat and the other boat which was intact. He took six men from the upturned boat. It was found that 10 men had been drowned from the upturned boat. The men who were rescued from the upturned boat stated to me that some of the men were under the boat when she capsized, and were not seen again. The second officer jumped from the boat into the sea, and told the others it was best to try to swim clear of the fire, which threatened to envelop them, as they assumed the fire was then only 10 yards from them. The boat then drifted away faster than the men could swim, and they were unable to reach the boat and were seen to drown by the rescued men.

I could attach no blame to anyone for this disaster, and had it not been for the heroic manner in which the Coast Guard went in and out of the fire to rescue the loss of life would have been much greater; and I take this opportunity to congratulate and thank them for their heroic work of rescue, and their kindness and attention to all after the rescue.

U. S. S. MINNESOTA,
3 October, 1918.

From: Commanding officer.
To: Commander Battleship Force One.
Subject: Report of damage sustained by striking mine.

1. At 3.15 a. m., September 29, 1918, when this ship was proceeding on course 13° (true), speed 96 revolutions, and was 20.5 miles from Fenwick Island Shoal Light

Ship, bearing 346° (true), a heavy explosion under the starboard bow, about abreast frame 11, occurred.

2. At this time I was in the chart house examining the chart. I immediately repaired to the bridge and took charge. Collision and torpedo defense quarters had been sounded and officers and men were repairing rapidly and quietly to their stations. The ship had settled by the bow without appreciable list. Early reports showed that the ship was intact abaft frame 16 but that forward of that frame all compartments were probably flooded. The shoring of the water-tight bulkhead at frame 16 was immediately started and pushed ahead as rapidly as possible. At 3.18 a. m. the engines were slowed to two-thirds speed (64 revolutions) to ease the pressure of bulkhead at frame 16. At 3.20 a. m. changed course to 270° (true) in order to get into shoaler water should the shored bulkhead fail. At 4.23 a. m., having reached the 10-fathom curve, changed course to 0° (true), and at 4.32 a. m. to 10° (true). Passed 2.7 miles to the westward of Fenwick Island Shoal Light Ship and proceeded to Delaware Breakwater via McCries Shoal gas and whistling buoy and the swept channel. Arrived off Delaware Breakwater at 9.30 a. m.; took on board pilot and proceeded to navy yard, Philadelphia, where arrived about 7.45 p. m., and was successfully docked at 9.30 p. m.

3. When the dock had been unwatered, it was found that on the starboard side, between frames 5 and 16, and from the lower edge of the armor belt to the keel, the ship's structure was practically obliterated. The skin plating had been ruptured and blown in past the centerline, the forward and after portions folding in sharply over the edges of the bulkheads at frames 5 and 16. Compartments A-3, 4, 5, 21, 36, and 37 are practically obliterated. A-38 is badly dished in and corresponding compartments on the port side are no longer water-tight. The protective deck is intact. A detailed examination has been made by the yard authorities and estimates of time and material for necessary repairs are being prepared.

4. At the time of the explosion the sea was smooth and the night dark, the waning moon, about two and one-half hours high, being obscured by clouds. The visibility was such that the U. S. S. *Israel*, the escorting destroyer, was visible when about 800 yards distant.

5. No one saw any trace of a submarine or a periscope nor was the wake of a torpedo near the site of the explosion seen by any one either before or after the explosion occurred, and I am of the opinion that the damage was caused by the explosion of an anchored mine. There is but one piece of testimony that might indicate that the cause was a torpedo. A few minutes after the explosion occurred and while the course was being changed to west (true), L. O. Griggsby, electrician, second class, who was stationed at No. 7 searchlight, reported the wake of a torpedo crossing the stern from starboard to port. He is quite positive that he saw this wake, though no one else observed it. If there was such a wake it should have been seen by the *Israel*, as it must have passed very close to her. She made no report of sighting such a wake, and as, after escorting this ship to Delaware Breakwater, she proceeded on other assigned duty, I have had no opportunity to get information from her upon this point.

6. Notwithstanding Griggsby's testimony, I am of the opinion that the cause of the damage was the explosion of an enemy mine. Fortunately, it is believed that the cause can be definitely determined by a thorough examination of a nearly complete composition casting found by the yard authorities in the damaged section of the ship. This casting has all the appearances of being one of the bushings into which the protruding horns of a German mine are screwed. Fragments of steel to which the casting was evidently brazed are attached to it. The color of the metal of the casting indicates a copper content much lower than any alloy used in the United States Navy. The internal screw threads are sufficiently intact to enable a determination to be made whether or not the threads are metric or English standard.

J. V. CHASE.

[1st indorsement.]

UNITED STATES ATLANTIC FLEET,
BATTLESHIP FORCE ONE,
U. S. S. "MINNESOTA," FLAGSHIP,
6 October, 1918.

From: Commander Battleship Force One.
To: Commander in Chief.
Subject: Report of damage sustained by striking a mine.

1. Forwarded.

2. The *Minnesota* was proceeding in accordance with prescribed routing instructions; there was no loss of life; the efficient condition of the ship as regards watertight integrity was demonstrated.

3. Under normal conditions, investigation by means of a court of inquiry of all the circumstances attendant upon this casualty would be held. It would, however, seriously interfere with important operations to order a court of officers of appropriate rank at the present time; therefore, in view of the facts set forth above, unless otherwise directed by the department, a court of inquiry will not be ordered.

4. The ability of the ship to proceed to port after sustaining so severe an injury reflects credit upon the officers and crew of the *Minnesota* and her efficient condition as to water-tight integrity.

A. W. GRANT.

U. S. S. "MINNESOTA,"
9 October, 1918.

From: Commanding Officer.
To: Commander Battleship Force One.
Subject: Supplemental report on damage sustained by *Minnesota* September 29, 1918.
Reference: (a) Report of damage sustained by striking a mine October 3, 1918.
Inclosures: (6) Statement of L. O. Griggsby, El. 2cl.
  " " A. E. Lynn, Sea. 2cl.
  " " E. J. Meyer, Yeo. 1cl.
  " " L. S. R. Steadman, Cox.
  " " W. Kent, Sea. 2cl.
  " " A. W. Singer, Sea.

1. I have to submit the following report supplementing and modifying paragraph 5 of reference.

2. In paragraph 5 of reference it is stated that L. O. Griggsby, El. 2cl., reported the wake of a torpedo crossing the stern from starboard to port, but no one else observed this wake. A more thorough investigation than had been possible at the time reference was written shows that five other men state that they observed a torpedo wake crossing from starboard to port. The statements of all six men are inclosed.

3. An examination of these statements indicates that whatever it was that these six men saw, they probably all saw the same thing. Two of the men were on lookout watch at the time of the explosion, the other four were awakened by the shock of the explosion. If these men did see a torpedo wake, it is evident from their statements that the torpedo had no direct connection with the explosion, as when they saw the wake the ship must have been at least 1,000 yards from the scene of the explosion.

4. It will be noted that four of these men state that at the time they observed the wake the ship was swinging to the right. As a matter of fact no such change of course was made, the only change of course being to the left, when the course was changed to west (true). This change of course to the left was made just about the time the report of the torpedo wake reached the bridge, my recollection being that the ship had begun to swing to the left when the report reached me. At that time the *Israel*, which had been on the port quarter when the explosion occurred, was coming up rapidly on the starboard side.

5. It was about this time that a dark object on the port bow was reported from the forward netting, and I directed the *Israel* to investigate this object. She turned passed under the stern, and proceeded off the port bow.

6. This ship continued to turn to course west (true), as I deemed this the best course to pursue under the circumstances, for the ship was thus being brought parallel to the reported torpedo wake and heading for the dark object, should it prove to be an enemy submarine. As a matter of fact I did not believe either report to be correct.

7. Through a duplication of orders, the siren was sounded a second time. This duplication was caused by a misunderstanding of a report which led me to believe that the general alarm had been sounded but the siren had not been blown. This second blast was about three minutes after the first blast.

8. After careful consideration of the inclosed statements, I still doubt very seriously if a torpedo wake was really seen and believe that what was seen was some commotion in the water caused by the *Israel*, combined possibly with the débris that must have been washed from the wrecked storerooms in wake of the explosion. As for the dark object reported on the port bow, nothing came of it and it apparently disappeared. I do not believe it had any real existence.

9. The fragment found by the yard authorities in the damaged section of the ship has been photographed and forwarded by the commandant to the Office of Naval Operations. It is hoped that an examination of this fragment will determine definitely the cause of the damage to this ship.

J. V. CHASE.

OCTOBER 6, 1918.

From: Commandant, Fifth Naval District.
To: Chief of Naval Operations.
Subject: American S. S. *San Saba*, formerly S. S. *Colorado*, 2,458 tons gross, owned by the Mallory Line until taken over by the United States Railroad Administration.

1. The above vessel left New York October 3, 1918, at 5 p. m., bound for Tampa, Mobile, with a general cargo. The master was Capt. B. G. Birdsall.

2. Just prior to the sinking her course was from Ambrose Light, vessel sailing south by west ¼ west. At 11.30 p. m., October 3, 1918, she had Barnegat on four points at 12.25 a. m.; October 4, 1918, Barnegat was abeam. At 12.30 a. m., her course was changed to southwest, and 15 minutes later while on this course she was struck. Ship had not been zigzagging. At 12.45 a. m. the vessel was struck amidship well below the water line with such force that she practically broke in two and sank in five minutes, being completely submerged by 12.50 a. m., with her colors flying. There was no moon, and the vessel was under full way when she was struck.

3. As stated by the second officer in inclosure (A) at 12.30 a. m. October 4, 1918, he sighted a very dim green light two points to the port bow about 500 feet distant; after the vessel was struck this light disappeared, and because of this circumstance second officer is convinced that the light came from an enemy submarine and was exposed with the intent of deceiving the *San Saba*. It is felt, however, that this opinion is not conclusive, as the light may have come from a sailing vessel which, warned by the destruction of the *San Saba* and assuming there was an enemy submarine, extinguished her light and escaped without attempting to render assistance to the crew of the *San Saba*. No signals were seen other than the above light to indicate the presence of a submarine. At the time the *San Saba* was struck another vessel heading north one point to the starboard bow, about one-quarter of a mile distant from the *San Saba*, changed her course and headed for the beach. No signals passed between this vessel and the supposed submarine.

4. The *San Saba* was not fitted with wireless, and the only secret code or papers aboard were the routing instructions which went down with the ship.

5. The second officer, figuring from memory, stated that officers and crew totaled 34 persons. This will be verified by Mr. John Staples, assistant marine superintendent,

Pier No. 36, North River, N. Y., who has the crew list and insurance papers. At the time the vessel sank there was no chance to launch the boats or get buoys, and it is believed that many were killed by the force of the explosion, which was so great that the belief is entertained that it came from an anchored mine. It will be noted in the third answer to inclosure (A) the second officer expressed himself as having "heard a heavy noise knocking on the ship's side which followed with an explosion a minute or so afterwards." There was in all probability a shorter lapse of time than the minute described by the second officer between his first hearing the knocking and the subsequent explosion. This was probably the mine bumping along the bottom of the vessel from the bow back to amidship where the explosion took place.

6. Referring to inclosure (D), Adolph Beer, the second officer; Edwardo Simona, seaman; and Pedro Aceredo, coal passer, are the only survivors known to us. Mr. Beer sustained himself by means of a life buoy, and was taken up, according to his own statement, at 4 p. m., by the Norwegian S. S. *Breiford*. The other two men, according to their statements, sustained themselves on an improvised life raft made in the water from wreckage, and were taken up at 4.30 p. m. by the S. S. *Breiford*. These two men further stated that two other members of the crew shared their life raft, but that one died from exposure at 6 a. m. and the second at noon on October 4. These three survivors as noted in reference (E) left Norfolk for New York via the New York, Philadelphia & Norfolk R. R. at 6 p. m., October 5, 1918.

On November 9, 1918, the U. S. S. *Saetia*, one of the naval overseas transportation ships of 2,873 gross tons, owned by the United States Shipping Board, bound from France to Philadelphia, with 10 officers and 74 enlisted men, one Army officer acting as quartermaster, a total of 85, struck a mine 10 miles SSE., magnetic course, Fenwick Island Shoal, from the statements of the members of the crew, about 8.10 or 8.30 a. m. Lieut. Commander Walter S. Lynch, the commanding officer of the U. S. S. *Saetia*, says he was in the wheelhouse when the accident occurred and that he went immediately to the side of the ship and saw that the explosion occurred abreast No. 3 hatch, and that the boats were gotten away immediately, or in about five minutes after the explosion. Sixty-six men were in boats 1, 2, 3, and 4, and 19 men on two life rafts. The papers of the ship were placed in a weighted bag and thrown overboard, as the captain believed the ship had been torpedoed by a submarine.

The ship was returning to the United States in ballast. The chief engineer was injured and the barber (a seaman) sustained a sprained back; two other men were hurt. One had his head split, and the other a split nose—making three men injured slightly and the chief engineer seriously. The chief engineer was in his room; the explosion took place right under his room, and the débris thrown up wounded him. He thinks himself a piece of torpedo went through his shin. No other fragments of a torpedo were found.

Lieut. J. W. Flemming, executive officer of the *Saetia*, placed the confidential papers of the ship in a weighted bag and threw it overboard.

Two of the men, Ensign E. E. Cornell and C. E. America, an oiler, are certain they saw the conning tower of a submarine not more than 200 feet away. However, it is thought probable that they saw part of their own wreckage, and that the ship was sunk by a mine. A total of 85 survivors were later accounted for.

On October 27, 1918, about 10 p. m., the *Chaparra*, Cuban steamship of 1,505 gross tons, with a cargo of sugar, bound from Cuba to New York, was blown up by a mine 10½ miles south by east off Barnegat Light. The crew of 11 men came in the Inlet with the captain in one of their own boats; the balance of the crew landed on North Beach, Coast Guard Station 112.

Capt. Jose Vinolas, the captain of the *Chaparra*, testifies that he is a native of Barcelona, Spain; that he was the captain of the *Chaparra*, and that she was flying the Cuban flag, her owner being Empresa Naviera de Cuba, S. A., Habana, Cuba. That they had a full cargo of sugar consisting of 14,000 bags. That the agents for the ship in New York were Manuel Caragol & Son. That they sailed from Cardenas, Cuba, on October 22, 1918, bound for New York. At the time of the ship's destruction her location was: South 60°, 10 miles from Barnegat, making 8 miles an hour. That on the night of October 27, at 10 p. m., they felt a heavy blow just forward of the bridge on the port side; there was a terrific explosion, and the vessel was fairly lifted out of the water. At the same time a column of water was thrown up which covered the bridge. The vessel listed to port and capsized, sinking within 2½ minutes. They only had time to launch two boats from the starboard side, and managed to save 23 of the crew of their 29. That he fears that the 6 missing men were killed. That they made for Barnegat Light, Station 113, and landed about 8 p. m. on October 28. They were picked up at that place by a boat which took them to Barnegat. The weather was clear with a moderate sea. Saw no submarine. There were various other vessels in the vicinity which were not molested, which leads him to believe that the ship struck a mine. Ship's papers went down with the ship.

The testimony of Capt. Vinolas is corroborated by the members of his crew, all of whom agree that the *Chaparra* was sunk by a mine.

MINE-SWEEPING SHIPS.

The mine-sweeping operations on the European side of the Atlantic are dealt with in another paper. For this duty on the Atlantic coast of the United States the following vessels were employed:

MINE-SWEEPING SHIP.

Name.	S. P. No.	Length.		Draft.	
		Ft.	in.	Ft.	in.
FIRST DISTRICT.					
Easthampton	573	168	8		
Long Island	572	164	4	13	
Lapwing	Navy.	180		9	9½
Surf	341	128	5	13	
Crest	339	125		13	
Breaker	1707	119	8	13	
Billow	1704	119	8	13	
Starling (formerly Petrel)	2981	141	5	13	6
Ibis (formerly Sea Gull)	3051	141	5	13	6
SECOND DISTRICT.					
Macomber, B. F.	980	138	5	12	
Whitecap	340	143		13	5
Comber	344	143		13	5
Lawrence	858	157	8	10	
Price	839	125	5	8	8
Pocomoke	265	115		8	6
Ardent	280	106	5	7	
Mansfield	691	100		10	
THIRD DISTRICT.					
Spray	2491	126	5	22	
Ripple	2439	126	5	22	
Foam	2496	126	5	22	6
Seneca	427	150		12	
New England	1222	130		9	8
Lowell	504	119	4	9	
Coney	346	112		14	
Freehold	347	110	1	11	
Aurora	345	110		13	
Knickerbocker	479	110		11	
Tasco	502	109		12	
Newark	266	107		13	
Crawford	366	100	2	11	
Fulton	247	93	3	12	1
Pentucket	Navy.	92	6	8	9
P. R. R. No. 9	679	92		13	
Cayuga (formerly Powhatan)	Navy.	101		10	
FOURTH DISTRICT.					
Delaware	467	140		11	4
Garner	682	140		14	
McKeever Bros	683	136		12	
S. W. McKeever	1169	136		12	
E. J. McKeever	684	136		10	
Breakwater	681	105		11	
Brown	1050	103		10	
Fearless	724	103		9	6
Vester	686	96	4	8	
FIFTH DISTRICT.					
Spartan	366	105		10	
S. T. No. 2	267	101		11	
Bellows	323	162		14	
Kajeruna	389	153		6	
Struven	332	152		9	5
Messick	322	145		12	
McNeal	312	140			
Margaret	328	128		12	
SIXTH DISTRICT.					
Alaska	3035	131	8	10	
Adams	400	113	3	13	
Ranger	369	137	4	12	
Montauk	392	121		10	
EIGHTH DISTRICT.					
Chame	Army.				
Mariner	Army.				
Engineer	Army.				
Farragut (emergency)	Navy.				

In general, the scheme carried out on the Atlantic coast was to keep constantly swept clear of mines a certain number of channels leading into the principal ports. This mine sweeping was continuous and carried on in connection with the routing of vessels. As an illustration the port of Boston had three channels of approach. The routing officer selected one of these as the channel of exit or entrance for a specified time and this was made in the secret routing instructions issued to the captain of each vessel. This information being given to the commandant of the district, that particular channel of entrance was swept constantly and always immediately in advance of any important vessel or vessels that were leaving or entering port. When the entrance channel was changed by the routing officer the mine-sweeping operations moved with the change. All this work was precautionary, and did not become of real importance until the arrival of the first German submarine on this coast.

MINE-SWEEPING OPERATIONS ON UNITED STATES ATLANTIC COAST.

7 FEBRUARY, 1919.

1. On 18 November a message was received from Admiral Sims, giving location of mine fields laid on Atlantic coast by Germans. These fields are shown on charts Nos. 524 and 3924 in yellow.

2. On November 27, a second message was received from Admiral Sims, giving location of mine fields laid by Germans on the Atlantic coast. This differed somewhat from the first message in that field were shown in the first message that were not in the second message. Four German chartlets were sent, showing locations of mines in second message. These fields are shown on charts Nos. 524 and 3924 in red.

3. On 16 January, a third message was received from Admiral Sims stating that it was complete German information relative to mine fields on Atlantic coast. These are shown on charts Nos. 524 and 3924 in blue. Chartlets were received on February 3 showing the location of these fields. All of the fields given in this last message were also given in both other messages and the number of mines was given in some cases.

4. These fields were as follows:
    No. 1: Northeast of Fire Island Lightship. Number of mines not given.
    No. 2: Off Barnegat Light. Number of mines, 9.
    No. 3: South of Fenwick Island Shoal Lightship. Number of mines, 7.
    No. 4: South of Winter Quarter Shoal Lightship. Number of mines, 8.
    No. 5: Adjoining No. 4, and shown as a very small field, marked on German chartlets as 8–a. Number of mines given by message, 8. Not given on chartlet.

No. 6: Off Chesapeake Bay Buoy 2cB. Number mines given by message, 6. Not shown on chartlet.

No. 7: Off Wimble Shoal Buoy. Number mines, 9.

5. All of these areas, and all of the areas given in other two reports, have been carefully swept.

6. Mines have been found as follows:

Area No. 1: Fire Island.

	Number.
San Diego—Sunk 19 July	1
20 July—Destroyed	3
5 August—Found on Fire Island	2
5 September—Found on Fire Island	1
8 September—Found on Sandy Hook	1
Total	8

Area No. 2: Barnegat.

	Number.
7 September—Mine cut loose by U. S. S. South Carolina	1
8 September—Destroyed 14.5 miles NE. Brigantine Shoals Buoy	1
4 October—U. S. S. San Saba sunk	1
10 October—Destroyed by U. S. S. Teal	1
12 October—Destroyed by U. S. S. Teal	1
14 October—Destroyed by U. S. S. Teal	1
16 October—Destroyed by U. S. S. Freehold	1
27 October—U. S. S. Chaparra sunk	·1
Total	8

German report give nine mines in this field.

Area No. 3: South of Fenwick Island Lighthouse.

	Number.
29 September—U. S. S. Minnesota mined	1
9 November—U. S. S. Seatia sunk	1
9 January—Destroyed by U. S. S. Teal	1
12 January—Destroyed by U. S. S. Teal	1
13 January—Destroyed by U. S. S. Teal	1
14 January—Destroyed by U. S. S. Teal	1
20 January—Destroyed by U. S. S. Teal	1
Total	7

German report gave seven in this area.

Area No. 4: South of Winter Quarter Shoal Lightship.

	Number.
23 November—Destroyed by U. S. S. Rail	4
24 November—Destroyed by U. S. S. Rail	3
Total	7

S. S. *Inland* reported sinking one mine 11 miles SW. Winter Quarter Shoal Lightship 15 January. If this report is correct, it would make eight mines accounted for in this field. German report gave eight mines in this field.

Area No. 5: South of Winter Quarter Shoal Lightship.

No mines have been found in this field, although it has been carefully swept.

138   GERMAN SUBMARINE ACTIVITIES ON ATLANTIC COAST.

Area No. 6: Off Chesapeake Bay Buoy 2CB.

	Number.
22 June—Two miles from Virginia Beach Buoy, destroyed	1
5 July—Lat. 36° 38' N., 75° 44' W., destroyed	1
31 July—Found ashore at Gargathy Inlet	1
18 August—Lat. 36° 08' N., 75° 34' N., destroyed	1
18 August—Four miles off Cape Henry Buoy 2CB, destroyed	1
9 September—Lat. 36° 52' N., long. 75° 44' W., destroyed	1
9 September—Found ashore Coast Guard Station No. 168	1
Total	7

None of these mines were swept up. Those destroyed were found floating or ashore. From German reports, six mines were planted in this area. The mine found at Gargathy Inlet might be credited with this field or the Overfalls field.

Area No. 7: Wimble Shoal.

	Number.
15 August—S. S. Mirlo sunk	1
18 August—Destroyed by U. S. S. Teal	2
25 August—Destroyed by U. S. S. Teal	2
30 August—Destroyed by U. S. S. Teal	2
5 September—Destroyed by U. S. S. Teal	3
Total	10

German reports gave nine mines in this field.

Area No. 8: Off Overfalls Lightship.

This field was not shown on any German chartlet, although one message from Admiral Sims states "across mouth of Delaware River 2 miles east of Overfalls Light."

	Number.
3 June—S. S. Herbert Pratt sunk	1
3 June—Destroyed	2
3 June—Destroyed	1
9 June—Destroyed	1
16 August—Destroyed 5 miles from Five Fathom Bank Lightship	1
10 June, 1919—Found ashore Coast Guard Light No. 140	1
Total	7

The mines swept up in this area were not across the entrance of Delaware, but were on a line about S. by E. from Overfalls Light.

7. Besides these reported areas, the following mines have been reported:

	Number.
20 September—Cut loose by P. V., not destroyed; lat. 40° 48' N., long. 70° 33' W. Reported by S. S. Plassey (doubtful)	1
9 September—Reported by steamship sunk south of Cape Hatteras	1
8 October—Reported by steamship sunk south of Cape Hatteras, lat. 33° 20' N., long. 76° 18' W	1
18 September—Sunk by rifle fire off Halifax	1
10 October—Landed at St. Margarets Bay	1
21 October—Washed ashore Sable Island	1
Total	6

8. The grand total of all mines found is as follows:

	Number.
Outside reported fields	6
Vicinity Overfalls Lightship	7
Vicinity Wimble Shoal	10
Vicinity Chesapeake Bay	7
Vicinity Winter Quarter Shoal Lightship	9
Vicinity Fenwick Island Shoal Lightship	7
Vicinity Barnegat	8
Vicinity Fire Island Lightship	8
Total	62

Of these, three mines were found off Nova Scotia, leaving 57 on the United States Atlantic coast.

9. Besides these mines which have been sunk, reports of mines sighted drifting have been received to the number of 29. While these reports of drifting mines could not be authenticated, only those that the source was considered reliable have been counted.

10. In view of the above, and the fact that all fields reported have been carefully swept, and some of them several times, it is believed that the United States Atlantic coast may be declared clear of mines, and sweeping discontinued.

TABLE No. 1.—*Vessels destroyed by the submarines acting on the surface, using gunfire and bombs, in western Atlantic.*

(Vessels American unless otherwise noted.)

Name.	Class.	Tons.	Gunfire or bomb.	Date.	Position.
Hattie Dunn	Sch	435	B	May 25	37° 24′ N., 75° 05′ W.
Hauppauge (salved)	do	1,446	B	do	37° 27′ N., 75° 09′ W.
Edna	do	325	B	do	37° 30′ N., 74° 52′ W.
Isabel B. Wiley	do	776	B	June 2	39° 10′ N., 73° 07′ W:
Jacob M. Haskell	do	1,778	B	do	Barnegat Light, E. by S., 50 miles.
Edward H. Cole	do	1,791	B	do	Barnegat Light, 50 miles SE. of.
Winneconne	S. S.	1,869	B	June 2	39° 26′ N., 72° 50′ W.
Texel	do	3,210	B	do	38° 58′ N., 73° 13′ W.
Carolina	do	5,093	G	do	38° 57′ N., 73° 06′ W.
Samuel C. Mengel	Sch	915	B	June 3	38° 08′ N., 73° 35′ W.
Eidsvold (Norwegian)	S. S.	1,570	G	June 4	37° 12′ N., 73° 55′ W.
Edward R. Baird, jr	Sch	279	B	do	37° 35′ N., 74° 00′ W.
Vinland (Norwegian)	S. S.	1,143	B	June 5	36° 32′ N., 73° 58′ W.
Pinar Del Rio	do	2,504	G	June 8	36° 16′ N., 73° 50′ W.
Vindeggen (Norwegian)	do	3,179	B	June 8–10	36° 25′ N., 73° 20′ W.
Henrik Lund (Norwegian)	do	4,322	B	June 10	36° 30′ N., 71° 29′ W.
Samoa (Norwegian)	Bk.	1,138	G	June 14	37° 30′ N., 72° 10′ W.
Kringsjaa (Norwegian)	do	1,750	G	do	38° 02′ N., 71° 40′ W.
Chilier (Belgian)	S. S.	2,966	B	June 22	39° 30′ N., 53° 40′ W.
Augvald (Norwegian)	do	3,406	G	June 23	38° 30′ N., 53° 42′ W.
Marosa (Norwegian)	Bk	1,987	B	July 7	40° 00′ N., 50° 35′ W.
Manx King (Norwegian)	Sch	1,729	B	July 8	40° 00′ N., 52° 00′ W.
Perth Amboy	Tug.	435	G	July 21	Coast Guard No. 40 W. (T), 3 miles.
Lansford	Bge	830	G	do	3 miles from Orleans, Mass.
Barge No. 403	do	422	G	do	Do.
Barge No. 740	do	680	G	do	Do.
Barge No. 766	do	527	G	do	Do.
Robert and Richard	Sch	140	B	July 22	Cape Porpoise, 60 miles SE.
Porto (Portuguese)	Bk	1,079	{B / G}	July 27	38° 25′ 36″ N., 61° 46′ 30″ W.
Dornfontein (Canadian)	Sch	776	Burned	Aug. 2	44° 17′ N., 67° 00′ W. (burned).
Muriel	do	120	B	Aug. 3	Seal Island E. (T), 45 miles.
Rob Roy	G. S	112	B	do	Seal Island E. (T), 35 miles.
Sydney B. Atwood	Sch	100	B	do	Seal Island E. (T), 30 miles.
Annie Perry	do	116	B	do	Do.
Nelson A. (Canadian)	do	72	B	Aug. 4	Shelbourne, SE. 25 miles.
O. B. Jennings	Tanker	10,289	G	do	36° 40′ N., 73° 58′ W.

TABLE No. 1.—*Vessels destroyed by the submarines acting on the surface, using gunfire and bombs, in western Atlantic*—Continued.

Name.	Class.	Tons.	Gunfire or bomb.	Date.	Position.
Agnes G. Holland (Canadian).	Sch.....	100	B.......	Aug. 5	Lehave Banks, 15 miles SE. of.
Gladys M. Hollett (Canadian).	...do....	203	B.......	...do....	Do.
Stanley M. Seaman.........	...do....	1,060	B.......	...do....	34° 59′ N., 73° 18′ W.
Merak...................	S. S.....	3,024	B.......	Aug. 6	34° 57′ N., 75° 40′ W.
Diamond Shoal L. S........	C.G.Ves.	590	G.......	...do....	Near Cape Hatteras, approximately 35° 05′ N., 75° 10′ W.
Sydland (Swedish).........	S. S.....	3,031	B.......	Aug. 8	41° 30′ N., 65° 22′ W.
Katie L. Palmer...........	G. S.....	31	B.......	Aug. 10	41° 45′ N., 67° 10′ W.
Reliance..................	...do....	19	B.......	...do....	41° 45′ N., 67° 10′ W.
William H. Starbuck.......	...do....	53	B.......	...do....	41° 45′ N., 67° 10′ W.
Progress..................	...do....	34	B.......	...do....	41° 45′ N., 67° 10′ W.
Aleda May................	...do....	31	B.......	...do....	41° 45′ N., 67° 10′ W.
Mary E. Sennett...........	...do....	27	B.......	...do....	41° 45′ N., 67° 10′ W.
Earl and Nettie............	...do....	24	B.......	...do....	41° 45′ N., 67° 10′ W.
Cruiser...................	...do....	28	B.......	...do....	41° 45′ N., 67° 10′ W.
Old Time.................	...do....	18	B.......	...do....	41° 45′ N., 67° 10′ W.
Dorothy B. Barrett........	Sch.....	2,088	{G....... B.......}	Aug. 14	38° 54′ N., 74° 24′ W.
Madrugada (Brazilian).....	G. S.....	1,613	Burned.	Aug. 15	37° 50′ N., 74° 55′ W.
San Jose (Norwegian)......	S. S.....	1,586	B.......	Aug. 17	42° 10′ N., 64° 42′ W.
Nordhav (Norwegian)......	Bk......	2,846	B.......	...do....	35° 42′ N., 74° 05′ W.
Triumph (Canadian).......	S. T	239	C.......	Aug. 20	60 miles S. by W. of Cranberry Island (T) (captured).
Lucille M. Schnare (Canadian).	Sch.....	121	B.......	...do....	Cape Canso, N. ½ E. (T), 52 miles.
Frances J. O'Hara, jr......	...do....	117	B.......	...do....	Do.
A. Piatt Andrew...........	...do....	141	B.......	...do....	Do.
Uda A. Saunders (Canadian).	...do....	124	B.......	...do....	44° 31′ N., 60° 30′ W.
Pasadena (Canadian).......	...do....	119	B.......	...do....	55 miles SSE. from Cape Canso, Nova Scotia.
Sylvania..................	...do....	136	B.......	Aug. 21	Cape Canso, SE. by E. 90 miles.
Diomed (British)..........	S. S.....	7,523	G.......	...do....	40° 43′ N., 65° 15′ W.
Notre Dame de Lagarde (French).	F. V.....	145	B.......	Aug. 22	45° 32′ N., 58° 57′ W.
Bianca (salved) (Canadian)	Sch	408	B.......	Aug. 24	43° 13′ N., 61° 05′ W.
E. B. Walters (Canadian).	...do....	126	B.......	Aug. 25	46° 33′ N., 57° 33′ W.
C. M. Walters (Canadian).	...do....	107	B.......	...do....	46° 33′ N., 57° 33′ W.
Verna D. Adams (Canadian).	...do....	132	B.......	...do....	46° 33′ N., 57° 33′ W.
J. J. Flaherty.............	...do....	162	B.......	...do....	46° 33′ N., 57° 33′ W.
Eric (British).............	S. S.....	583	B.......	...do....	Gallantry Light, SE. by E. 70 miles.
Gloaming (Canadian)......	Sch.....	130	B.......	Aug. 26	46° 02′ N., 57° 35′ W.
Rush.....................	S. T	162	B.......	...do....	44° 30′ N., 58° 02′ W.
Potentate (Canadian)......	Sch.....	136	B.......	Aug. 30	50° 30′ N., 47° 00′ W.
Elsie Porter (Canadian)....	...do....	136	B.......	...do....	50° 30′ N., 47° 00′ W.
Gamo (Portuguese)........	...do....	315	B.......	Aug. 31	46° 00′ N., 32° 00′ W.
Constanza (Danish)........	...do....	199	B.......	Sept. 11	62° 30′ N., 35° 00′ W.
Kingfisher................	S. T	353	B.......	Sept. 20	43° 31′ N., 61° 53′ W.
Industrial (British)........	S. V.....	330	B.......	Oct. 4	37° 57′ N., 66° 41′ W.
Stifinder (Norwegian)......	Bk......	1,746	B.......	Oct. 13	37° 22′ N., 53° 30′ W.

TABLE No. 2.—*Vessels destroyed by the submarine submerged and firing torpedoes.*

(Vessels American unless otherwise noted.)

Name.	Class.	Tons.	Date.	Position.
Harpathian (British).........	S. S.....	4,588	June 5	36° 30′ N., 75° 00′ W.
Dwinsk (British).............	...do....	8,173	June 18	38° 30′ N., 61° 15′ W.
Tortuguero (British)..........	...do....	4,175	June 26	55° 50′ N., 15° 30′ W.
Tokuyama Maru (Japanese)..	...do....	7,029	Aug. 1	39° 12′ N., 70° 23′ W.
Luz Blanca (Canadian).......	...do....	4,868	Aug. 5	43° 48′ N., 63° 40′ W.
Pennistone (British)..........	...do....	4,139	Aug. 11	39° 50′ N., 67° 25′ W.
Sommerstadt (Norwegian)...	...do....	3,875	Aug. 12	40° 10′ N., 72° 45′ W.
Frederick R. Kellogg.........	...do....	7,127	Aug. 13	12 miles N. of Barnegat Light.
Bergsdalen (Norwegian)......	...do....	2,550	Aug. 27	45° 10′ N., 55° 10′ W.
Shortind (Norwegian)........	...do....	2,560	Sept. 2	45° 15′ N., 30° 00′ W.
Leixoes (Portuguese).........	...do....	3,345	Sept. 12	42° 45′ N., 51° 37′ W.
Ticonderoga.................	U. S. S...	5,130	Sept. 30	43° 05′ N., 38° 43′ W.
Alberto Treves (Italian)......	S. S.....	3,838	Oct. 3	38° 20′ N., 67° 10′ W.
Lucia.......................	S. S.....	6,744	Oct. 17	38° 05′ N., 50° 50′ W.

TABLE No. 3.—*Vessels damaged or destroyed by mines.*

Name.	Class.	Tons.	Date.	Position.
Herbert L. Pratt (salved)....	Tanker.	7,145	June 3	Overfalls Lightship, N. 45° W. (T), 2½ miles.
San Diego (salved)...........	U. S. S..	13,680[1]	July 19	40° 30′ N., 73° 00′ W.
Mirlo (British)...............	S. S.....	6,978	Aug. 16	35° 30′ N., 75° 18′ W.
Minnesota (salved)..........	U. S. S..	17,650[1]	Sept. 29	38° 05′ N., 74° 05′ W.; made port, Philadelphia, Pa.
San Saba.....................	S. S.....	2,458	Oct. 4	39° 40′ N., 73° 55′ W.
Chaparra (Cuban)............	...do....	1,505	Oct. 27	S. 60° E., 10 miles from Barnegat.
Saetia........................	...do....	2,873	Nov. 9	E. from Ocean City, Md., about 10 miles SSE. (magnetic) from Fenwick Island Lightship.

[1] Displacement.

An analysis of the above tables is of considerable interest. Of the vessels attacked by the submarine on the surface, 62 were sailing vessels, tugs, barges, and motor boats, and 17 were steamers. Of the sailing vessels, there will be noted that many of them were very small, schooners from 100 tons up, besides a number of motor boats varying between 18 and 117 tons.

It will be noted that the vessels torpedoed were all steamships from moderate to large size. It is apparent that the submarine intended to take no chances, and where the vessel appeared large enough to probably be armed the torpedo was resorted to, whereas the small helpless craft was openly attacked and ruthlessly destroyed.

Of the vessels destroyed or injured by mines all were large vessels.

The German campaign, by means of submarines on the Atlantic coast of the United States, so far as concerned the major operations of the war, was a failure. Every transport and cargo vessel bound for Europe sailed as if no such campaign was in progress. All coastwise shipping sailed as per schedule, a little more care in routing vessels being observed. There was no interruption to the coast patrol which, on the contrary, became rather more active. The small vessels of the submarine chaser and converted yacht types, armed with very small guns but provided with depth charges, scoured the coast regardless of the fact that the enemy submarines were equipped with ordnance very much heavier than their own. There was no stampede on the Atlantic coast; no excitement; everything went on in the usual calm way and, above all, this enemy expedition of the Atlantic coast did not succeed in retaining on the Atlantic coast any vessels that had been designed for duty in European waters.

APPENDIX.

NAVY DEPARTMENT,
OFFICE OF NAVAL OPERATIONS,
Washington, 6 February, 1918.

From: A special board to formulate a plan of defense in home waters.
To: Chief of Naval Operations.
Subject: Defense against submarine attack in home waters.
Reference: (a) Opnav. letter No. ——— of February 1, 1918, convening Board.

1. Pursuant to instructions, reference (a), the Board convened at 10 a. m., Monday, 4 February, 1918, all members present except Lieut. Commander Foy, who was present beginning with the afternoon session. As a result of its deliberations, the Board submits the following report:

BASIS OF DISCUSSION.

2. The Germans have completed a number of cruising submarines of large radius and large capacity, and these may be used on our coast with a view to divert some of our military activity away from European waters. The constant increase of anti-submarine forces abroad may compel an enemy effort to cause such a diversion, and the comparative openness of American waters offers a good field for submarine activities. Information is indefinite as to the number of enemy submarines possibly intended for American waters, but an approximation is sufficient for discussion. The salient features of the situation are therefore taken to be as follows:

GENERAL SITUATION.

3. A division of four submarine cruisers, each armed with 6-inch guns, 36 mines, and 16 torpedoes, and capable of at least one month's activity on our coast, may appear in American waters without warning.

4. Their aim will be to destroy shipping, interrupt the transport of troops and supplies to Europe, interfere with our coastwise shipping, by these means causing the recall from abroad of some of our naval force for defense of home waters. Bombardment of coast towns may also be done, with a view to heighten popular demand for local protection, and thereby embarrass the naval administration.

5. They will employ mines, guns, torpedoes, and bombs. Their principal activities may be expected to be directed against the main shipping centers—Halifax, New York, Hampton Roads, and Florida Straits. At the same time, by activity of some kind in several localities so separated as to suggest the presence of a large force, they may expect to produce a maximum popular disturbance early in their campaign.

GENERAL POLICY.

6. The general policy of the United States is to send the maximum possible force abroad for offensive operations in the active theater of war. This policy the Board has kept constantly in mind to the end that there might be no weakening of it.

7. With regard to any force still retained or in the future to be held in American waters which might be suitable abroad, the Board has been governed by the consideration that trans-Atlantic transit, the security of which is the chief task of the

naval force based on America, depends for its success upon a sufficient guard in American as well as in European waters. The force retained in American waters can not with reasonable military prudence be reduced below the minimum required for meeting the emergency here being considered. It has devolved upon this Board to determine what that minimum is; and such determination should be held to against the repeated urgings, to send all force abroad, of individuals who have not fully considered the situation as a whole. In the course of our discussions this principle had repeatedly to be adverted to and reaffirmed. Emphasis is laid upon it as the basis of any plan for defense against hostile operations near our coast.

Policy in the Face of Submarines.

8. In the event of actual submarine hostilities on this coast, first disclosed perhaps by the sinking of a steamer by a mine, what shall be the policy as to shipping? Shall it continue, with the least possible interruptions, or shall it be held in port until the enemy submarines shall have been located and destroyed? The latter course would be to surrender at once to the enemy a large measure of success in his purpose.

9. It is recognized that to keep on sending out shipping may involve the loss of some vessels soon after departure from our ports; we are, notwithstanding, convinced that this course should be pursued. To hold vessels in port until all is clear will encourage the enemy, both near and abroad; it will help prolong his period of activity on our coast and will demoralize and confuse our arrangements on shore far more than would the loss of one or two vessels. Abroad the suspension of arrivals for several weeks would have an effect serious beyond calculation. On the other hand to continue with our sailings boldly, unshaken in our general offensive policy, would, hearten our own people while giving no ground to the enemy submarine. The escort with our convoys would force the submarines to take a chance for every sinking they might attempt. From the first disclosure of their presence their accomplishing anything in our waters should become increasingly difficult, and this can only come about by our taking the strong line of action.

10. On this point it is therefore the decision of the Board that we should keep on sending shipping out with the least possible delay, at the same time taking all possible offensive measures to remove the danger.

11. The measures necessary to put into effect the foregoing policy divide under two general heads—control of shipping and military offensive.

Control of Shipping.

12. After discussing the several questions involved successively, the Board came to the following conclusions:

Outbound shipping.

(*a*) That where mines have appeared, outbound shipping should be routed clear of them through a swept channel.

(*b*) That shipping should use swept channels as soon after the sweeping as circumtances permit.

(*c*) That coastwise shipping should proceed at night and independently. (See change.)

(*d*) That ocean shipping should proceed in convoys.

(*e*) That the convoys should be as large as the available escort permit.

(*f*) That convoys should be preceded to the 50-fathom curve by four submarine chasers equipped with listening attachment. (See change.)

(*g*) That air scouts should patrol the convoy's intended course, at least out to the 50-fathom curve, from the convoy's departure until it clears 50 fathoms or darkness comes on. (See change.)

(h) That convoys should be accompanied by an ocean escort, by an antisubmarine escort to the 50-fathom curve, and by one or more escorting submarines for lookout. (See change.)

(i) That the ocean escort should be a cruiser, or a converted merchant vessel in naval commission, armed with guns of 5-inch or larger caliber.

(j) That the antisubmarine escort should consist of submarine chasers armed with depth bombs and guns up to 3-inch caliber. (See change.)

(k) That the antisubmarine escort for a convoy should be the number required by approved instructions in force at the time.

(l) That the escorting submarines with a convoy should precede it, running awash, to keep lookout for enemy submarines and warn and divert the convoy before the enemy submarine can sight it. (Omit; see change.)

13. Considering a suggestion that interference with shipping would be made more difficult by sending convoys out of more ports than are so used at present, it was concluded that available escort vessels were too few, that land transportation would be disarranged, and that harbor facilities would be taxed too much beyond their normal capacity, to offer any success for such a measure. Accordingly,

(m) The dispatch of convoys should be limited to New York and Hampton Roads, as at present.

14. The foregoing applies mainly to the area between Nantucket Shoals and Cape Hatteras. Shipping out of the Gulf, including the important fuel-oil supply, has not as yet been convoyed and escort force is not available to establish such a convoy service.

15. A division of submarines and an aviation station are located at Key West, and dependence must be placed upon these and upon local and passing traffic and the coastwise lookout service for information of hostile submarines in the vicinity; and in such event, shipping out of the Gulf of Mexico should be routed south of Cuba. (See change.)

16. In the event of submarines operating against shipping coming from the canal shipping may be routed via Cape Horn; but action as to this would be too much subject to the particulars of the situation at the time for any more definite conclusion by this Board. (Omit; see change.)

INCOMING SHIPPING.

17. In order to route incoming shipping clear of submarine dangers, it is the consensus of the Board that the best means would be return convoys. This would insure the correct receipt of and compliance with routing instructions. Not enough cruisers being available to convoy return shipping, however, there is no choice but that—

(n) Return shipping to the United States must be independent of convoys. (See change.)

18. Considering the great extent of coastal waters inside the 50-fathom curve, it will be at best possible only to keep one avenue of approach to New York and one to Hampton Roads sufficiently swept for a practical degree of safety from enemy mines. Our sweeping task is lessened by the fact that only a small number of mines can be brought over by submarines. Judging by the latest experience abroad, these may be planted in small groups in several widely separated locations. There being only a few mine sweepers available, they can be employed to the best advantage by *searching out* a route clear of mines rather than by attempting to keep several fixed routes *swept clear*. In searching formation sweepers can cover more ground than in sweeping formation. The Board concludes, therefore—

(o) That incoming shipping should be routed into port through approach channels that have been found by searching or sweeping to be safe.

SECRECY IN ROUTING.

19. To the end that vessels may be warned daily of the positions of submarines and mines and receive directions for their movements—

(p) Return shipping to the United States should be controlled by radio from the United States.

20. To provide for the necessary secrecy of such radio control—

(q) Each belligerent vessel should carry a commissioned communication officer of her own or of United States nationality. Such officer would be in charge of codes, would decipher code messages and transmit them to the master of the vessel, but would have no authority over nor responsibility for the vessel. He need have no seagoing experience, but must be trustworthy and of sufficient education; hence to supply these communication officers, our trained personnel need not be drawn upon.

21. The foregoing provision must be undertaken immediately, to be available for use when wanted; but wholly apart from its value in emergency, the Board strongly recommends its adoption as a measure that will greatly promote the safe routing of ships in the war zone and thereby reduce tonnage losses.

22. Until commissioned communication officers shall have been established on board belligerent vessels, as provided in paragraph (q) above, other means to facilitate communication with incoming ships are recommended to be established, consisting of a system of secret routing for ships approaching this coast similar to the method in use in the war zone. The Board does not consider this as an alternative but only as a temporary means, pending the adoption of the commissioned officer system, which alone of the two has the requisite reliability and flexibility.

MILITARY OFFENSIVE.

23. The foregoing measures cover the procedure necessary to carry out the policy recommended affecting shipping, namely, to continue sending it out with the least possible interruption. These measures alone constitute one means of combating enemy submarines both actively, by resisting their attacks upon convoys, and passively, by wearing out their endurance, ultimately depriving them of their main object—breaking the supply abroad. But active measures to remove the submarines from our waters are necessary, in addition, lest their stay be prolonged to our disadvantage and the attendant risk to shipping continue long enough to have serious internal effect in this country.

FIXED AND LOCAL DEFENSE.

24. Connected with measures of active offense the subject of purely passive defensive measures were considered. Fixed fortifications under the Coast Artillery should be sufficient to prevent the actual penetration of our interior waters. In addition to this, all districts have patrols at the entrance to principal harbors, and in the second, third, and fifth districts there are guns afloat in the old battleships *Massachusetts*, *Indiana*, and *Iowa*. These means the Board considers sufficient to frustrate any attempt which might be made to enter interior waters.

25. Request has been made of the War Department to supplement the forces of the naval districts employed in coast defense by one or two gun batteries at salient points along the coast which might be bombarded. While such an attack might cause no great material damage, popular clamor might compel some military dispositions seriously affecting the active theater of operations. The War Department has replied, however, that no guns can be employed for this purpose.

SUBMARINE NETS.

26. Submarine nets were considered as part of fixed defenses. As to offshore nets outside New York and Hampton Roads and Long Island Sound, even if the material

were available, the operation of planting them is too extensive to be undertaken within a short time; and even when in place, the nets are of small effect unless thoroughly patrolled, not to mention the effort and material required for upkeep.

(r) The Board concludes, therefore, that no outside nets should be considered, but that inside nets as maintained or planned by the Coast Artillery, and at Base Two and Cape Henry by the Navy, should be retained, and that these nets, together with fixed fortifications and harbor patrols, will afford sufficient security against any hostile attempt to enter a principal harbor.

MINES.

27. Mines which are submerged at a depth which is dangerous to surface craft, including submarines (subsurface mine fields), would be a greater embarrassment to our own vessels in the situation under consideration than to the enemy's. We can not afford to endanger or restrict the movements of our own vessels, which are at best very limited in number, and there being no hostile surface vessels involved, the Board concludes—

(s) That no subsurface mine fields should be included in the present plans. (See change.)

28. At present the Mark VI mine has no attachment for safety in case of shallow planting, and the mines of earlier marks are not capable of deep planting without modification of the depth-regulating apparatus. Even with such modification, they could not be planted at a rapid rate. These mines also have no safety provisions against shallow planting. As a whole, therefore, we have no mines suitable for deep mine fields at present. A safety attachment for the Mark VI mine is being developed, and mines of that mark are being manufactured in considerable number, so that within several months we may have a supply which could be used in emergency for deep mine fields on our own coast, though destined for another project abroad.

29. The free operation of our own submarines would, however, be endangered in the vicinity of deep mine fields, and hostile submarines may be expected to operate far enough offshore to be clear of any deep fields large enough to embarrass them, unless we used a number of mines beyond any possibility of supply. The chance of deep mine fields contributing materially to the destruction of enemy submarines is remote on account also of the small number of submarines that may be expected to operate. The Board therefore concludes that—

(t) Unless hostile activities on our coast be prolonged beyond control by other measures, no deep mine fields should be planted; but

(u) That naval districts be prepared to plant mines and that steps be taken to make mines available for planting a deep barrier across the approaches to New York Harbor and Hampton Roads. And, further (see change),

(v) That districts should be prepared to announce fictitious mine fields in the event of the emergency contemplated actually arising and to route shipping accordingly.

30. As a whole, the passive defenses of the first, second, third, and fifth districts are deemed sufficient for the defense of the principal harbors in those districts.

ACTIVE OFFENSIVE.

31. The purpose of measures of active offense is to locate and destroy the submarines.

32. The principal operations of these submarines must be conducted in the offing of New York, off the Capes of the Chesapeake, and in the Florida Straits and Yucatan Channel. In order to continue their operations beyond their self-contained capacity, the enemy submarines must replenish from some near-by base or by some means of supply from our coast or some neutral source.

INFORMATION SERVICE.

33. To locate the submarines we have an organized lookout service in operation along the coasts in the several naval districts and also a secret service of sufficiently

wide extent and connections. These should be warned to be on the lookout for evidences of any use of our coasts and of any support to enemy submarines from on or near our coast.

34. The same applies to the possibility of the enemy's use of a base in the Bahamas. Connection of our intelligence service with that of the British in the Bahama Islands should be sufficient provision to secure timely information. In this connection it is stated by the commander of squadron 2, cruiser force, that a reconnoissance of the Bahama Islands shows little suitability of that region for use as a submarine base.

AIR PATROL.

35. The Naval Air Service, in addition to assisting the escort of convoys, may contribute materially to the locating of submarines by air scouting off our coast, including the use of kites and dirigibles, especially between Nantucket Shoals and Cape Hatteras. It is assumed that this may and will be done should the contemplated emergency arise.

ACTIVE FORCES.

36. The situation has not yet sufficiently developed to enable the Board to do more than outline the offensive action that may be taken. The conclusion was reached—

(*aa*) That provision should now be made for forces to be available where likely to be needed, to detect and locate enemy submarines, to act upon information of their whereabouts, and to be capable of attacking a submarine if encountered.

37. The kind of force that should accompany convoys has already been stated. In addition, it is the Board's conclusion—

(*bb*) That, in addition to harbor and inshore vessels, there should be a force of destroyers and of submarines ready to act upon information of hostile submarines near our coast.

(*cc*) That the strength of these should be, in the first naval district, 2 destroyers, 1 submarine; third naval district, 4 destroyers, 5 submarines; fifth naval district, 4 destroyers, 5 submarines.

38. The possibility of there being more submarines capable of service at the New London and other bases, and of more destroyers being under shakedown, after the building program shall have begun to yield more frequent deliveries, was taken into account, as also the submarines at Key West and Panama and the vessels already in the several districts. The forces named in paragraph (*cc*) above are the minimum increase needed.

CONTROL OF ACTIVE FORCES.

39. The lookout service and reports of coastwise and other passing traffic first come under the cognizance of the naval districts, and these districts will have at disposal the forces intended to act according to the situation that may arise. The success of measures against submarines in the majority of cases will probably depend on the celerity with which forces act on information received. This indicates that their direction and control should be in the hands of the respective naval district commandants, and the Board so recommends.

PROVIDING THE NECESSARY FORCES.

40. Adverting to the policy laid down in paragraph 7, the Board, examining the sources that could be drawn upon for the force specified in paragraph (*cc*), concluded that the best practical plan was to utilize new destroyers and new submarines during the shakedown period before departure for European waters.

41. Considering first the destroyers, this would involve a delay at first, but this is unavoidable if adequate provision is to be made for the contingency under con-

sideration. Besides, the delay is not so long as at first apparent. Not less than two weeks is the probable minimum required by the average new destroyer for preliminary shakedown. To this some few days more may be needed for new fittings constantly being added, which would be installed on board on this side instead of abroad. During the time so spent the destroyer would be available for emergency if here; but if abroad she would not be operating so no operating time is lost on this account. Further, by a somewhat longer shakedown time on our coast, together with a quick run across instead of a slow passage for shakedown en route, the ultimate date of beginning service in the war zone would be little affected. The same applies to the submarines.

42. The Board concluded, therefore—

(*dd*) That new destroyers should remain on our coast for one month shakedown after commissioning, to be available for service in the event of the appearance here of hostile submarines; but that not more than nine at one time need be so detained if prepared earlier to sail for distant service.

(*ee*) That the nine destroyers so detained shall be stationed one in the first, and four each in the third and fifth naval districts, the commandants of which shall be instructed to use them as necessary in the event of hostile submarines appearing on this coast; otherwise not to employ them, but instead to allow them all possible freedom in their training for active service.

(*ff*) That to provide the necessary submarines for the emergency service contemplated, new submarines should have a shakedown period of two months; their training course not to be interrupted but to continue in its normal course from its usual base; but upon the appearance of hostile submarines, one division to be escorted to New York and one division to Hampton Roads; further, while based on these places, to continue their training to such extent as the situation may permit; the respective naval district commandants to observe the same attitude as toward destroyers, stated in paragraph (*ee*).

43. Still other forces are required, which, with available sources, may be stated briefly:

(*gg*) Participation by any force from the Atlantic Fleet, other than the Cruiser Force as now employed in convoy duty, is not counted upon.

(*hh*) A force of 30 submarine chasers each, based on New York and on Hampton Roads, will be needed for convoy escort and listening service. To provide these, the earliest deliveries intended for other districts should be diverted to the third and fifth districts until the necessary total numbers are present in these districts.

(*ii*) One destroyer and one submarine permanently employed in experimentation are counted upon, with one new destroyer under paragraphs (*dd*) and (*ee*), to make up the force for the first naval district.

(*jj*) In order to accomplish the sweeping task without delaying shipping, in or outbound, there must be based at New York and Hampton Roads, sweepers enough to keep in service two sweeping groups of three pairs each. For this there must be 18 or more mine sweepers at each place named. As neither the third district nor the fifth has this number, the Board recommends that sweepers from the first and second districts be added to those of the third district when the occasion arises, and, similarly, those from the fourth district to go to the fifth district.

(*kk*) For the air service to be performed, it is estimated that a force of 40 airplanes will be needed at Rockaway Inlet and at Hampton Roads in order to insure 16 planes being serviceable for escort duty; and this number should be made available. (See change.)

WEAKNESS OF DISTRICT VESSELS.

44. The armament of such vessels of the naval districts as are seaworthy is too light for engaging a single submarine with success, except by surprise. It is therefore recommended—

(*ll*) That in view of the possible appearance of submarines armed with 5 or 6 inch guns, the armament of district vessels be replaced by larger calibers as soon as practicable, but not to the deprivation of suitable armament for vessels navigating the war zone.

AID TO NAVIGATION.

45. In order to increase the navigating difficulties of submarines, especially in fog and darkness, and also to prevent the converging of shipping at a point favorable for submarines to operate, the Board recommends—

(*mm*) That immediate steps be taken to install on board all outside lightships on the Atlantic Coast radio and listening equipment;

(*nn*) And that, upon the appearance of a hostile submarine in American waters, all submarine signal bells be stopped, the bells and whistles on outside buoys silenced, and Nantucket Shoal lightship be withdrawn. (See change.) (See additions (*oo*) and (*pp*).)

46. The Board has included in this report only such detail as has seemed necessary to make its recommendations clear, to show the extent to which existing dispositions have been taken into account, to make a decision where there has been or may be doubt or wide difference of opinion, and especially to strengthen the statement as to the minimum of increase in force necessary to retain on this side. In view of existing machinery for executing plans, it seems inadvisable to go further into details.

(Signed) M. JOHNSTON,
Rear Admiral, U. S. Navy.
PHILIP ANDREWS,
Captain, U. S. Navy.
S. S. ROBINSON,
Captain, U. S. Navy.
L. R. DE STEIGUER,
Captain U. S. Navy.
R. R. BELKNAP,
Captain, U. S. Navy.
L. MCNAMEE,
Captain, U. S. Navy.
J. R. Y. BLAKELY,
Captain, U. S. Navy.
S. P. FULLINWIDER,
Commander, U. S. Navy.
J. V. BABCOCK,
Commander, U. S. Navy.
E. J. FOY,
Lieut. Commander, U. S. Navy.

Approved as changed by modifications, etc., appended.

W. S. BENSON.

NAVY DEPARTMENT,
OFFICE OF NAVAL OPERATIONS,
Washington, March 6, 1918.

The foregoing plan, "Defense Against Submarine Attack in Home Waters," with the following alterations, modifications, or changes, is approved. Steps will be taken immediately to put it into effect.

MODIFICATIONS AND CHANGES OR ALTERATIONS—OUTBOUND SHIPPING.

PAR. 12 (*c*). That the best practice is to have the coastwise shipping proceed by day, hugging the shore and keeping within the 5-fathom curve, or as near it as practicable. Also, since it is the policy of the shipping committees charged with such work to allocate the smallest and least valuable ships to the coasting trade, it, as a matter of expediency, should be the policy to protect said shipping by the means within the capacity of the naval districts through which the coastwise shipping passes rather than to attempt to divert guns from ships in the trans-Atlantic trade or to allocate cruisers for the protection of our coastwise trade, except in such cases where the districts could not afford protection or the guns were readily available. That if it were found expedient to route coastwise ships at night that they should sail independently, being routed with due regard to the warnings received of the location of enemy submarines.

PAR. 12 (*f*). Change to read: That convoys should be preceded to the 50-fathom curve or as far beyond as necessary by four submarine chasers equipped with listening attachments.

PAR. 12 (*g*). Change to read: That air scouts should patrol the convoys' intended course out at least to the 50-fathom curve and as far beyond as circumstances permit, or until darkness comes on.

PAR. 12 (*h*). Omit the words "and by one or more escorting submarines for lookout." It is the policy to use our submarines offensively against hostile submarines, and their movements are influenced by the movements of hostile submarines, not by the movements of our convoys.

PAR. 12 (*j*). Add at the end of paragraph: "and also of destroyers if advisable."

PAR. 12 (*l*). Omit entirely.

PAR. 15. Last two lines, change to read: "shipping out of the Gulf of Mexico should be routed north or south of Cuba as circumstances existing at the time renders most expedient."

PAR. 16. Held to be not sound, as the delay thus caused to shipping practically reduces its efficiency to a lower limit than the actual submarine sinkings could impose.

PAR. 17 (*n*). Add the words "until such time as convoys can be established."

PAR. 27 (*s*). That in view of the slight advantages to be derived as compared to the inordinate risk to shipping, the subsurface mine will not be used offensively against hostile submarines. That it is legitimate to use it defensively, but that such use should be confined to the purpose of barring entrance and exit to our principal shipping ports and confined to the lowest limits compatible with a fair degree of safety. That even when a defensive mine field is laid, a clear and ample passage must be left for the transit of shipping, and this passage must under no circumstances be mined, but be patrolled and protected by other means. That all mines upon being detached from their moorings must become innocuous. That the three places to be considered now as coming within the scope of defensive mining are New York, capes of the Chesapeake, east entrance to Long Island Sound.

PAR. 29 (*u*). After the words Hampton Roads, add: "But that owing to the great demand for mines abroad this step be not considered now."

PAR. 43 (*kk*). Read that a force consisting of at least one squadron of 20 airplanes will be needed at each station (Rockaway Inlet and Hampton Roads), and that this number should be made available as soon as practicable, not to interfere with the European program.

PAR. 45 (*nn*). Omit the words "and Nantucket Shoal Lightship be withdrawn."

PAR. 45. Add new paragraph: (*oo*). "Be prepared upon special order of the Navy Department to withdraw all light vessels on the Atlantic coast, but this will be done only when the necessity is strongly apparent."

PAR. 45. Add new paragraph: (*pp*). "Establish listening stations at the entrances to Chesapeake Bay, New York, and the east end of Long Island Sound. If these stations prove effective and are needed, to extend the system to other important localities."

(Signed)   W. S. BENSON.

APPENDIX.

28754–26:146.
Op–36.

NAVY DEPARTMENT,
Washington, March 13, 1918.

[Memorandum for all divisions of Office of Naval Operations.]

Subject: Execution of a plan for defense against submarines in home waters.

1. In accordance with the attached plan and approved modifications, the following parts thereof are assigned to the divisions of this office for information and action. Where a part has been assigned to more than one division, the officers in charge will cooperate in its execution in accordance with the duties of their respective divisions.

2. Provisions of the plan that require the action of any bureau will be prepared by the head of the division concerned and transmitted to the bureau after signature by the Chief of Naval Operations.

Operations Division.—Assistant for operations, paragraphs 6, 7, 10, and 45; overseas transportation, paragraphs 12 (c) (d) (e), 13 (m), 17 (n), 19 (p), and 22; ship movements, paragraphs 12 (i), 19 (p), 36 (aa), 37 (bb) (cc), 39, 42 (dd) (ff), 43 (gg) (hh) (ii) (jj); submarine detection, paragraphs 12 (j), 36 (aa), 37 (bb) (cc), 42 (dd) (ee) (ff), 43 (hh) (ii) (jj), and 45 (mm) (nn) (pp).

Material Division.—Paragraphs 12 (i) (j), 26 (r), 27 (s), 29 (t) (u), 36 (aa), 43 (ii) (kk), 44 (ll), 45 (mm) (pp).

Intelligence Division.—Paragraphs 32, 33, and 34.

Communications Division.—Paragraphs 19 (p), 20 (q), and 21.

Naval Districts Division.—Paragraphs 12 (a) (b) (c) (f) (g) (h) (j) (k), 15, 18 (o), 24, 26 (r), 27 (s), 29 (t) (u) (v), 32, 33, 34, 35, 37 (bb) (cc), 39, 42 (dd) (ee) (ff), 43 (hh) (ii) (jj) (kk), 44 (ll), 45 (mm) (nn) (oo) (pp).

Aviation Division.—Paragraphs 12 (g), 15, 35, 36 (aa), and 43 (kk).

(Signed)   W. S. BENSON.

Op–23.

28 MARCH, 1918.

From: Chief of Naval Operations.
To: Commandant, first, second, third, fourth, fifth, sixth, seventh, and eighth naval districts.
Subject: Plan for coastwise shipping in case of submarine activities on this coast.

1. It is requested that the commandant of each naval district forward to the department (operations) general recommendations on the above subject and detailed recommendations as it concerns his district. It is desired that there be taken into consideration all local conditions affecting the plan, such as the prevalence of fogs and particularly unfavorable weather at certain seasons; the facilities for coastwise shipping entering harbors under all conditions of tide, night, etc.; character of the coastal waters, whether coasting may be done in less than 10 fathoms; the offshore areas in which there may be danger of colliding with outbound convoys at night, etc.

2. Outlines below as a guide is a plan under consideration by the department.

(a) To all customs officials, shipowners, and others connected with operating vessels in coastwise trade will be sent out immediately a circular letter stating that in the event of reports being received of submarine activities on this coast upon notification the control of all shipping will immediately pass into the hands of the Navy. Coastal vessels may expect radio war warnings to be sent out in plain English giving notice of the presence of submarines and ordering all coastal vessels within designated districts to put into the nearest port for orders. The limits of the naval districts will be defined and the captains of the vessels will be instructed to ask for instructions from the naval district commandant, whose telegraph address and telephone number will be given.

(b) Until the actual presence of submarines on this side, coastwise shipping is to follow the normal routes and schedules.

(c) Acting upon warnings received of the location of enemy submarines, shipping will be routed in those districts, where it may be necessary, along the following general plan:

(1) In all cases the control of shipping within a district will be in the hands of the district commandant in order that the proper coordination may be obtained along the whole coast. This control will follow a general doctrine, and the commandant of each district will be informed of the control of these districts adjacent to his district.

(2) The best practice is to have coastwise shipping proceed by day, hugging the shore and keeping within the 5-fathom curve or as near to it as practicable. Also, since it is the policy of the shipping committees charged with such work to allocate the smallest and least valuable ships to the coasting trade, it, as a matter of expediency, should be the policy to protect such shipping by means within the districts through which the coastwise shipping passes.

(3) When it is found expedient to route coastwise shipping by night, it should proceed independently, being routed with due regard to the warnings received of the location of enemy submarine.

(4) *Districts 1, 2, and 3—New York and northward.*—All coastwise shipping bound to or from New York, proceed via Long Island Sound, keeping to the northern shore, and travel by night or day as far as New London.

Since it is impractical to follow the 5-fathom curve from New London northward, proceed (1) by day or night via Buzzards Bay and Cape Cod Canal, or (2) by day or night via Vineyard Sound, or (3) independently by night coasting when necessary to go outside.

Northward from Nantucket Shoals or Cape Cod Canal proceed independently by night coasting.

(5) *Districts 3, 4, 5, and 6—Between New York and Jacksonville.*—Shipping proceed by day, hugging the shore and keeping within the 5-fathom curve as near as it is practicable. This shipping will be protected by the means within the capacity of the naval districts through which it passes.

(6) *District 7—Jacksonville to Key West.*—The coast here is too steep to allow daylight coasting in less than 10 fathoms, and lack of sheltered anchorages will not allow night cruising from port to port (except for small craft that can use anchorages at Settlement Point, Bimini Islands, and Turtle Harbor).

The Florida Straits should then be made safe for traffic by having it convoyed through or by aircraft and destroyer patrol. Shipping out of the Gulf of Mexico should be routed north or south of Cuba as the circumstances existing at the time render more expedient.

(7) *Districts 7 and 8—Between Key West and Galveston.*—Same as New York to Jacksonville.

(8) *District 8—Between Galveston and Tampico.*—Night coasting.

Op-14-A-D 5/4.

NAVY DEPARTMENT,
OFFICE OF NAVAL OPERATIONS,
Washington, May 4, 1918.

TO ALL SHIPMASTERS AND SHIPOWNERS.
[Circular letter.]

THESE REQUIREMENTS ARE ENTIRELY OUTSIDE OF CUSTOMS CONTROL AND HARBOR REGULATIONS IN FORCE UNDER ORDER OF THE SECRETARY OF THE TREASURY.

1. In the event of enemy submarine activity on the Atlantic coast, the following steps will become necessary for the protection of shipping at sea and in order that shipping may be properly routed.

2. Upon notification by the Navy Department, the control of all shipping, coastwise and overseas, for routing and within the defensive sea areas and outside of harbors will be assumed by the Navy Department. This control will be exercised locally by the commandants of the several naval districts.

3. Before leaving port, masters of vessels must in all cases apply to the commandant of the district for orders and routing instructions.

4. Vessels at sea should be prepared to receive at any time radio instructions to put into the nearest port or some port other than port of destination for orders.

5. Orders to make port should be promptly carried out and arrival reported at once with request for further orders and route instructions.

6. In coastal waters and at sea the boundaries of the naval districts shall be considered to extend seaward as follows:

First naval district.—When north of the parallel of latitude of Chatham, Mass. (41° 41′), communicate with the commandant first naval district, Little Building, corner of Boylston and Tremont Streets, Boston, Mass. Telegraph address, Boston; telephone address, Beach 7620.

Second naval district.—When within the area bounded as follows, communicate with the commandant, second naval district: On the north by the parallel of latitude of Chatham, Mass. (41° 41′ N); on the east by longitude 67° 45′; on the south by a line passing west true from longitude 67° 45′ to Nantucket Shoals Light Vessel, thence to Montauk Point, thence to Bartlett's Reef Light Vessel south and west of the entrance to New London Harbor, address commandant second naval district, naval station, Newport, R. I.; telegraph address, Newport, R. I.; telephone address, Newport 27.

Third naval district.—When between latitudes of Chatham, Mass. (41° 41′), and that of Barnegat, N. J. (39° 45′), excepting the areas described for the second naval district, communicate with commandant third naval district, 280 Broadway, New York; telegraph address, New York, N. Y.; telephone address, North 8900.

Fourth naval district.—When between the latitude of Assateague (37° 50′) and Barnegat, N. J. (39° 45′), communicate with commandant fourth naval district, White Building, corner of Twelfth and Chestnut Streets, Philadelphia, Pa.; telegraph address, Philadelphia, Pa.; telephone address, Walnut 5060.

Fifth naval district.—When between the latitude of New River Inlet, N. C. (34° 30′), and Assateague (37° 50′), communicate with commandant fifth naval district, Citizens National Bank Building, Norfolk, Va.; telegraph address, Norfolk; telephone address, Norfolk 6200.

Sixth naval district.—When between the latitude of St. Johns River, Fla. (30° 22′), and New River Inlet, N. C. (34° 30′), communicate with commandant sixth naval district, Peoples Office Building, Charleston, S. C.; telegraph address, Charleston, S. C.

Seventh naval district.—When within the area to the southward and eastward of the latitude of St. Johns River, Fla. (30° 22′), and bounded on the westerly and southerly sides by a line running as follows: West on the latitude of Tampa to longitude 83°; thence south to the Island of Cuba; thence following the shore to Cape San Antonio; thence southeasterly to a point latitude 18° 35′ north, longitude 78° 25′ west; thence easterly passing to the southward of the Islands of Haiti and Porto Rico and St. Croix; thence northeasterly through Anegada Passage; thence 84° true, communicate with the commandant seventh naval district, naval station, Key West, Fla.; telegraph address, Key West, Fla.

Eighth naval district.—When within the Gulf of Mexico to the westward of the seventh naval district, the Yucatan Channel, and waters to the southward to latitude 18° 35′ and to the eastward to the limits of the seventh naval district, communicate with commandant eighth naval district, naval station, New Orleans, La.; telegraph address, New Orleans, La.

APPENDIX. 155

Fifteenth naval district.—When within the waters to the southward of latitude 18° 35′ north and to the westward of line passing from latitude 18°.35′ north, longitude 78° 25′ west to Cape Tiburon, Republic of Panama, communicate with commandant fifteenth naval district, Cristobal, Canal Zone; telegraph address, Cristobal, Canal Zone.

(Signed.)   JOSEPHUS DANIELS.

[Confidential.]

Op-14-A-D-5/6,
C-26-146.

MAY 8, 1918.

From: Chief of Naval Operations.
To: Commandants first naval district, second naval district, third naval district, fourth naval district, fifth naval district, sixth naval district, seventh naval district, eighth naval district, fifteenth naval district, commander in chief, United States Atlantic Fleet.
Subject: Dispositions for control of coastwise shipping in event of submarine activity off eastern coast of United States.
Reference: (a) C. N. O. let. March 28, 1918, Op-23. (b) Notice to shipmasters and shipowners, May 4, 1918. (c) C. N. O. let. May 6, 1918.
Inclosure: (A) Reference (b).

1. Until submarine activity develops in the western Atlantic, coastwise shipping will proceed along normal routes and schedules.

2. When necessity arises for the Navy to assume control of coastwise shipping, this will be done by the various commandants of naval districts upon receipt of a dispatch from the department (operations): "Assume control of coastwise shipping."

3. Unless further advised, commandants of naval districts will, upon receipt of the above dispatch, take action along the lines outlined in reference (a), paragraph 2 (c) (1–8), making adaptations required by local conditions. It is to be noted that this plan contemplates coastwise shipping sailing independently of convoy, being routed with due regard to warnings received of the location of enemy submarines.

4. Attention is invited to reference (b) inclosed. It is of the highest importance that district commandants should have all routing possibilities and the requirements of coastwise shipping and military and commercial requirements on shore fully developed and understood with the various parties interested. This in order that vessels diverted from regular routes in accordance with instructions, or arriving in port for orders, may suffer the least delay in obtaining routing orders.

5. District commandants will have the inclosed letter to mariners, reference (b), printed in sufficient quantity and cause them to be distributed to shipowners and shipmasters and to custom officers and captains of the port and others in such manner as to insure their reaching the various parties interested as promptly as possible.

(Signed)   W. S. BENSON.

INDEX.

A.

	Page
Aceredo, Pedro (San Saba)	133
Acushla, American gas screw	86
Adelheid, American s. s.	29
Advance, American s. s.	48
Agnes G. Halliard. (See Agnes G. Holland)	58
Agnes G. Holland, Canadian schooner	58
Ainsleigh, Charles (Lansford)	54
Alban, British s. s.	106
Albert W. Black, American gas screw	83
Alberto Treves, Italian s. s.	104
Aleda May, American schooner	82
Algeria, Swedish s. s.	96
Alicke, Rudolph (Ticonderoga)	110–111
Allied Intelligence Service	101
America, C. E. (Saetia)	134
American Telephone & Telegraph Co	120
Amirault, Louis (Katie L. Palmer)	89
Amphion, American s. s.	104
Analysis of tables	141
Andrews, Philip, Capt., U. S. N.	150
Annie Perry, American schooner	59-58
Ansaldo III, Italian s. s.	96
Anson M. Bangs, American tug	30
Appendix	143
A. Piatt Andrew, American schooner	66
Appleby, British s. s.	38
Arabian, U. S. tug	24
Aras, British s. s.	48
Arnauld de la Perière (U–139)	12
Atlantic Maritime Co. (Muriel)	57
Atlas Shipping Corporation	30
Augvald, Norwegian s. s.	49
Author, British s. s.	46

B.

Babcock, J.V., Commander, U.S.N.	150
Bagley, D. W., Lieut. Commander (Jacob Jones)	113
Ballested, Edward (Vindeggan)	45, 46
Barber, Capt. (Carolina)	36
Barge 403	54
Barge 740	54
Barge 766	54
Baron Napier, British s. s.	11, 82
Bastin, Rene H. (O. B. Jennings)	74, 75
Batt, Alfred E. (Diomed)	81
Beer, Adolph (San Saba)	133
Belknap, R. R., Capt., U. S. N.	150
Belliveau, Forman (K. L. Palmer)	90
Bencleuch, British s. s.	77
Bennett, H. H. (Herbert L. Pratt)	125
Benson, W. S., Admiral, U. S. N.	38, 150, 151, 152, 155
Bergsdalen, Norwegian s. s.	99
Bianca, Canadian schooner	97
Birch, Capt. (Moorish Prince)	108
Birdsall, B. G. (San Saba)	132
Blakely, J. R. Y., Capt., U. S. N.	150
Board recommendations for defense against submarines	38, 143, 151, 152, 155
Birmingham, U. S. S.	19
Blaine, Clyde (San Diego)	128
Blommersdijk, Dutch s. s.	22
Boundaries of naval districts	154
Breiford, Norwegian s. s.	133
Brewer, Capt. (Bussum)	127
Briarleaf, British s. s.	117
Bright, C. J., Lieut. (San Diego)	127
Bristol, American s. s.	34, 36
British Major, British s. s.	71
Brown, Capt. (Malden)	127
Bruce, Capt. Wallace (A. Piatt Andrew)	66
Bryssel, Danish s. s.	38
Bussum, U. S. S.	127

C.

Cable cutting	25
Cable cutting (U–151)	25, 119, 123
Cacique, American s. s.	45
Camilla Rickmers (Ticonderoga)	106
Carolina, American s. s.	36
Carty, Col. John J	120
C. C. Mengel & Bros	41
Central and South American Cable Co	120
Chaparra, Cuban s. s.	125, 134, 137

157

158 INDEX.

	Page.
Charts	In pocket.
Chase, J. V. (Minnesota)	130, 132
Chester, U. S. S.	113
Chilier, Belgian relief ship	49
Chope, Capt. (Llanstephan Castle).	46
Christine, American bark	18
Christy, H. H. (San Diego)	127
Chr. Knudsen, Norwegian s. s.	22
Circular letter to shipmasters and shipowners	153
City of Calcutta, British s. s.	48
Clan MacArthur, British s. s.	105
C. M. Walters, Canadian schooner.	69
Coast Guard Station No. 82	56
Coast Guard Station No. 83	46
Coast Guard Station No. 115	45
Coast Guard Station No. 179	129
Coastwise routing office	39
Coffey, M. (C. G. M., U. S. N.)	22
Colhoun, U. S. S.	56
Collister, Thomas (Keemun)	47
Colorado. (See San Saba)	132
Commandant 5th naval district	132
Commercial Cable Co	120
Constanza, Danish schooner	11, 106
Cook, F. L. (Madrugada)	94
Corinthian, American s. s.	87
Cornell, E. E. (Saetia)	134
Crenella, British s. s.	24, 123
Cretan, American s. s.	78
Cruiser, American Ga. s.	83

D.

D-2 (U. S. submarine)	19
Daniels, Josephus, Secretary of the Navy	155
Davis, Thomas E. (San Diego)	128
Davis, W. H. (J. M. Haskell)	33, 126
Defense against submarines in home waters	143
Defense against submarines in home waters—Alteration of plans	150
De Steiguer, L. R., Capt., U. S. N.	150
Derbyshire, British s. s.	62, 65
Deutschland	7, 15, 100
Diamond Shoal Lightship	75, 77
Dias, Manuel, Capt. (M. E. Sennet)	87
Diomed, British s. s.	75, 79
Dispatches from Force Commander, European waters	9
Disposition for control of coastwise shipping in event of submarine activity off eastern coast of United States	155

	Page.
District defense	9, 38, 152
Dochra, U. S. S.	49
Dodge, Capt. (F. P. Jones)	127
Doon, American bark	43
Dornfontein, British schooner	56
Dorothy B. Barrett, American schooner	93
Doucette, Fred (Aleda May)	83
Droscher, Kapitanleutnant (U-117)	82
Dwinsk, British s. s.	48

E.

Earl and Nettie, American Ga. s.	83
E. B. Walters, Canadian schooner.	69
Eckelmann, Eric, Kapitan leutnant (U-155)	18, 100
Edna, American schooner	24, 121, 123
Edward H. Cole, American schooner	34
Edward H. Cole Co	34
Edward R. Baird, jr., American schooner	42
Eidsvold, Norwegian s. s.	43
Elizabeth von Belgie (Belgian Relief ship)	59
Ella Swift, American schooner	44
Elsie Porter, Canadian schooner	99
Empresa Naviera de Cuba	134
Eric, British s. s.	68
Eva B. Douglas, American schooner	38
Evans, David (Pennistone)	61
Execution of a plan for defense against submarines in home waters	152

F.

Fairfax, U. S. S.	105
Fassett, J. A., Ensign, S. P. No. 507	38
Flemming J. W. (Saetia)	133
Florence Olson, American s. s.	56
Folkmans, Jens (Vindeggen)	45
Fooks, D. J. (Edw. R. Baird, jr.)	22
Force Commander European Dispatches	9
Forsyth, A. O. (Montoso)	100
Foy, E. J., Lieut. Commander, U. S. N.	150
F. P. Jones, American s. s.	127
Francis J. O'Hara, jr., American schooner	66
Frank H. Buck, U. S. S.	101

INDEX. 159

	Page.
Franz, Kapitanleutnant (U-152)..	106, 111, 113
Frederick R. Kellogg, American s. s.	92
Freehold U. S. S.	137
Frehe, Tarwald (Stifinder)	115
Fulcher, Lieut. (j. g.), (Ticonderoga)	109, 111
Fullinwider, S. P., Commander, U. S. N.	150
Furness Withy & Co., San Jose...	61
Fuylcher, Surgeon (U-152)	112

G.

Galveston, U. S. cruiser	70
Gamo, Portuguese schooner	101
George G. Henry, U. S. S.	106
George W. Truitt, jr., American schooner	47
German submarines—arrivals and departures	7
Gilmore, Capt. C. W. (Edna)	25, 27
Gladys Frehaleit (G. M. Hollett)..	58
Gladys M. Hollett, Canadian schooner	58
Gleaner, American gas screw	83
Gleaves, Albert, Rear Admiral, U. S. N	19
Glenlee, British s. s.	49
Gloaming, Canadian schooner	70
Gloucester, American s. s.	124
Golart, Joseph (Rush)	98
Goodspeed, American s. s.	88
Granpian, British s. s.	108, 111
Grant, Admiral A. W. (Minnesota).	9, 131
Grecian, American s. s.	33
Griggsby, L. O. (Minnesota)	130
Grostock, Harold (Samoa)	47
Gymeric, British s. s.	56

H.

Haggart, R. S. (U. S. S. Hull)	42
Hamburg, German cruiser	76
Hansen, George, Capt. (Sommerstadt)	91
Hansen, Hans T., Capt. Sam. C. Mengel	42
Hansen, Louis (Mariners Harbor)..	77, 79
Harpathian, British s. s.	44
Harris, Paul John, San Diego	128
Harrisburg, U. S. S	54, 70, 80, 124
Harry Lauder	112

	Page.
Hart, Walter M. (Bristol)	36
Hattie Dunn, American schooner.	24, 26, 121, 123
Hauppauge, Americans. v.	24, 26, 121, 123
Hawaiian, American s. s.	105
Heine, Chief Engineer (U-152)	112
Helen E. Murley, American Ga. s.	89, 91
Henley, U. S. S. destroyer	41
Henrik Lund, Norwegian s. s.	46
Herbert L. Pratt, American tanker	30, 41, 123, 125, 138
Herman Winter, American s. s.	61
Holbrook, Capt. (Hattie Dunn)	25, 26
Holte, S. E. (Marosa)	52
Hull, U. S. S.	42, 74
Huntress, British s. s.	23
Huntsend, British s. s.	45

I.

Industrial, British schooner	104
Inland, American s. s	137
Intelligence Section	9
Inter-Allied Radio Conference	121
Isabel B. Wiley, American schooner	27, 30, 121, 124
Israel, U. S. S.	130, 131

J.

Jacob Jones, U. S. S.	113
Jacob M. Haskell, American schooner	33, 121
Jacobsen & Thon (Samoa)	47
J. C. Donnell, American s. s.	24
Jerden, Wm. and W. S. (K. L. Palmer)	88
J. J. Flaherty, American schooner.	69, 70
J. L. Luckenbach, American s. s..	18
John J. Fallon, American schooner	99
Johnson J. (Eidsvold)	43
John Twohy, American s. s.	18
Johnson, M., Rear Admiral, U. S. N.	150
Jonancy, American s. s.	24
Joseph Cudahy, American tanker.	70

K.

Katie L. Palmer, American Ga. s.	82, 88
Kearsarge, U. S. S.	95
Keemun, British s. s.	46, 47
Kent, W. (Minnesota)	131
Kermanshah, American s. s.	72
Kerr Steamship Co. (Kermanshah)	72

	Page.
Kingfisher, U. S. S.	93
Kingfisher, steam trawler, American.	103, 125
Kirin Maru, Japanese s. s.	118
Knoeckel, J. (U-156).	61, 65
Knudsen, Waldemar (Winneconne)	31
Knudsen and Christiansund (Kringsjaa).	48
Koenig, Capt. Paul (Deutschland).	15
Kohler, Lieut. (U-151).	29, 35, 42, 48
Koln, German s. s. (See Amphion.)	104
Kophamel, Korvettenkapitan (U-140).	70
Kringsjaa, Norwegian bark.	48
Kronprinz Heinrich, German s. s.	114
Kroonland, U. S. S.	54

L.

L-5, American submarine.	46
Lackawanna, British s. s.	64, 75
Lacy, Albert (O. B. Jennings).	24
Lafrenz, Lieut. Commander (U-65)	122
Lake Bridge, U. S. S.	50
Lake Erie, U. S. S.	50
Lake Forest, U. S. S.	49
Lane, W. (captain of Eric).	68
Lansford, American barge.	54
Larson, Alexander (master Sydland).	59
Launo, G. (captain Eva B. Douglas).	38
Leary, C. F. (master Lucia).	104
Leixoes, Portuguese steamer.	102
Letter from Force Commander in European waters.	12
Linda, British schooner.	53
Llanstephan Castle, British s. s.	46
Loriat, Mr. (cable engineer).	120
Louisiana, U. S. battleship.	29
Lowrey, K. B. (Texel).	34
Lucia, U. S. A. C. T.	104, 118
Lucille M. Schnare, Canadian schooner.	66
Luckenbach Co.	81
Luz Blanca, Canadian tank ship.	58
Lynch, Walter S. (Saetia).	133
Lynn, A. E. (Minnesota).	131

M.

Madison, J. J., Lieut. Commander (Ticonderoga).	107
Madrugada, Brazilian motor schooner.	94

	Page.
Magnusdel, Gunwald (Kringsjaa).	48
Malden, American s. s.	127
Mallory, S. S. Co. (San Saba).	132
Manning W. J. (O. B. Jennings).	74
Mantella, British s. s.	45
Manuel Caragol & Son (Chaparra).	134
Manx King, Norwegian schooner.	53, 124
Mapleleaf, British s. s.	46
Marcussen, Sven (Nordhav).	95
Mariners Harbor, American s. s.	77
Marosa, Norwegian bark.	51
Marsh, C. C. (Captain U. S. N. retired).	5
Mary E. Sennett, American Ga. s.	82, 87
McClellan, U. S. A. C. T.	49
McDonald, George E. (Frank H. Buck).	101
McNamara, John (Pleiades).	82
McNamee, L., Capt., U. S. N.	150
Melitia, British s. s.	56, 71
Melville, U. S. S.	22
Mengel C. C. & Bros. (S. C. Mengel).	41
Merak, American s. s.	77
Merritt William (Dorothy B. Barrett).	93
Mesquita, Joseph P. (Francis J. O'Hara).	66
Messina, British s. s.	117
Meusel, Lieut. Commander (U-155)	18
Mexican U. S. S.	48
Mexico, American s. s.	31
Meyer, E. J. (Minnesota).	131
Mine-laying Operations.	122
Mine laying (U-151).	30, 41
Mine-sweeping Operations, Atlantic Coast.	136
Mine-sweeping ships (naval districts).	134
Minneapolis, U. S. cruiser.	50
Minnesota, U. S. S.	124, 125, 129, 137
Mirlo, British s. s.	125, 128, 138
Modifications and changes in plans for defense against submarine attack in home waters.	150
Mohawk, American s. s.	24
Monmouth, British s. s.	11, 101
Montau, C. P. O. (U-152).	112
Montcalm, Canadian s. s.	24
Montoso, American s. s.	100
Moorish Prince, British s. s.	108, 111
Muller, F. L. (Ticonderoga).	109, 111
Munson, Andrew (San Diego).	128

INDEX. 161

	Page.
Muriel, American schooner	57
Myhre, G. (Triumph)	65

N.

	Page.
Naval censorship	119
Naval districts, sea boundaries of	154
Nelson A., Canadian schooner	58
Nelson, Gustave (J. M. Haskell)	33
Nelson, H., Lieut. Commander (Dwinsk)	48
Nelson John (Reliance)	87
Nevasa, British s. s.	50, 104
Newby Hall, British s. s.	102, 125
Newcombe H. G. (Edward H. Cole)	34
New Hampshire, U. S. battleship	29
Newton, U. S. S.	76
New York and Porto Rico S. S. Co.	36
Nicholson, American whaler	44
Nickerson Eldridge (Muriel)	57
Nickerson, James (Reliance)	86
Nordhav, Norwegian bark	95
Nordstrom, George W. (O. B. Jennings)	73
North Sea Mine Barrage	70, 113, 119
Nostitz v. Korvettenkapitan, U-151	27
Notre Dame de 1 Garde, French schooner	67
Nyanza, American s. s.	23
Nyhus, Andrew A. (Marosa)	51

O.

	Page.
O. B. Jennings, American tank ship	73
Office of Naval Intelligence	119
O'Hara, Jack (K. L. Palmer)	88
Ohio, U. S. battleship	29, 30
Oldenburg v. Kapitanleutnant (U-156)	50
Oldham, Capt. (Relay)	120
Old Time, American Ga. s.	82, 87
Oliveisa, d', Jose Tude da Velha, captain of Porto	71

P.

	Page.
Pan-American Pet. & Trans. Co. (Fredk. R. Kellog)	92
Pasadena, Canadian schooner	66
Pastores, U. S. S.	79
Patterson, U. S. S.	48
Patterson, G. E., Capt. (Briarleaf)	117
Paul Jones, U. S. S.	48
Pedersen, Alfred (Augvald)	49

	Page.
Pennistone, British s. s.	61, 65
Perth Amboy, American tug	54
Pierce, Mr. (cable engineer)	120
Pinar del Rio, American s. s.	45
Plan for coastwise shipping in case of submarine activities on American coast	152
Plassey, British s. s.	138
Pleiades, American s. s.	81
Pluos. (See Rush.)	98
Porto, Portuguese bark	71
Potentate, Canadian schooner	99
Potomac, British s. s.	44
Prairie, U. S. S.	48
Preble, U. S. coast torpedo vessel	41
Princess Matoika, U. S. S.	48, 118
Progress, American Ga. s.	82
Proteus, American s. s.	43
Publicover, Capt. (Uda A. Saunders)	67
Pyrrhus, British s. s.	92

Q.

	Page.
Quadros, Alvro P., Capt. (Rush)	98
Quinlan, Fred., crew (K. L. Palmer)	90

R.

	Page.
Radioleine, French tanker	42, 43
Radio Service (adequate if cables had been destroyed)	121
Rail, U. S. S.	137
Randwijk, U. S. S. (formerly Dutch)	46
Reginolite, British s. s.	104
Relay, American cable vessel	120
Reliance, American Ga. s.	83, 86
Rheinhard, W. M., master (Elsie Porter)	99
Rijndijk, U. S. S.	88
Ringleman, Gustav (Ticonderoga)	106, 109
Risberg, Eric, Capt. (Algeria)	96
Robert and Richard, American schooner	55
Rob Roy, American schooner	57
Robinson, S. S., Capt., U. S. N.	
Rochet, James F. (San Diego)	128
Rondo, U. S. S.	100
Rose, American schooner	55
Rose, Hans, Lieut. (U-53)	18, 113
Rouse, Frederick (Madrugada)	94

INDEX.

	Page.
Rush, American steam trawler	98
Russell, Edward (K. L. Palmer)	87, 88, 90

S.

Saetia, U. S. S.	125, 133, 137
Sam C. Mengel, American schooner.	41
Samoa, Norwegian bark	42
Sanchez, R. A. (Wm. H. Starbuck)	85
San Diego, U. S. S.	54, 57, 124, 125, 126, 137
Sanghove, Clifford T. (Ticonderoga)	108
San Jose, Norwegian s. s.	60, 65
San Saba, American s. s.	32, 124, 125, 132
Santiago, American s. s.	31
Saunders, M. H. (Edna)	25, 28
S. C. No. 234 (U. S.)	46
S. C. No. 294 (U. S.)	117
Schuill, Marsi ("Rose")	55
Schwarz, Lieut. (U-152)	112
Seaborne, F. O. (Newby Hall)	102
Seidlitz, German s. s.	76
Shipping	8
Shortind, Norwegian steamer	101
Simona, Edwardo (San Saba)	133
Sims, Admiral W. S.	12, 136, 138
Singer, A. W. (Minnesota)	131
Small, C. A. (Edna)	24
Smith, R. Lawrence (Hauppauge).	26
Smith, Robert H. (Kermanshah)..	72
Sodral, Norwegian s. s.	46
Solberg, Norwegian s. s.	99
Sommerstadt, Norwegian s. s.	91
Sorkness, Norwegian bark	53
South Carolina, U. S. S.	46, 137
Special board to formulate plan of defense in home waters	10, 143
Special Planning Board of Feb. 6, 1918	38, 143
S. P. No. 507 (U. S. S.)	38
Standard Refinery Co. (Pratt)	123
Stanley M. Seaman, American schooner	75, 77
Staples, John	132
Steadman, L. S. R. (Minnesota)	131
Stephano, British s. s.	22
Steps taken by Navy Department to protect shipping	8, 38
Stifinder, Norwegian bark	112, 115
Strathmore, British s. s.	22
Stringham, U. S. S.	79
Submarine mines, Atlantic coast, United States	125
Sucena, Joaquim F. (Leixoes)	102
Susquehanna, U. S. S.	50
Swain, Charles H. (Annie Perry)	58
Sweeney, Capt. (Hauppauge)	25, 66
Sydland, Swedish, Belgian Relief ship	59
Sylvania, American schooner	66
Sydney B. Atwood, American schooner	57

T.

T. A. Scott, jr., American s. s.	17
Table, arrivals and departures of German submarines	7
Table No. 1, vessels destroyed	139, 140
Table No. 2, vessels destroyed	140
Table No. 3, vessels destroyed	141
Tampa, U. S. S.	113
Tapley, J. P. (Perth Amboy)	55
Tappley, Geo. S. (Ticonderoga)	109
Tasida, Jos. (Rush)	98
Taunton, Norwegian s. s.	95
Taylor, U. S. S.	128
Teal, U. S. S.	137, 138
Telles, Joseph (Rush)	98
Temple, E. Dorr, American s. s.	56
Texel, American s. s.	34
Thespis, British s. s.	96
Thomas, Frazier O., M. M., 2d class	128
Thomassen, Thom. I (Isabel B. Wiley)	30
Thorbyonsen, Capt. Hans, San José	60
Ticonderoga, U. S. S.	100, 106
Tingey, U. S. S.	60
Tokuyama Maru, Japanese s. s.	73
Tortuguero, British s. s.	50
Triumph, Canadian trawler (steam)	65
Turner, W. M. Seaman (Ticonderoga)	109

U.

U-15, French submarine	122
U-53, German submarine.	7, 8, 13, 18, 113
U-65, German submarine	122
U-117, German submarine	7, 60, 82, 124, 128

INDEX.

	Page.
U-139, German submarine	7, 8, 12, 102
U-140, German submarine	7, 70, 99
U-151, German submarine	7, 10, 23, 123
U-152, German submarine	7, 16, 106
U-155, German submarine	7, 18, 100, 118, 125
U-156, German submarine	11, 50, 75, 124
Uberaba, Brazilian s. s.	79
Uda A. Saunders, Canadian schooner	66, 69
Umbria, Italian s. s.	73
Una P. Saunders. (See Uda A. Saunders.)	66
U. S. Hydrographic Office	5
U. S. Railroad Administration	132

V.

	Page.
Velha, Jose Tude d'Oliveisa, da captain of Porto	71
Verna D. Adams, Canadian schooner	69, 70
Vindeggen, Norwegian s. s.	45, 46
Vinland, Norwegian s. s.	44
Vinolas, Jose, captain (Chaparra)	134
Von Nostitz und Janckendorf (U-151)	23
Von Schrader, Commander (U-53)	113
Von Steubon, U. S. S.	48

W.

	Page.
Wagadesk, Norwegian s. s.	18
Walters, Capt. Cyrus (E. B. Walters)	69
Walters, Capt. Wilson (C. M. Walters)	69
War Ranee, British tank ship	82
War Warnings	8
Wasch, H. (Winneconne)	32
West Haven, U. S. S.	70
West Point, British s. s.	22
Wharton, Robt. A. (Robert and Richard)	56
White, C. H. (Fredk. R. Kellog)	92
Wilkins, John W. (S. C. Mengel)	42
Wille, Lieut. (U-152)	112, 114
William H. Starbuck, American Ga. s	82, 85
Williams, W. R. (Mirlo)	128
Willie, G., Canadian schooner	68
Willoughby, Edw. J. Carpenter, Ticonderoga	109
Wilson, President Woodrow	42, 56, 57, 88
Winneconne, American s. s.	27, 31, 32, 121, 124
Winsborg, T. L. (Hauppauge)	25
Wireless	9

CHART NO. 1

German Submarine Activities in the Western Atlantic Ocean, 1918

TO ACCOMPANY
MONOGRAPH NO. I
"German Submarine Activities on the Atlantic Coast of the United States and Canada"

NAVY DEPARTMENT
Office of Naval Records and Library
Historical Section

1920

GERMAN SUBMARINE ACTIVITIES

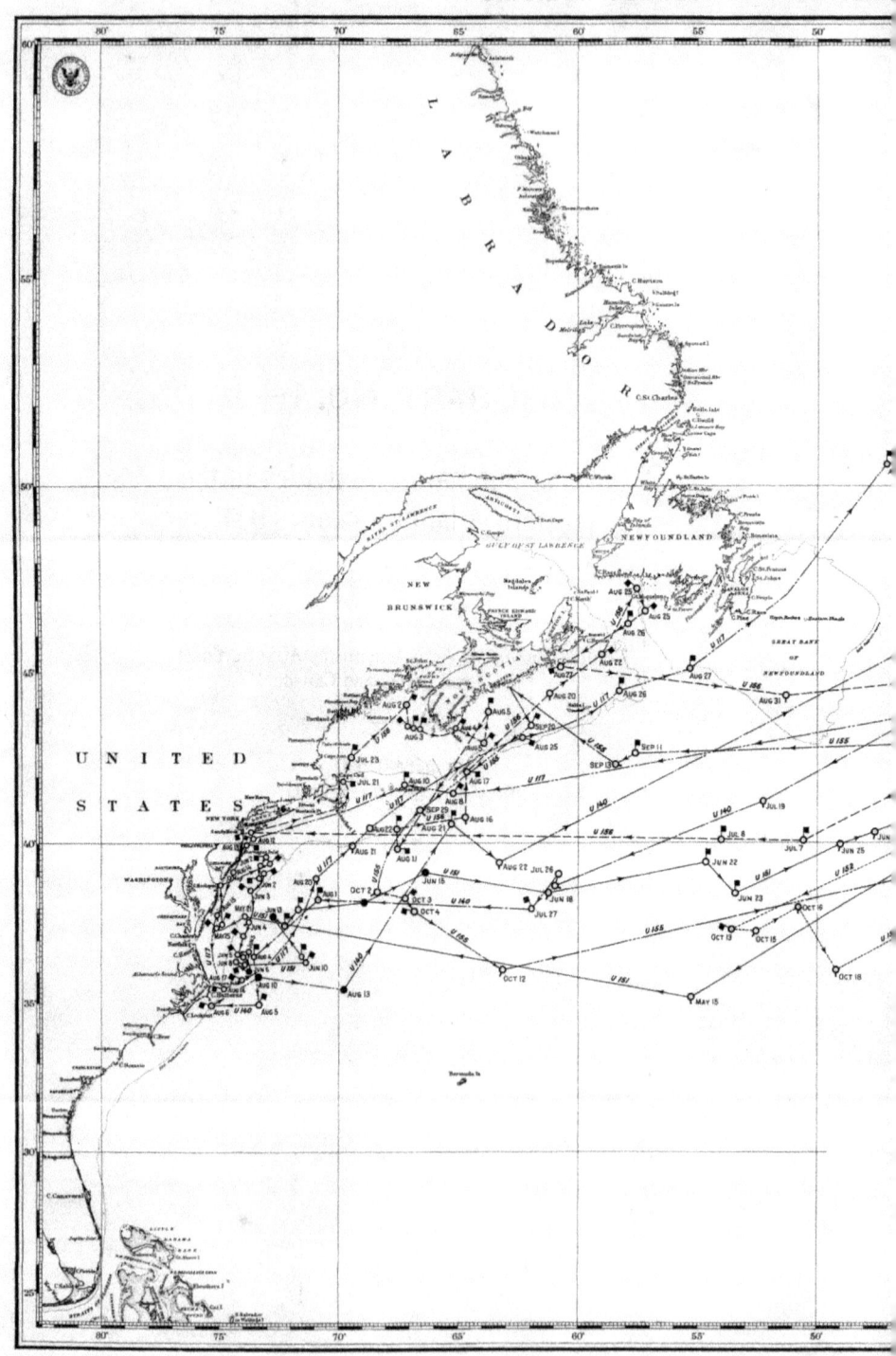

WESTERN ATLANTIC OCEAN, 1918

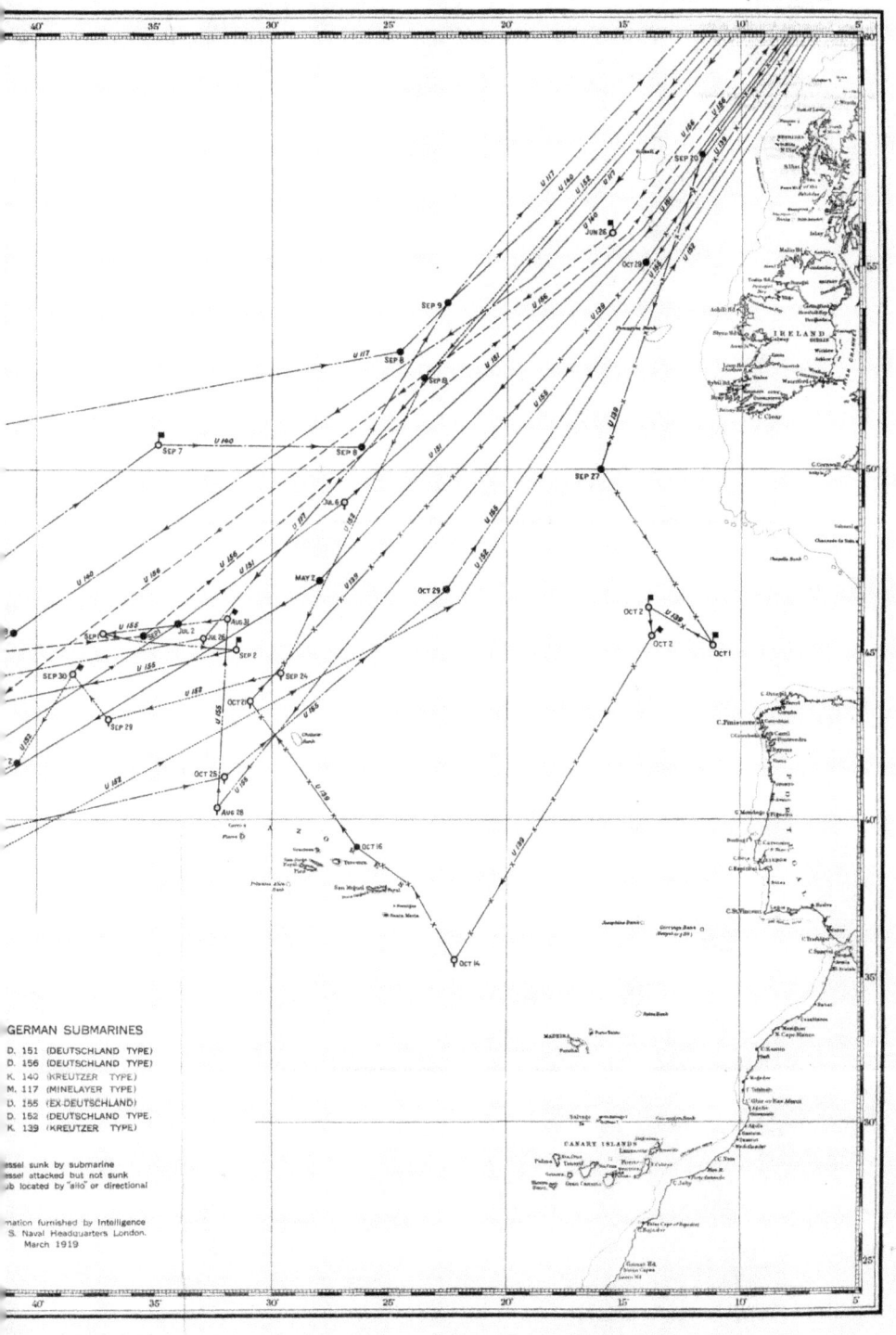

GERMAN SUBMARINES

D. 151 (DEUTSCHLAND TYPE)
D. 156 (DEUTSCHLAND TYPE)
K. 140 (KREUTZER TYPE)
M. 117 (MINELAYER TYPE)
D. 155 (EX-DEUTSCHLAND)
D. 152 (DEUTSCHLAND TYPE)
K. 139 (KREUTZER TYPE)

ssel sunk by submarine
ssel attacked but not sunk
ub located by "allo" or directional

mation furnished by Intelligence
S. Naval Headquarters London.
March 1919

Chart No. 2

Summary of Enemy Mining Activities on United States Atlantic Coast

TO ACCOMPANY
MONOGRAPH No. 1
"German Submarine Activities on the Atlantic Coast of the United States and Canada"

NAVY DEPARTMENT
Office of Naval Records and Library
Historical Section

1920

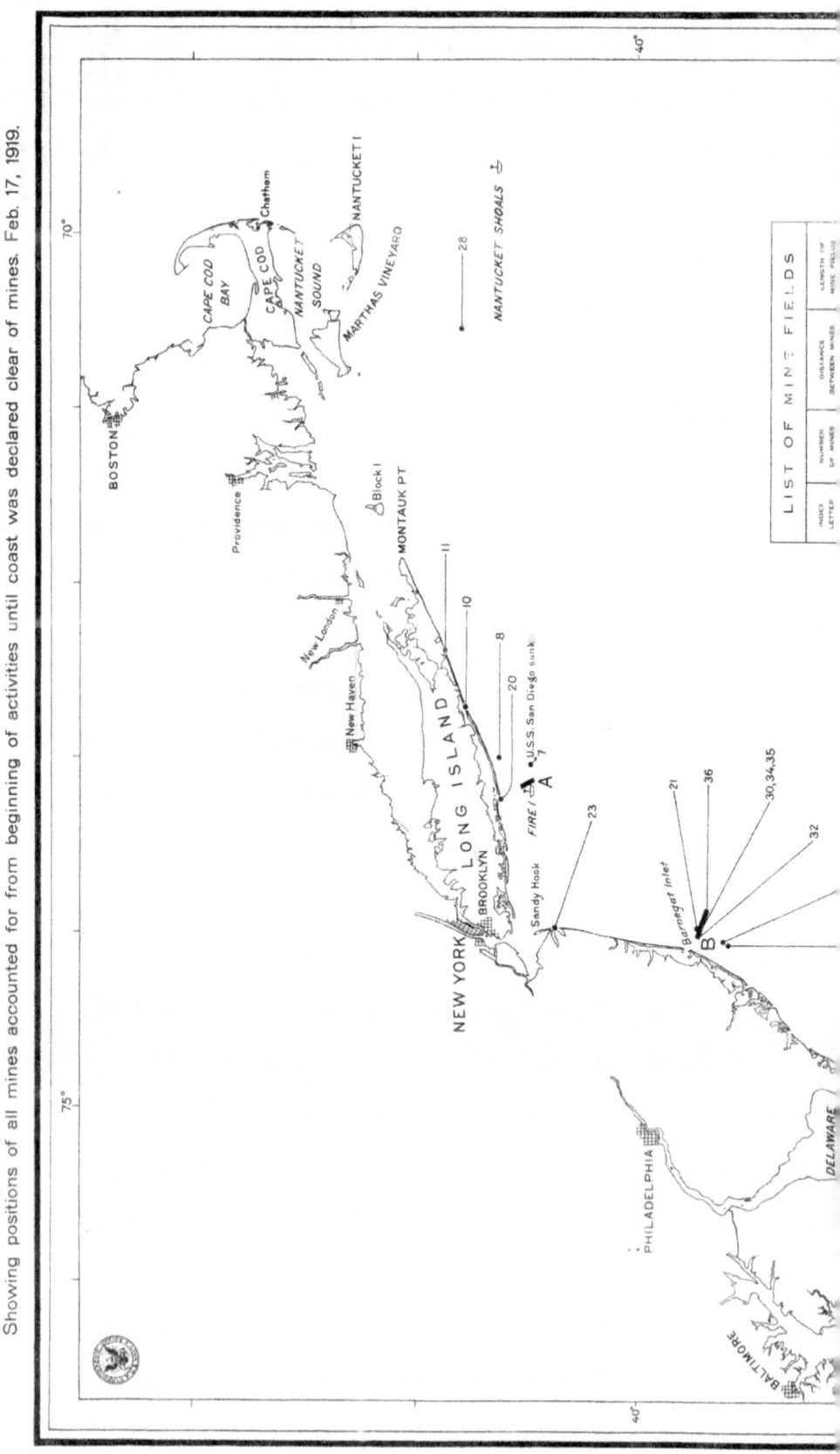

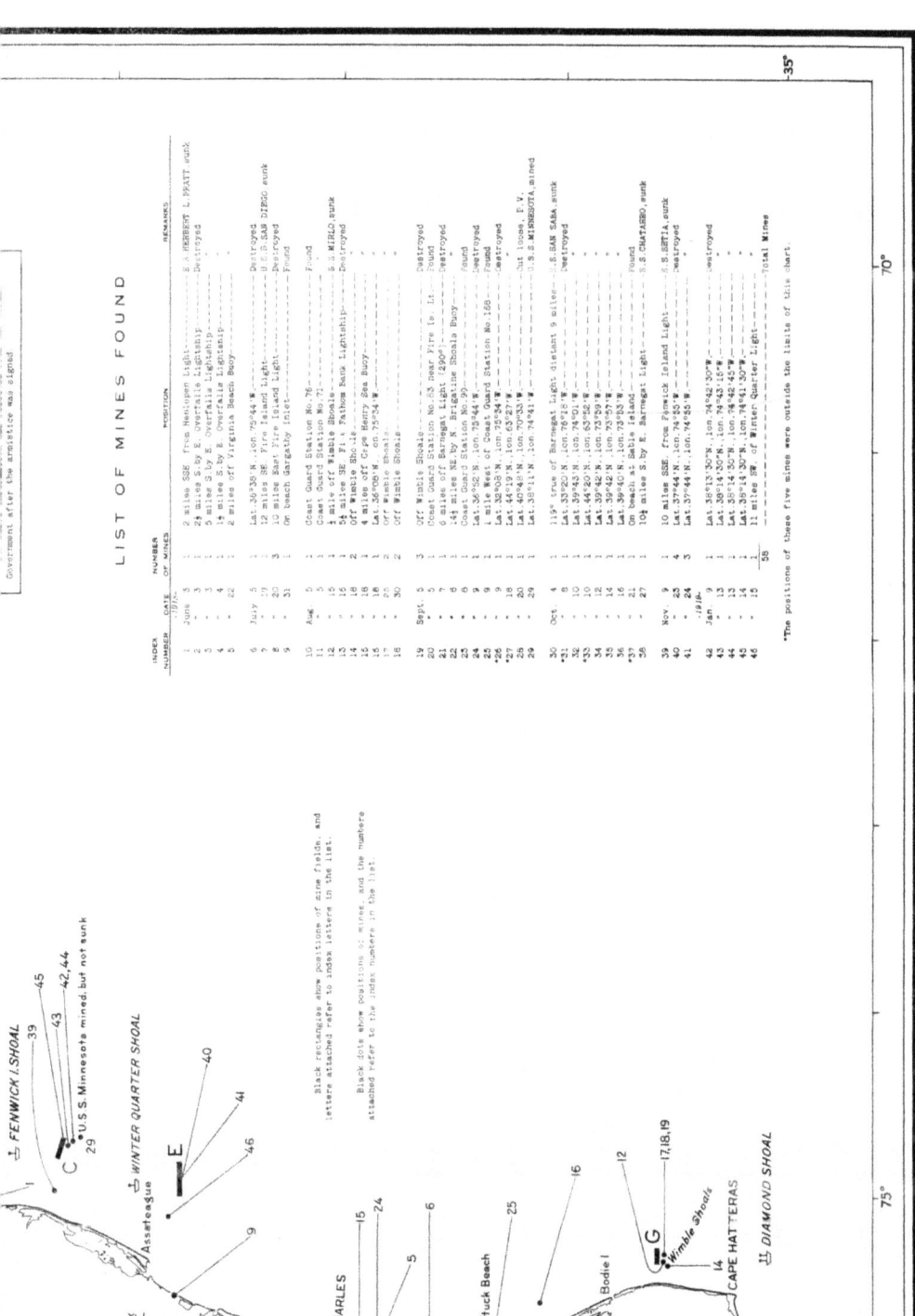

Government. After the armistice was signed.

LIST OF MINES FOUND

INDEX NUMBER	DATE 1918	NUMBER OF MINES	POSITION	REMARKS
1	June 3	3	2 miles SSE from Nantucket Lightship	S.S.HERBERT L.PRATT sunk
2	" 3	3	2½ miles S. by E. Overfalls Lightship	Destroyed
3	" 3	1	5 miles S. by E. Overfalls Lightship	"
4	" 3	4	1½ miles S. by E. Overfalls Lightship	"
5	" 5	22	2 miles off Virginia Beach Buoy	"
6	July 5	5	Lat. 36°35'N., lon.75°44'W.	Destroyed
7	" 19	29	12 miles SE Fire Island Light	U.S.S.SAN DIEGO sunk
8	" 20	3	10 miles East Fire Island Light	Destroyed
9	" 21	31	On beach Gargathy Inlet	Found
10	Aug. 5	5	Coast Guard Station No. 76	Found
11	" 15	15	Coast Guard Station No. 71	"
12	" 15	1	1 mile off Wimble Shoals	S.S.MIRLO sunk
13	" 18	18	5½ miles SE Fl. Fathom Bank Lightship	Destroyed
14	" 15	18	Off Wimble Shoals	"
15	" 16	2	4 miles off Cape Henry Sea Buoy	"
16	" 18	18	Lat. 36°06'N. on 75°54'W.	Found
17	" 10	30	Off Wimble Shoals	"
18	"	2	Off Wimble Shoals	"
19	Sept. 5	3	Off Wimble Shoals	Destroyed
20	" 7	1	Coast Guard Station No.68 Near Fire Is.	Found
21	" 8	1	6 miles off Barnegat Light 1290°	Destroyed
22	" 6	6	4½ miles NE by N Brigantine Shoals Buoy	"
23	" 9	1	Coast Guard Station No.99	Destroyed
24	" 9	2	Lat. 36°52'N. lon.75°44'W.	Found
25	" 9	9	1 mile West of Coast Guard Station No.168	Destroyed
*26	" 18	1	Lat. 32°03'N., lon.75°34'W.	Cut loose, F.V.
*27	" 18	20	Lat. 44°19'N. lon.63°27'W.	U.S.S.MINNESOTA,mined
28	" 20	1	Lat. 40°48'N. lon.70°33'W.	"
29	" 29	1	Lat. 38°01'N. lon.73°41'W.	
30	Oct. 4	1	115° true of Barnegat Light distant 9 miles	U.S.SAN SABA sunk
*31	" 8	1	Lat. 33°20'N. lon.76°18'W.	Destroyed
32	" 10	10	Lat. 39°43'N. lon.74°01'W.	"
*33	" 10	1	Lat. 44°20'N. lon.63°52'W.	"
34	" 12	12	Lat. 39°42'N. lon.73°29'W.	"
35	" 14	14	Lat. 39°42'N. lon.73°57'W.	"
36	" 14	1	Lat. 36°40'N. lon.73°33'W.	Found
*37	" 21	1	On beach at Sable Island	"
38	" 27	1	10½ miles S. by E. Barnegat Light	S.S.CHATARIO sunk
39	Nov. 9	1	10 miles SSE. from Fenwick Island Light	S.S.SETIA sunk
40	" 23	4	Lat. 37°44'N. lon.74°45'W.	Destroyed
41	" 24	3	Lat. 37°44'N. lon.74°55'W.	"
	1916			
42	Jan. 9	1	Lat. 38°13'30"N. lon.74°42'30"W.	Destroyed
43	" 13	13	Lat. 38°14'30"N. lon.74°43'15"W.	"
44	" 13	13	Lat. 38°14'30"N. lon.74°42'45"W.	"
45	" 14	14	Lat. 38°14'30"N. lon.74°41'30"W.	"
46	" 15	15	11 miles SW of Winter Quarter Light	"
		56		Total Mines

*The positions of these five mines were outside the limits of this chart.

Black rectangles show positions of mine fields, and letters attached refer to index letters in the list.

Black dots show positions of mines, and the numbers attached refer to the index numbers in the list.

www.ingramcontent.com/pod-product-compliance
Lightning Source LLC
Chambersburg PA
CBHW070550160426
43199CB00014B/2447